Southern Africa in Crisis

Southern
Africa
in **CRISIS**

Edited by

GWENDOLEN M. CARTER

and

PATRICK O'MEARA

Indiana University Press

BLOOMINGTON   AND   LONDON

Published in Canada by Fitzhenry & Whiteside Limited, Don Mills, Ontario

Manufactured in the United States of America

Library of Congress Cataloging in Publication Data

Main entry under title:
Southern Africa in crisis.
Bibliography
Includes index.
1. Africa, Southern—Politics and government—
1975-   —Addresses, essays, lectures.   2. Africa,
Southern—Foreign relations—Addresses, essays, lectures.
3. World politics—1975-1985—Addresses, essays, lec-
tures.   I. Carter, Gwendolen Margaret, 1906-
II. O'Meara, Patrick.
DT746.S58   1977   320.9'68'06   76-48534
ISBN 0-253-35399-8   1 2 3 4 5 81 80 79 78 77

Cover photograph and frontispiece courtesy of the United Nations.
Cover: J. P. Laffont, photographer.
Frontispiece: Y. Nagata, photographer.

CONTENTS

PREFACE

The need to provide background and insight into the rapidly changing international situation in Southern Africa led both the director of Indiana University Press, John Gallman, and the editors of this volume to decide to prepare with maximum speed a volume of essays by recognized authorities on each of the countries of that area. The purpose of this book is to enable students and the general public to focus on the most significant features of the widely varying situations within Southern Africa and their essential interrelationship. In the interests of directness and clarity, footnotes have been dispensed with.

We would like to express our appreciation to all those who have supported us in preparing this volume in record time. The contributors have put aside important responsibilities or simply added the preparation of their sections to already fulltime work because they agreed with us on the importance of the project. The African Studies Program at Indiana University, and in particular, Alice Young, Susan Myers, Mary Pigozzi, and Anne Fraker, and the Press itself have lent invaluable aid. We are indebted to Cathryn L. Lombardi for the map work. To all those who have been involved we extend our very warm thanks in the knowledge that they agree with us that an understanding of the factors involved in the struggle for power in the last white minority-controlled part of the world is of deep significance to us all.

Gwendolen M. Carter
Patrick O'Meara

Southern Africa in Crisis

Introduction

The International Dimension of the Crisis in Southern Africa

COLIN LEGUM

SOUTHERN AFRICA IS experiencing a shift of power of historic importance. Just how far or fast the shift will go—or how much violence and
disruption it will entail—is still impossible to predict, except in two major
respects. First, it is already clear that it is only a matter of time before black
power replaces white power throughout the entire region. The replacement
of white power will inevitably result in the ending of Western dominance
in that part of the world, but this does not necessarily mean that anti-
Western governments will emerge in the southern tip of Africa. This prospect represents a total reversal of the situation that had existed until as
recently as 1974. The second predictable factor is that this decisive change
will occur within the next five to ten years, making the coming decade a
period of turbulent crises and upheavals.

This revolutionary change in Southern Africa should not be viewed as
simply another isolated episode in modern history; it is part of an important
series of related events in what might best be described as the Post-Imperial
Era, which began after World War II and the end of which is not yet in
sight.

The Post-Imperial Era is one of those watersheds in history when the old balance of power shifts decisively and when new forces and ideas take shape —as in the periods now known as the Industrial Revolution, the Renaissance, and the Hundred Years' War. The generations who lived through those important periods were unable at that time to see the separate episodes occurring in their time as belonging to a single historic process of change; but it is already possible for our own generation to relate the four great changes that have been occurring in our lifetime as part of a rapid process of change which is producing an entirely different international system.

The first of these changes has been the erosion of the position of Western dominance in international affairs that began after World War II. Until then the ability of the Western nations, individually or in alliances, to impose their will on the non-Western world was virtually unchallengeable. All the great power struggles of the European Imperial Era were fought out among the Western nations themselves in their rivalries for primacy among the major powers.

The Industrial Revolution of the late eighteenth century had given the West a head start over the rest of the world in the ability to create new wealth and to accumulate greater military power, which resulted in the expansion of European imperialism and the rise of the United States of America. However, the technological advances that flowed from the Industrial Revolution have increasingly ceased to remain an exclusively Western possession, and imperial possessions have become a liability instead of the asset they once were.

What we are now witnessing is the recession of the West's dominant (and domineering) power. The loss of empire is but one facet of this changing power; another is the decline in Western confidence of its own role and of its future, resulting in the anxious search within Western society for ways of transforming its power for different purposes, as exemplified by the current concern about the benefits and disadvantages of the affluent industrial society and the spoliation of the environment.

Above all, this is a period struggle to establish a new equilibrium in the balance of world power between the older, dominant forces and the new challengers. This redistribution of power and of resources is being achieved only gradually, so far mainly by nonviolent methods. But every now and again there are violent interludes when one or another of the Western nations forgets, or ignores, the reality of its lost ability to impose its will on parts of the non-Western world, as these nations had been accustomed to doing for so long; this produces what can only be described as aberrations. Examples of such aberrations are the United States' involvement in war in Vietnam, Britain's disastrous Suez operation, France's miserable struggle in Algeria, Portugal's stubborn resistance in Africa, and, on a lower scale, the recent episode in Angola.

All these attempts at using military and/or economic coercive power ended in failure for the Western nations. It is significant, too, that contributory factors to this failure were the disagreements within the Western community whenever one of its errant members engaged in such an operation, and the bitter internal divisions within the nations engaged in such foreign enterprises. The old era of "patriotism," "my country right or wrong," "for King and Country" already begins to look strangely old-fashioned.

The second decisive change in this new era has been the rise of the Soviet Union (though not of international communism) as a serious challenging world power—not yet equal to that of the West, but strong enough to force acceptance of the Soviets as one of the two superpowers. This has produced a dual response: collective Western defense through such alliances as NATO; and a policy of detente to minimize the risks of a new world war. Though not yet industrially a match, Soviet military strength has begun to measure up to that of the West. The rise, for the first time, of the Soviet navy as a world sea power is one significant feature of this changing balance of power.

The third significant change has been the emergence of China as a potential world power for the first time in history. Though militarily less of a challenge to the West than the Soviet Union, its economic potential has at long last begun to be mobilized and its influence has begun to spread through most areas of the world.

However, despite the rise of these two great communist powers, the possibility of their forming part of an alliance against the "capitalist West" has been aborted by their historic suspicions of each other. The Sino-Soviet rivalry is a crucial element in the worldwide struggle for the redistribution of power and resources.

The fourth great change—also for the first time in history—is the emergence of the Third World as a major factor in world affairs. Mostly former colonial dependencies, the nations of the Third World are by no means a cohesive force, nor are they likely to become so except when it comes to particular issues such as those which may deeply affect the independence of these younger states, the aspirations of nationalisms still struggling for liberation from the colonial past, and, especially, the unequal relations in the prevailing system of world trade. Thus the concept of the new international economic order represents an important shared aspiration of the developing nations, while the movement of nonaligned nations is an expression of their aspiration toward independence, globally, from either of the major military power blocs.

It is because of these shared interests that, for example, the Palestinians can demand a state of their own and can count on almost unanimous backing from the Third World, and that the liberation movements in Southern Africa can rely on, at the very least, their moral support.

Africa is an important element of the Third World. In some ways the continent is perhaps the most closely knit unit within this grouping, with loyalties that cut across such distinctions as "Arab" and "black" Africa— at least on issues that smack of "colonial relationships" or "Western bullying." They are more ambiguous, and more careful, in their dealings with Moscow, mainly because the Soviet bloc is seen as a potential ally in conflicts with Western powers affecting African interests. Relations with Peking are much less ambiguous and less certain than with the Soviets since the Chinese are felt to be a part of the Third World in everything except size. The fact that China does not form part of a military bloc strengthens this feeling; but because of its open rivalry with the Soviet Union, the Third World countries, not wishing to become aligned with either side, treat the Chinese as only "honorary" members of their club.

These four major forces—the West, the Soviet bloc, China, and the Third World—engage at different levels in the struggles to achieve a different political and economic equilibrium in the evolving world order. Sometimes two or more of these forces may be engaged on the same side (three of them in the case of the Arab-Israeli conflict); at other times they might find themselves ranged against each other—as in Angola, where China's position was little different from that of the United States and one half of the African states. However, on the issues bearing on the crisis in Southern Africa there is a strong unity of purpose among the Third World, the Soviet Union, and China, at least about major objectives if not about tactics. This collective alliance—notwithstanding the fact that the Soviets and the Chinese maneuver against each other for influence within this grouping—is committed to the single objective of ending white power in the subcontinent.

The Western nations, who were once openly, or ashamedly at best, identified with the white-ruled nations of Southern Africa, now find themselves trapped in an ambiguous position because of their past policies. While steadily moving closer to the African side, the Western nations (with the exception of Sweden) remain undecided whether or not to make the kind of commitment against the present rulers of Pretoria that has long ago been made by Moscow and Peking. For the latter, of course, the decision was easier, since China had nothing to lose and much to gain from the ending of white supremacy in the African subcontinent. In the years immediately ahead, as the Southern Africa crisis deepens and as the "communist threat" is perceived as becoming more menacing (i.e., that the communist nations will come to be looked on as friendly allies by Africans because of their support for liberation movements), Western policies will predictably change, as they have already begun to do. The timing of this change of attitude could have a major bearing on the shape of the African subcontinent when it, too, finally emerges as a part of the Third World.

The roots of the present crisis in Southern Africa lie in the past when European conquest and expansion subjected the indigenous peoples to a status of second-class citizenship. South Africa's modern black nationalist movement, dating from 1912, was among the earliest manifestations of the anticolonial struggles. But when, after the end of World War II, independent African states began to stretch virtually all the way from the Mediterranean to the banks of the Zambezi River, the liberation movement became blocked by the powerful resistance of the white-ruled societies headed by South Africa. The Zambezi became the Great Divide between black- and

Arab-ruled Africa and the white-ruled states, forming a kind of Mason-Dixon Line between the new nationalisms of the north and the older nationalisms of the south.

For the ebullient black nationalists symbolically united under the banner of Pan-Africanism and organically linked in the Organization of African Unity (OAU), the setback on the banks of the Zambezi came to represent a special challenge to their unfinished revolution. For the tough defenders of the white redoubt, the challenge was seen as a life-and-death struggle in the defense of their centuries-old way of life. No compromise was possible between these two historic forces.

A few dents had been knocked in the white defense system to the south of the line of confrontation when, in the mid-1960s, the three former British High Commission Territories—Botswana, Lesotho, and Swaziland—became independent; otherwise the line held fast until 1974. Up to that point the white defenders were able to maintain their position through a loose but tough alliance system of military and economic power between the Republic of South Africa, the white rebel regime of Rhodesia, and Portugal's colonial empire, centered principally in Angola, Mozambique, and, further to the north, in Guinea-Bissau.

Up to 1974 it still seemed to many, especially in the Western world, that the military and economic power of this triple alliance could hold out for long enough to see the flames of militant Pan-Africanism doused by the cold realities of the post-independence problems that are the inevitable lot of all nascent nation-states. The disintegration of the evolving African system was being freely predicted in the 1950s and 1960s, and there was a strong belief that more moderate black leadership would emerge, more concerned with economic priorities and with the urgent task of building their own new institutions than with external "adventures" in support of liberation movements.

So confident were a majority of the Western decision-makers in the accuracy of this forecast that they continued at an accelerating rate to pour new investments into Southern Africa, especially South Africa. Western defense planners continued to base their future strategy on the assumption that in the event of war the white-ruled states would remain an important bastion for the Western alliance.

As late as 1970 the American President (on the advice of Henry Kissinger) decided as a matter of deliberate policy to change the thrust of the previous Kennedy and Johnson administrations in order to "tilt the balance towards the whites" in Southern Africa. That grotesque miscalculation (set out in National Security Study Memorandum 39) rested on the stated assumption that the forces of black violence could not succeed; that white military and economic power could hold out; and that a much slower, more evolutionary process of change was likely.

Only six years later the author of NSSM 39, standing before an audience in Lusaka close to the Zambezi border, reversed that tilt in favor of supporting the idea of majority rule throughout the subcontinent. On that important occasion on April 27, 1976, Kissinger declared:

> Africa in this decade is a testing ground of the world's conscience and vision. That blacks and whites live together in harmony and *equality* is a moral imperative of our time. Let us prove that these roles can be realized by human choice, that justice can command by the force of its rightness instead of by force of arms.

Yet it was precisely because of what Africans had achieved *by force of arms* that Kissinger had finally been persuaded to move the problems of Southern Africa up from almost the very bottom of his list of international priorities to somewhere near the top. The crack in white power had finally been achieved exactly two years earlier—in April 1974—when the Portuguese colonial empire collapsed with dramatic suddenness following a military coup in Lisbon that ended the long years of Salazarism in Portugal.

Although the course of Portugal's colonial history was changed in its metropolitan capital, the impetus of the coup came from the twelve years of struggle against the liberation movements in Guinea-Bissau, Mozambique, and Angola. These guerrilla wars had not only wrecked Portugal's economy and paralyzed its once confident leadership; they had also worn out the Portuguese army, whose own commanders and men returned home frustrated and disillusioned with the wars of attrition they had been unable to win and, ironically, carrying home with them many of the ideas propounded by their enemy in the bush.

It was the realistic right-wing prime minister of South Africa, John Vorster, who was the first to grasp the true import of the collapse of Portugal's empire. On the morrow of that traumatic event Vorster spoke of South Africa having come to "a new cross-roads." With the collapse of one leg of the tripod on which the white power system had rested in the region, he saw that the second leg, Rhodesia, was no longer dependable. Accepting phlegmatically that South Africa must learn to live with the new Marxist regime of the Front for the Liberation of Mozambique (Frelimo) as its neighbor, Vorster realized the importance of extricating South Africa's military support forces from Rhodesia and of moving them south below the river frontier of the Cunene, between Angola and Namibia, and the Limpopo, between South Africa and Rhodesia. At the same time he sought to compensate for this setback by holding out his hand of friendship to black Africa with a promise to cooperate in achieving a negotiated settlement in Rhodesia to produce African rule there, and, moreover, by relenting in his republic's long defiance of international opinion over the right of Namibia (South West Africa) to its independence as a single, unified country. He was not forthcoming, however, over the possibility of meaningful change in his own apartheid republic.

South Africa's proffered hand of friendship was eagerly grasped, first by President Kenneth Kaunda of Zambia, and soon by other African leaders, notably by presidents Julius Nyerere of Tanzania, Sir Seretse Khama of Botswana, and Samora Machel of Mozambique. Thus was born the quartet of allies who were soon to become known as the front-line presidents, i.e., the leaders of the countries bordering closely on the Zambezi.

Three of these leaders (Machel had not yet become president of Mozambique) had been the signatories, along with another dozen East and Central African presidents, of the famous Lusaka Declaration of 1967, which had first held out the hand of friendship to white South Africa on condition that its leaders be prepared to negotiate for the peaceful transfer of power, over an undefined period, to African majority rule. The signatories of the Lusaka manifesto declared their preference for peaceful change in Southern Africa but warned that if this proved impossible they would have no alternative but to support an armed struggle.

Now, seven years later and with the armed struggle having proved successful in the Portuguese colonies, South Africa's prime minister finally took up the offer of the Lusaka Declaration; previously he had chosen to regard it as a threatening challenge. Although Vorster negotiated honestly and vigorously over the question of Rhodesia, he remained less forthcoming over Namibia, where he refused to deal with the guerrillas of the South West African People's Organization (SWAPO). Most tenaciously, Vorster rejected any solution other than separate development (apartheid) for South Africa. Nevertheless, the fruits of this attempt at negotiation did produce one important result: it removed South Africa's military support from Rhodesia at a time when the Zimbabwe People's Liberation Army (ZIPA) was beginning to take more effective shape from their bases in the newly liberated frontier state of Mozambique.

This attempt at negotiation between the two confrontation sides was shattered by the events surrounding the independence of Angola. There, in 1975, the People's Liberation Movement of Angola (MPLA) succeeded in winning power after a military struggle against its rivals, thanks largely to massive military support from the Soviet Union and Cuba. Their alliance proved too strong even against the ill-conceived military intervention by South Africa, which had mistakenly hoped for strong American backing in their effort to "stop communism from spreading down Africa."

During the Angolan crisis, probably for the first time in its modern history, an American administration had found itself prevented from pursuing a major foreign policy initiative by a Congress that had no taste for new foreign involvements in the aftermath of Vietnam.

The Angolan affair proved to be traumatic for South Africa as well as having several other major consequences. It was the first time that South Africa's powerful army had been used independently outside its own frontiers. Although only a tiny fraction of the army was committed to the intervention, and despite the fact that its commanders were severely limited in their freedom to fight according to well-established military principles, its defeat was seen by Africans (especially by black South Africans) as evidence of the vincibility of white military power. Black morale, already boosted by the independence of Mozambique, rose in South Africa—and nowhere more than among militant black youngsters, a generation made bitterly resentful by almost three decades of apartheid rule. On the other hand, white morale was badly shaken by what had happened in Angola and by the early signs of youthful black defiance at home.

For white South Africa the result in Angola had brought closer to reality two of its worst nightmares: the success of a black movement of violence and the "approach of the communists" to their borders.

For the Soviet Union their risky but successful intervention, thousands of miles from home, had at least three positive results. They had provided convincing evidence to other struggling liberation movements in Namibia, Rhodesia, and South Africa that Moscow could be relied on as a powerful ally in their own struggles. They had tested the limits of detente with the United States and found that they could engage in foreign intervention, as in Angola, without disrupting this diplomatic initiative. And they had prevented China from playing an effective role as a convincing ally of African liberation.

For China, Angola was a defeat. Up to then, the Chinese had been much more effective in the kind of support—military training, arms, and economic help—they were giving to liberation movements in the area. Having opted out of the power struggle in Angola (in compliance with a decision of the OAU demanding that no foreign powers should help any of the three rival Angolan movements), the Chinese saw their bitter enemy, the Soviets, score a major diplomatic victory.

In fact, as I have argued elsewhere,* the primary reason (though not the only one) for the Soviet Union's decision to intervene in Angola was determined less by a desire to undercut Western influence in Africa than by a wish to prevent the Chinese from playing a successful role in the subcontinent. Angola was another reminder of the important part that Sino-Soviet rivalry plays, especially in the Third World, in determining the respective foreign policies of the communist powers.

For Western Europe, their relative inactivity in Angola only emphasized the swiftness with which these recently dominant colonial powers were withdrawing from their former imperial concerns, at least insofar as military commitments are concerned.

*After Angola: The War Over Southern Africa (New York: Africana Publishers, and London: Rex Collings, 1976).

For Africans—at least for the majority of their leaders—Angola rekindled anxieties about the ease with which major powers could intervene when they chose in Africa's internal affairs. Their Monroe-like doctrine of "Hands off Africa" was severely jolted. The OAU found itself divided exactly in half in its response to the Soviet/Cuban intervention, a result produced only because of the South African army's intervention on the side opposed to that supported by Moscow and Havana. For most Africans, white South Africa represents the greater danger in the continent because of their own commitments to the unfinished revolution.

And for the United States, or at least for President Ford's administration, the Angolan episode represented a setback to American and Western power and international interests. The reaction of the administration was colored even more by the fact of the Cubans' role than by that of the Soviets.

Nevertheless, it was the upset in Angola that launched Washington on a new course. It led to Kissinger's discovery of the importance of Africa. Making his first official visit to Africa, in April 1976, he announced:

> I have come to Africa because in so many ways the challenges of Africa are the challenges of the modern era. Morally and politically, the drama of national independence in Africa over the last generation, has transformed international affairs.

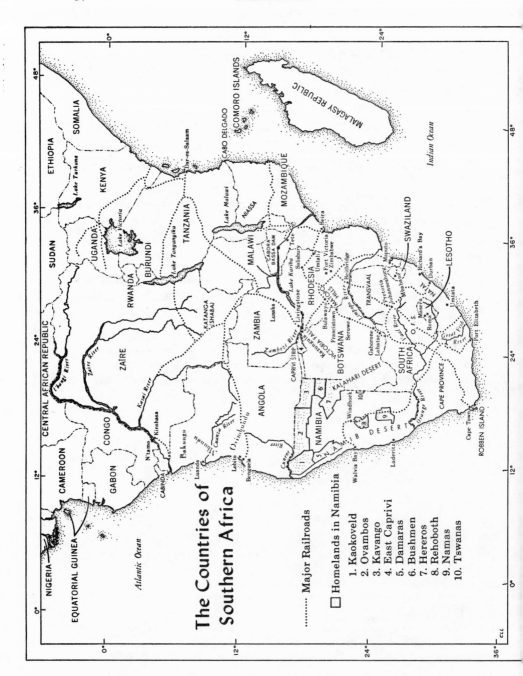

The Countries of Southern Africa

.... Major Railroads

☐ Homelands in Namibia

1. Kaokoveld
2. Ovambos
3. Kavango
4. East Caprivi
5. Damaras
6. Bushmen
7. Hereros
8. Rehoboth
9. Namas
10. Tswanas

[1]

Rhodesia

From White Rule to Independent Zimbabwe

PATRICK O'MEARA

ON SEPTEMBER 24, 1976, Prime Minister Ian Smith conceded the necessity of moving Rhodesia to majority rule and thus in effect might have
opened the way for the establishment of the new state of Zimbabwe. A small
body of whites, never totaling more than five percent of the population, has
controlled this large and well-endowed country from 1890. Rhodesian society has been polarized between a powerful white minority and an African
majority that has been virtually excluded from effective political participation. For whites, Rhodesia has proved to be a country of privilege and ease,
while for Africans it has been one of subservience and frustration. White
settlers displaced African institutions and replaced them with a modern
state in which Africans provided cheap labor and were separated from the
white community either in reserves or in specially defined sections of the
urban areas.

On November 11, 1965, Rhodesia declared itself independent because
Great Britain was unwilling to grant it independence unless significant
political rights, leading to majority rule, were extended to Africans. The

white Rhodesian government has never received international recognition, not even from South Africa, and has been beleaguered by sanctions organized by the United Nations at Britain's request, demands for an acceptable constitutional settlement, and escalating guerrilla warfare.

From the 1920s African nationalist movements have unsuccessfully attempted to secure changes in discriminatory legislation, to obtain better allocation of land, and to gain a fair share of an economy designed by the dominant white minority. It was not until after the Portuguese coup in April 1974, and the ensuing independence of Mozambique and Angola, that nationalist pressures in the form of guerrilla raids from both Mozambique and Zambia placed white supremacy in jeopardy. Africans have never been reconciled to their subordinate position in a country in which they are the overwhelming majority. The current crisis in Rhodesia is not of recent origin but has been evolving and increasing in intensity over much of the past half century. Today the major obstacle to the achievement of a settlement remains the central contradiction of safeguarding entrenched white interests while at the same time providing opportunities for full African political participation.

In 1976 the intervention of Prime Minister B. John Vorster of South Africa, whose country controls the rail lines by which Rhodesia reaches the outside world, and the United States secretary of state, Henry Kissinger, led to Ian Smith's historic announcement.

How has this small white population remained in power for so long? By what means has it excluded Africans? How have Africans responded to their predicament? At what point and under what conditions will Rhodesia be transformed into the independent nation of Zimbabwe? The answers to these questions must be sought in history. Part of that history is embedded in the Zimbabwe ruins near Fort Victoria, whose size and form indicate a high level of African civilization. It is not without reason that the two major African nationalist movements in Rhodesia named themselves Zimbabwe African People's Union (ZAPU) and Zimbabwe African National Union (ZANU), and that Africans have chosen the name Zimbabwe for their country when it achieves majority rule and independence. The whites, in contrast, named the land they entered in 1890 after Cecil Rhodes, then

Prime Minister of the Cape and an economic and political entrepreneur in Southern Africa. The distinction between these two names is itself a commentary on the history of the past eighty-six years.

THE ARRIVAL OF THE WHITES

Cecil Rhodes first began to make plans for opening up the region in 1878, but he did not feel it was time for him to act until 1888, after Portugal's claim in 1887 to all of the interior between Angola and Mozambique. He was motivated by a combination of personal gain, the advancement of the British empire, and the pressures of the Portuguese. Rhodes's agents immediately attempted to obtain treaties from Lobengula, the king of the Ndebele, one of the major ethnic groups in the area. The Rudd mineral concession granted by Lobengula in 1888, though later repudiated by him, gave Rhodes a monopoly of the mineral rights in Lobengula's kingdom. A year later Cecil Rhodes and his associates obtained a royal charter to form the British South Africa Company (BSA). The charter authorized the company "to settle and administer [an area] immediately to the north of the South African Republic and west of the Portguese Dominions." A deeply disturbed Lobengula wrote to Queen Victoria on August 10, 1889: "The white people are troubling much about gold. If you have heard that I have given my whole country to Rhodes, it is not my words. I have not done so, Rhodes wants to take my country by strength."

In 1890 a pioneer column consisting of two hundred settlers and five hundred police reached the site of the future capital of Rhodesia, Fort Salisbury. This occupation by white settlers marks the beginning of the period of sustained conflict between black and white. The Ndebele rebelled against white rule and were defeated in 1893. In 1896 they rebelled again and were once again defeated. Lobengula had fled after the first defeat and subsequently died; to prevent the reemergence of a strong centralized Ndebele state the company refused to recognize any successor in his place. Acting independently of the Ndebele, the Shona, the most numerous ethnic group in the area, also rebelled and were defeated between 1896 and 1897. By 1904 there were 12,000 settlers in Rhodesia and by 1911, 24,000—most of whom were primarily engaged in one form of agriculture or another. For the first fifteen years of its rule the British South Africa Company expected that enough gold would be found to justify its large investment for administration and development. But the company had overestimated the wealth of central Africa, which was far from being a second great gold reef as the Witwatersrand in South Africa, and obtained little profit from its struggling settlement. In addition there were frequent disputes with the settlers, who felt that their interests were kept secondary to company profits. Nonetheless, when the twenty-five-year term of the British South Africa Company's charter expired in 1914, the settlers chose to support the continuation of charter rule for another ten years rather than to join the newly established Union of South Africa or to press for self-government.

In 1921 a royal commission, the Buxton Commission, was appointed to look into the possibility of responsible government and a new constitution for Rhodesia. It suggested that a referendum should be held among the whites on whether there should be continuation of British South Africa Company rule, union with South Africa, or self-government. There was much to be said for the incorporation of Southern Rhodesia into the Union of South Africa. Rhodesia had been colonized from the south; both shared the same legal system based on Roman-Dutch Law; and there was a continuous railway line between the two countries. Fearing too close an alliance with the Afrikaners of South Africa, a small majority of the whites, 59.4 percent from a total of 14,763 votes, favored self-government.

Company rule was dissolved and Rhodesia was formally annexed to the British Crown. From this point on, its constitutional status was the ambiguous one of a self-governing colony, governed in effect by a white minority.

Under the 1923 constitution, a Crown-appointed governor acted on the advice of the Rhodesian ministers except in regard to certain legislation pertaining to the "indigenous population," over which the British retained a veto. The British had power only to prohibit openly discriminatory legislation but because of this Rhodesians had to exercise restraint. The existence of the reserve powers maintained the nonracial character of the electoral roll, however, and preserved limited individual freedoms in Rhodesia.

The character of white society had been shaped by several factors: the settlers' struggle against a hostile environment; their conflict with the Ndebele and Shona; their fight for political self-determination; and the fact that

African interests were not to be primary in the development of the area. The early conflict situation was replaced by a form of paternalism in which the African was invariably the servant rather than the master, the employee rather than the employer, and thus Rhodesia could be referred to as a composite society only in economic terms.

Although Rhodesia decided not to join South Africa in 1923, South African influences have been important. Afrikaners remain a unified and significant pressure group in a predominantly English-speaking country, and they are strongly opposed to policies of African advancement.

By the late 1930s, Godfrey Huggins (later Lord Malvern) and his United Party, which ruled from 1933 to 1956, had evolved a "double pyramid" policy that stressed the separate development of whites and blacks, who were to have an ultimate meeting at a distant future on the national level. By the late 1940s, Huggins had moved away from the "double pyramid" policy although many of its principles remained in Rhodesian thought and political action. In pursuance of this policy the government established separate areas for development of the different racial groups. The Land Apportionment Act of 1930 (recommended by the Morris Carter Commission) excluded Africans from permanent rights to land in European areas and reserved less than half of the colony's land for Africans. The 1923 constitution had set aside close to twenty-one million acres for African use and occupation; the most favorable land was set aside for white use. The Industrial Conciliation Act of 1934 created a color bar to entering skilled employment.

As early as 1924 the possibility of some form of political union between Northern and Southern Rhodesia and Nyasaland had been discussed. It was felt that association would not only bring together cheap labor from Nyasaland, minerals from Northern Rhodesia, and technical skill and capital from Southern Rhodesia, but that it would also consolidate the small white populations in these countries. The Hilton-Young Commission of 1929, which investigated the possibility of closer relations, however, stressed "the paramountcy of native interests." A conference held between Northern and Southern Rhodesia at Victoria Falls in 1935 requested the appointment of a commission to study the possibility of amalgamation "in principle," but despite serious consideration no action was taken on the matter because the conference felt that the discriminatory policies of Southern Rhodesia would clash with Britain's commitment to Africans in Northern Rhodesia and Nyasaland.

Shortly before the end of World War II, Huggins once again took up the idea of federation. Despite opposition to amalgamation by white Southern Rhodesians, who feared that the greatly increased proportion of Africans to whites in such a federation might bring about "the Gold Coast ideas" of African domination, there had been a subtle change in white Rhodesian thinking. Economic development and urbanization made complete separation less attractive for Rhodesians. The growing interdependence of black and white necessarily modified the "two-pyramid" scheme. In essence, while political control had to remain in white hands, black-white interaction on an economic and a limited social level was acceptable.

The Central African Federation came into being in 1953 as a result of urging by whites in both Southern and Northern Rhodesia and the compliance of the British Conservative government. But as the decade moved on, the rate of progress toward multiracialism both in the Federation and in Southern Rhodesia became an issue of concern to the latter's whites. The key word in the political vocabulary of the Federation was "partnership." For the British government it implied ultimate equality for the Africans. For Huggins, who called it "a very blessed word," it was the "partnership of the [black] horse and the [white] rider." For most Africans it meant a still uncertain future.

THE ISSUE OF THE FRANCHISE IN SOUTHERN RHODESIA

In the Southern Rhodesian political sphere, Huggins' move into federal politics in 1953 resulted in the election of a new prime minister, Garfield Todd, a former missionary from New Zealand. The Southern Rhodesian political system had been white-dominated from 1924 to 1957, with inputs and outputs primarily determined by and for the interests of the white minority. In terms of party politics, Southern Rhodesia was clearly a one-party system. Todd introduced limited reforms while prime minister. In particular in 1956 he appointed Sir Robert Tredgold to head a commission to reconsider the question of franchise rights, a key issue for political power. In 1958 Todd supported a revised franchise that involved the voter registration of all male Africans with ten years of education.

When Southern Rhodesia had been granted a form of representative government in 1898, Proclamation 17 contained the color-blind franchise taken from the Cape under which the same qualifications applied equally to white and black. In practice the qualifications excluded most Africans. By 1911 there were only fifty-one Africans on the voters' roll. In 1912 the qualifications were raised: a voter had to fill out the whole claim form himself and, if asked to do so, had to write fifty words of English dictation. The minimum property ownership was raised to £150 and the minimum annual wage to £100. The 1923 constitution made no changes in the franchise. In 1928, however, the dictation clause was removed, possibly because of the increase in the number of white immigrants from Europe, but the financial restrictions were sufficient to exclude most Africans. In 1951 the means requirement was increased to an income of £240 per annum and occupation of property valued at not less than £500. The prospective voter also had to be able to complete and sign the necessary forms and speak and write in English.

Partly because of the revised franchise, though more specifically because of personality differences with his cabinet, Todd was replaced by Sir Edgar Whitehead after a special party congress in February 1958. Todd remains a controversial figure in Rhodesian politics; while he tried to introduce some significant reforms, he was at the same time responsible for repressive legislation such as the Public Order Act. Sir Edgar Whitehead became prime minister of Rhodesia at the time when the federal structure was breaking up.

In 1961 Whitehead introduced a new constitution for Rhodesia. It was proposed in an effort to appease African discontent and in an attempt to clarify Rhodesia's constitutional problems. The 1961 constitution introduced a dual-roll voting system instead of a common roll. Voters with higher qualifications were placed on an A roll and those with lower qualifications went on a B roll. Most whites were on the A roll but the majority of Africans were eligible only for the B roll. Franchise proposals formulated on numerous occasions, such as these A and B voters' rolls, with differing weight attached to African and white votes cast, were either efforts to appease Britain or to pacify African discontent and always fell far short of providing full African political participation.

AFRICAN NATIONALIST RESPONSES

African nationalist movements had long operated within the political system and tried to bring about reforms on a constitutional basis. However, since the white establishment was reluctant to broaden its bases of support so as to include Africans, a rigid and permanent dichotomy developed over time. Not only was the white power structure unwilling to permit increased African participation, but it also limited channels of protest and opportunities for political mobilization. Ultimately, therefore, the nationalists moved outside of what they saw as a restricted political system.

One of the earliest African organizations, the Rhodesian Native Association (RNA), concentrated its activities in Mashonaland. It operated on behalf of an educated elite, and it was concerned with constitutional politics. Indeed, in 1920 even the chief native commissioner saw it as a "reputable organization." The RNA was concerned with obtaining "certificates of exemption" to free educated Africans from the operation of the pass laws, which obligated all male Africans over the age of fourteen to carry registration certificates, and it also planned to send a delegation to interview General J. C. Smuts, the prime minister of South Africa, and to oppose the incorporation of Rhodesia into the Union; its leaders were anxious to see a continued British presence and were against links with South Africa.

Like the RNA, the Rhodesia Bantu Voters' Association (RBVA), founded in July 1923 under the chairmanship of Ernest Dube, saw itself operating in order to change rather than to supplant the political system. These associations were run by and appealed to the new African elite, who were greatly concerned to gain from the whites social recognition as "advanced natives" in contrast to the "uneducated masses."

In the 1940s African nationalist activities began to take the form of party politics for the first time; the Reverend T. D. Samkange assumed the leadership of what has now come to be known as "the old ANC"—the old African National Congress—which sought the repeal of discriminatory legislation, such as the pass laws, but had limited success in achieving its ends.

In Rhodesia, as in other parts of Africa, World War II led to increased African urbanization and an expanded African political consciousness. The British African Voice Association was formed in 1947, and until it was banned in 1952, it was led by Benjamin Burumbo. The organization operated mainly in the urban centers of Salisbury and Bulawayo and conceived of itself in constitutional terms, focusing on the social, economic, and industrial needs of Africans. It saw itself as an intermediary between the white government and the Africans.

In the early 1950s powerful labor movements dominated African politics, especially the Reformed Industrial Council of Unions (RICU) under the leadership of Charles Mzingeli. Joshua Nkomo, currently the leader of ZAPU, was at the time general secretary of another union, the Railway African Workers Union. The African Teachers' Association had members such as Ndabaningi Sithole, who was to become the original leader of ZANU; Robert Mugabe, currently the leader of ZANU and highly respected by the guerrillas; and Leopold Takawira. Ultimately the union movements failed because the white power structure refused to participate in any form of bargaining with them and used force whenever they felt the movements were going beyond defined limits.

In August 1955 the Youth League (YL) was established by Edson Sithole, with James Chikerema as president. At first it planned to infiltrate secretly into urban and rural areas, but George Nyandoro of the Capricorn Africa Society advocated mass activities to bring pressure on the government. A mass bus boycott in Harare Township in Salisbury was successful. On September 12, 1957, the leaders of the Youth League called a meeting of organized African political groups. As a result of this meeting, a new African National Congress (ANC) was born under the leadership of Joshua Nkomo. It emphasized a nonracial political philosophy and white Rhodesians were welcome to join. The ANC operated in both urban and rural areas and was particularly successful in mobilizing African farmers in 1959 against the Native Land Husbandry Act in what it referred to as "Operation Sunrise." The act ran contrary to the concept of communal ownership and to the status of cattle within traditional society.

Sir Edgar Whitehead banned the ANC in February 1959 because of its potentially strong rural base. The ANC had provided a means of political expression and marked the beginning of a process of mass political education for Rhodesian Africans. Sir Edgar Whitehead maintained that while he could imagine an African political party that showed no trace of extremism, he felt as soon as it became nationalist it would almost inevitably become militant.

On January 1, 1960, Michael Mawema formed the National Democratic Party (NDP); it was essentially the ANC under a new name. According to Mawema, the NDP sought majority rule, higher wages for Africans, land for people displaced by the Native Land Husbandry Act, facilities for the education of African children, and better housing in the urban areas. The NDP had to operate under severe disadvantages: its members were forbidden to organize in the rural areas, mass meetings were discouraged by different municipalities, members of the executive were harassed by both the police and the provisions of the Law and Order (Maintenance) Act. African leaders were beginning to realize that none of the reforms for which they were pressing, particularly majority rule, could be achieved without real political power and that as long as the white minority had control of the sources of power, they could not achieve their ends. In December 1961 the National Democratic Party was reorganized as the Zimbabwe African People's Union (ZAPU) under the leadership of Joshua Nkomo.

THE BREAKUP OF THE FEDERATION

In 1960 the Monckton Commission held that no form of association between the three territories was likely to succeed unless Rhodesia was willing to make drastic changes in its racial policies. The recommendation of the Monckton Commission was simply that Rhodesia was to put its constitutional house in order before the dissolution of the federation. The right-wing Dominion Party in Rhodesia rejected further black-white compromises and renewed its demands for secession from the federation and for Dominion status, essentially independence, for Rhodesia alone.

Meetings between the Rhodesian government, the British government, and the nationalists took place in February 1961. At first they resulted in an agreement on the new constitutional proposals, but after consulting with members of the National Democratic Party executive, Joshua Nkomo, its leader, withdrew his support and the NDP decided not to participate in the October election. The nationalists felt that the 1961 constitution, with its emphasis on income and educational franchise qualifications, made it impossible for Africans to achieve majority rule for a great number of years, if ever; only about 608,000 of Southern Rhodesia's approximately 3,970,000 Africans were in paid employment in 1963, even less than the 622,000 in mid-1962. The average African wage in 1964 was $315 a year, while the average white wage was approximately $3,300. Current average earnings for whites are $8,278 and for Africans, $758.

The Dominion Party, at this time led by William Harper, saw itself as a white party holding back the African threat. Several African nations were becoming independent and white refugees were entering Rhodesia from the Congo. Thus the Dominion Party felt that the future of white civilization depended on the result of the 1961 referendum. Harper was particularly opposed to the presence of African members in the Rhodesian Parliament and the possibility of African cabinet ministers. Sir Edgar Whitehead had proposed that if he won the election, there would be one African cabinet minister, and by the following election, possibly between three and six such ministers. Harper maintained that "to have Africans in this House at this stage is going to damage the structure of European tenure in this country. Whether one likes it or not, European tenure is sensitive to the fact that the African has not proved his case to take part in the administration of the country as a whole." Harper thus voiced the more obvious aspects of Rhodesian intolerance. Whitehead's UFP lost the 1962 election because of the controversy surrounding the new constitution and because of African opposition to the proposals.

In 1963 the Rhodesian Front Party (RF) came to power. This was the year of the breakup of the Central African Federation, and the grant of independence to Nyasaland (as Malawi) and Northern Rhodesia (as Zambia) was soon to be made. The ideology of the Rhodesian Front Party made any form of direct cooperation with black governments impossible. It also saw itself holding the line against "communist infiltration" down the African continent. Southern Rhodesia had benefited considerably from the federation, but the costs for the continued alliance were considered too high, leaving aside the question of whether or not the new black governments themselves wanted to continue the federation. The breakup resulted in Southern Rhodesia's receiving many of the benefits of the federation; for example, all federal military equipment was returned to it. The demise of the federation ushered in the new era of white extremism in Rhodesia.

RHODESIA'S BID FOR INDEPENDENCE

One of the first acts of the new Rhodesian prime minister, Winston Field, was to take up negotiations with the British Labour prime minister, Harold Wilson, on the future status of Rhodesia and in particular on the question of independence. British conditions for granting independence were enumerated in five principles—the NIBMAR Principles: No Independence Before Majority African Rule—which were to become the stumbling block to all future negotiations. They included the principle of unimpeded progress toward majority rule, guarantees against retrogressive amendments to the constitution to retard African advancement, an increase in African political representation, and an end to racial discrimination.

Within the year Winston Field had been eased out as prime minister. In a prepared statement Field said that "serious disagreements had arisen" and Ian Smith was in power, summoning the "Spirit of '96"—1896, the year in which the pioneers had defeated the Ndebele. The main obstacle to independence was the British Labour government, which had been elected in October 1964. White Rhodesians had long been suspicious of the British Labour Party, particularly because in the 1930s Labour had fostered the concept of "the paramountcy of native interests," which Rhodesians regarded as a betrayal. With Smith as prime minister, a Unilateral Declaration of Independence became a definite possibility. There were many, including Sir Edgar Whitehead, who were alarmed at the prospect of such a drastic step and who stressed the economic isolation that might follow such a declaration; even South Africa cautioned against UDI.

A referendum on the question of a declaration of independence based on the 1961 constitution gave Ian Smith a majority of 89 percent, and in a general election in May 1965 the Rhodesian Front Party won all fifty A-roll seats. White opposition parties, such as the Rhodesia Party and later the Centre Party, were only to play a minor role in Rhodesian politics. Smith now had a solid public support for leverage in negotiating with Britain. Following the 1965 election Whitehead's party was eliminated. However, Africans elected to the Legislative Assembly on the B roll came together to form the United People's Party—thirteen parliamentarians elected with a total of less than eight hundred votes.

With the backing of a party highly organized at the grass-roots level, which had won national elections in 1962 and in 1965, Ian Smith felt confident in pursuing a UDI. He countered the British NIBMAR Principles with five of his own. They included a statement on Rhodesia's unwillingness to accept the principle of unimpeded progress toward majority rule. On November 11, 1965, Rhodesia declared itself independent.

Britain's immediate response to the UDI was to declare the Rhodesian actions void and to ask the Commonwealth to help suppress the revolution. In addition the foreign secretary, Michael Stewart, flew to New York on November 12, the day after UDI, and addressed the Security Council. The Council decided to condemn UDI. It called on states not to recognize the illegal Smith regime and required all member states to impose selective economic sanctions, which prohibited investment or transfer of funds to Rhodesia.

Britain incorrectly assumed that there would be significant internal opposition among both Africans and whites toward the Rhodesian Front Party and a UDI, and that sanctions would force white Rhodesians to accept British terms for independence. The immediate effect of sanctions on Rhodesia caused a lack of oil, financial difficulties as a result of foreign exchange controls, restrictions on imports, and travel difficulties for Rhodesian citizens; tobacco was, perhaps, the hardest hit industry.

In efforts to resolve the Rhodesian crisis, Harold Wilson met Ian Smith in 1966 on the H.M.S. *Tiger* and again in 1968 on the H.M.S. *Fearless.* Although the two prime ministers arrived at working documents, the constitutional crisis was not settled. It appeared that Smith's mandate to negotiate was limited, and once he referred the proposals back to the Rhodesian Front, they were rejected even though the terms of the agreement by no means sought majority rule but were variations on the 1961 constitution. It is now apparent that in these efforts Smith was playing a diplomatic game in order to buy time.

A new constitution, accepted in a referendum in June 1969 with 54,724 votes in favor and 20,776 against, reinforced a segregated society in which the possibility of majority rule was all but eliminated. On March 1, 1970, Rhodesia declared itself a republic, claiming to end its "80-year link with the British Crown." The Land Tenure Act of 1969 redivided Rhodesia into two parts: 45 million acres for Africans and 45 million for whites. The 1961 constitution had set up tribal trust lands which expanded the reserves by 19 million acres. By the end of 1966, tribal trust lands were 40,020,000 acres of a total Rhodesian area of 96,600,000 acres.

Under the 1969 constitution there were to be ten chiefs elected by the National Council of Chiefs to the Rhodesian Senate. The chiefs have mainly provided some legitimacy for the preexisting government policy or served in ceremonial roles. Although chiefs differ in power, influence, and authority, it can be said that Rhodesian chiefs rarely tend to be political or social innovators; that they owe their allegiance to the white power structure which ratifies their appointments and pays their salaries; and that they have alienated large numbers of their traditional supporters.

ZAPU VERSUS *ZANU:* THE NATIONALISTS SPLIT

While white politicians were seeking to perpetuate white rule, the African nationalists were seriously divided. Shortly after the banning of ZAPU in 1963, Nkomo decided that because of increasing limitations placed on nationalist activities, a government-in-exile would be more effective, and he therefore moved the ZAPU executive to Dar es Salaam. This move from Rhodesia antagonized some members of the party executive who felt that the struggle should be in Rhodesia. In July leaflets were circulated in Highfield suggesting the need for a new party. On August 9, 1963, Ndabaningi Sithole announced the formation of the Zimbabwe African National Union (ZANU) and was joined by Leopold Takawira, Morton Malianga, Robert Mugabe, and others. ZANU's aims included the establishment of a nationalist, democratic, socialist, and Pan-Africanist republic; adult suffrage; repeal of all color discrimination and repressive laws; national control of all land with the government as the people's trustee; amnesty for all political prisoners; free health service and unemployment relief; and compulsory secondary education to the level of form two.

ZANU attracted African intellectuals and aimed at "a grass-roots alliance organization of peasants, peasant farmers, businessmen, students, the chiefs and headmen and the professional men and women." Nkomo, nevertheless, still retained mass support because of his remarkable ability to reorganize ZAPU (the permanent staff of ZAPU remained loyal to him) and on his ability to draw large crowds of followers. The intensity and depth of ethnic divisions is hard to gauge; the executives of both organizations are not strictly divided along ethnic lines, but constituencies tend toward such a division. ZAPU operates out of Bulawayo, an Ndebele stronghold, and ZANU has a substantial Shona membership. Further, as part of their policy of divide and rule, white Rhodesians have deliberately promoted the dangers of ethnic conflict. Distrust does exist between ethnic groups, but it is simply not comparable to the Nigerian situation, which resulted in the Biafran civil war. Many ZAPU supporters were concerned about the split because they felt that African unity was essential, and they tried to avoid this first major division in African politics. Although the split was based on personality differences, it also marked the beginning of a new phase; the key issues of where the struggle was to be waged (whether within Rhodesia or from outside), the quality of leadership, and the nature of ideology, can be seen as a prelude to subsequent guerrilla activities. The tensions between ZANU and ZAPU continued when these organizations were forced to operate from outside of Rhodesia despite several efforts to bring them together.

In November 1963 Nkomo was banned from attending all meetings for three months and the People's Caretaker Council (PCC), which was a short-term replacement for ZAPU, was banned from organizing meetings. In February 1964 more than one hundred nationalists were restricted to Wha Wha. In March the Law and Order (Maintenance) Act was amended so as to extend detention without trial from ninety days to one year. In April, shortly after Ian Smith became prime minister, Nkomo, Msika, and Josiah Chinamano of the PCC executive were restricted to a remote area, Gonakudzingwa. Subsequently other leaders of both the PCC and ZANU were placed in restriction or detention. Lusaka now became the base from which the PCC and ZANU began to plan and execute guerrilla activities.

From 1965 some Africans participated in parliamentary opposition parties such as the United People's Party, the National People's Union, and the Centre Party. They operated strictly within the political system and their members were rejected by the nationalists.

In 1971 the Front for the Liberation of Zimbabwe (FROLIZI) was formed in an effort to inspire the young with a new spirit of resistance and to form a new military fighting force. The executive of FROLIZI included Shelton Siwela, James Chikerema, George Nyandoro, and Nathan Shamuyarira. FROLIZI supporters were to be absorbed into ZAPU, and later many of its leaders backed the Muzorewa wing of the African National Council.

A new generation of Africans eager to shift the emphasis from the political sphere to guerrilla warfare was becoming involved. With a predominant Shona membership, ZANU operated in an area where it was possible for guerrillas to hide in the villages and merge into the local environment. In 1973 there were successful combined efforts by ZANU and Frelimo (Front for the Liberation of Mozambique), especially in the northeastern part of the country.

THE PEARCE COMMISSION AND THE AFRICAN
NATIONAL COUNCIL

By the end of 1971 Rhodesia had survived six years of UDI. It had a declining export market, a shortage of skilled labor, and a dearth of foreign exchange. The presence of a Conservative government in Britain led to a new round of negotiations with a British representative, Lord Goodman. In addition, in 1971 the Byrd amendment permitted the United States to resume the importation of chrome, regarded as a strategic mineral despite a stockpile of 1.3 million tons. This was approved in the United States Senate and later in the House of Representatives. The United States thus broke the sanctions imposed by the U.N. Security Council in 1965, albeit on a limited basis, thereby giving the Rhodesian government the right to claim a breakthrough in sanctions at a strategic time in negotiations with Britain.

The agreement worked out by Lord Goodman and ratified by Sir Alec Douglas-Home included, on paper, electoral arrangements to produce an African parliamentary majority in the distant future. Rhodesia had to declare its intention to make progress toward ending racial discrimination and to accept a new declaration guaranteeing individual rights and freedoms. The proposals provided a complicated formula for a gradual increase in African political involvement and opened the way for a possible African government at some far distant future date. In December 1971 the British House of Commons approved the government's plan for a settlement in Rhodesia by a vote of 297 to 269. Sir Alec Douglas-Home told the House that "in conscience" he did not believe "better terms could have been negotiated" because he felt that "Britain's influence was running out." The terms were only in the form of a proposal, and everything now depended on the findings of a commission headed by Lord Pearce, formed to test opinion on the plan.

Analysis of the terms of the 1971 proposals indicated a considerable willingness on Great Britain's part to compromise. The proposed terms were far from the guarantees of the relatively liberal 1961 constitution, which permitted whites and blacks to register on a common roll under the same financial and educational qualifications and which promised eventual majority rule. Indeed, the accepted formula left the white government with considerable influence over African representatives, particularly since two of every four African seats were to go to traditional chiefs. The major concession Ian Smith made was to abandon his public commitment that Africans would never achieve more than parity in representation in Parliament, although this was to be at a distant time, and to allow at least some African voters to be registered on a common voters' roll with whites.

The presence of the Pearce Commission in Rhodesia in the early part of 1972 precipitated significant African political activity. African distrust and suspicion erupted because of the impending settlement; many Africans realized that a "yes" vote would lead to the entrenchment of the Smith regime and would end Britain's involvement in Rhodesian politics.

The African National Council (ANC) was formed in 1971 to mobilize African opposition to the proposals of the Pearce Commission. Bishop Abel Muzorewa, a bishop of the Methodist Church in Rhodesia, maintained that Great Britain was now merely consulting African opinion in order to give some form of respectability to an already concluded deal. The bishop thus perceived the founding of the organization as a result of spontaneous African concern in both urban and rural areas following the publication of the White Paper on the Pearce Commission. The primary thrust was to organize strong opposition to the Pearce Commission: "The Constitutional provisions are so full of reservations and escape clauses, the declaration of rights are so open to abuse, as to render the document meaningless. For every right there is a restriction which renders it void. The road to majority rule is boobytrapped every inch of the way."

The ANC of the 1950s had been an important mass movement, and the naming of the African National Council (ANC) was a conscious effort to recall the unified nationalist thrust before the split between ZANU and ZAPU. The ANC rejected a settlement with Britain on the proposed terms, attempted to fuse the followers of the two former nationalist organizations that were still operating outside the country, and planned to operate in both rural and urban areas to obtain African trade union support and the support of the African Christian churches.

Active participants in the ANC included several prominent African nationalists such as Eddison Zvobgo, formerly a member of ZANU; Edson Sithole, formerly a member of the ZANU executive; Josiah Chinamano, a former member of the ZAPU executive and a close adviser of Nkomo; and Michael Mawema and Simon Moyo, former members of ZANU.

Thus, the choice of the name African National Council, and in particular the abbreviation ANC, had obvious significance; the organizers intended it to act as a reminder of the long tradition of African nationalist politics, and specifically the African National Congress.

The Pearce Commission Report, released in May 1972, gave a clear "no" vote to the settlement proposals. Lord Pearce and the commissioners concluded that neither intimidation nor ignorance had made it impossible for Africans to form a judgment on the acceptability of the proposals. The commission reported that it was satisfied that the proposals were fully and properly explained to the people of Rhodesia and that those who gave an opinion had understood the terms well enough to enable them to pass judgment. From this point there was a recognition by African leaders that they were now an important and active political force in Rhodesia; Bishop Muzorewa emphasized that this was the first time in ten years that Africans had actively participated in the Rhodesian political process. Furthermore, the commission stated that far from being a country of placid politics, Rhodesia was in fact "alive with political activity at the grass roots."

A new era in nationalist Rhodesian politics opened in December 1974, when Nkomo, Sithole, and Muzorewa met with Ian Smith in a railway carriage on the bridge across the Zambezi, which links Rhodesia and Zambia. The nationalists entered the carriage from the Zambia end, and Smith and his party entered from the Rhodesian side. South Africa, keenly aware that the white redoubt was crumbling, had begun to play a bigger role in the Rhodesian issue, as had also the four front-line presidents of Tanzania, Zambia, Mozambique, and Botswana. Because of South African pressures Sithole had been released from prison and Nkomo from detention. Prime Minister Vorster had negotiated with President Kaunda to bring the meeting about; however, because of nationalist divisions and Smith's intransigence, the talks were unsuccessful. In September 1975 Nkomo's uneasy alliance with Muzorewa ended when Nkomo tried to take over the leadership of the ANC. Robert Mugabe, who had opposed ZANU joining the ANC in 1974, left Rhodesia for Mozambique in 1975 and after establishing close ties with the guerrillas became a spokesman for their operations.

1976—YEAR OF CRISIS

The year 1976 has proved to be a critical year in Rhodesia's history. It was marked by the escalation of guerrilla activities in rural areas, by attacks in white urban areas, and by pressures for settlement from the United States and South Africa with the effective backing of Britain and the other eight nations of the European community. The front-line presidents of Tanzania, Mozambique, Zambia, Botswana, and Angola also played a forceful role in fostering guerrilla activities and in delicate diplomatic negotiations. Guerrilla activity, which had centered on the northeastern part of Rhodesia, spread to the southeastern part of the country and along the border with Mozambique. It also became apparent that Zambia was permitting guerrillas to operate along its border with Rhodesia, and numerous instances of guerrilla activity in the south and west of the country indicated that the war zone had also spread to these areas.

The prime minister's office announced that the guerrilla war zone had almost doubled in size since the beginning of the year and that the escalation of the war had forced an increase of 60 percent in security forces, mainly from the call-up of civilians. The Rhodesian government also started to recruit army volunteers in the United States, Britain, France, and West Germany to supplement its armed forces. On Easter Sunday three South African motorcyclists were killed and one person was wounded by guerrillas who were mistaken for Rhodesian policemen on the road from Fort Victoria to Beitbridge on the South African border. This crucial road, eighty-five miles inland from Mozambique, is the main highway for tourists and for the transportation of gasoline and supplies from South Africa. On the same day guerrillas mined a section of the important rail link to South Africa at Rutenga. The state of emergency which had been in effect since November 1965 was renewed for another year. While no part of Rhodesia has ever been under guerrilla control, the civilian and military injuries and the loss of life from their activities have created considerable tension. Furthermore, according to the last government report, there were 680 political prisoners in Rhodesia.

National service for white school-leavers was extended from twelve to eighteen months and men between twenty-five and thirty-eight were liable for call-up for continuous service for eighty-four days. National service demands severely disrupted the business sector because of the small available pool of white manpower. This call-up not only has had a disruptive effect on the economy of Rhodesia, but has had a profound impact by making whites question whether Rhodesian society justifies such a sacrifice. The Rhodesian government introduced legislation under which Africans could be drafted into the armed services for the first time. Currently 60 percent of the army consists of African volunteers, including two battalions of the Rhodesian African Rifles. In addition, a sizable portion of the police force is black. Those Africans drafted into the army would not necessarily have to engage in combat but would release more whites to do so. Plans were also under way to train a selected group of Africans for combat positions, thus pitching blacks against blacks in a civil war situation.

The decision to reimpose censorship was another indication of the seriousness of the crisis; the Rhodesian Front government established a National Security Committee under the emergency powers regulations to prohibit the publication and broadcasting of news on defense, public safety, public order, or the economic interests of the state.

The 1976 budget tabled in the Rhodesian parliament by Finance Minister David Smith allocated $152 million for defense and security, an increase of 40 percent over 1975 and of almost 300 percent since the fighting began in 1972. A further $24 million for additional security spending during the year was also set aside. The police allocation was $63 million. Defense now replaced education as the second largest item of government expenditure. An important feature of the budget was the reduction of emigrant allowances from $8,000 to $1,600 and travel allowances from $700 to $440. The 10 percent war-tax, first imposed in 1975 on corporations and individuals, was also renewed.

By mid-1976 there were fifty "protected villages" in areas of guerrilla activity in Rhodesia and more than 100,000 Africans living in them. The first of these villages were set up in 1974, and more were established with the increase in the number of guerrillas crossing over the Mozambique border. The Rhodesian Government claimed that these stockaded villages with their strict curfew laws, registration of all persons over the age of thirteen, and control of everyone entering or leaving the camps protected Africans from guerrilla attacks. However, the government's main purpose was to prevent guerrillas from gaining a foothold among the African people and to separate them from vital bases of support, since many rural Africans had provided food, supplies, cover, and even new recruits. The International Committee of Jurists maintained that the villages were overcrowded, had poor sanitation facilities, were disruptive of traditional African culture, and caused considerable discontent.

In March, following an incident of "hot pursuit" by Rhodesian forces into Mozambique, President Samora Machel announced that he was closing the border with Rhodesia and that Rhodesian government property within Mozambique would be seized. Rhodesia lost one sixth of its railway rolling stock, worth about $46 million, and access to the port of Maputo (Lourenço Marques), which had once dealt with more than 80 percent of Rhodesia's foreign trade. Ian Smith maintained, however, that this dependence already had been reduced to 20 percent. All Rhodesian exports and imports now had to go through South Africa, thus making Rhodesia more vulnerable to South African pressures.

In August a large mechanized Rhodesian force penetrated twenty-five miles into Mozambique and raided a base camp again in hot pursuit of a group of combined guerrillas and Frelimo forces, which it maintained was responsible for killing five Rhodesian soldiers in a mortar attack across the border. The Rhodesians claimed that they killed more than three hundred guerrillas, thirty Frelimo soldiers, and ten civilians. A Mozambique source placed the deaths at 670. Investigation by the United Nations High Commission for Refugees maintained that the Rhodesians had destroyed a U.N. refugee camp and not a guerrilla base. The Rhodesian government, however, insisted that it had "irrefutable evidence" that the camp was a guerrilla base. The Rhodesians received world criticism for this action, which was regarded as rash and provocative; internally white Rhodesian extremists greeted it with enthusiasm.

The cumulative effect of the prevailing tensions resulted in the fact that for the first half of 1976 Rhodesia registered a net loss of 2,280 white emigrants compared to a net gain of 1,600 for the same period in 1975. A substantial number of Portuguese refugees from Mozambique are now resident in Rhodesia, but the number of these refugees that is reflected in the white population figures is not clear.

The "Third Force" (a term first used by President Julius Nyerere of Tanzania) based in Mozambique was responsible for the intensification of guerrilla operations in Rhodesia. In December 1974 the African National Council (ANC) became the umbrella organization for ZANU and ZAPU under the leadership of Bishop Muzorewa. ZANU, which was then under the leadership of the Reverend Ndabaningi Sithole, had received assistance from the Chinese, the Organization of African Unity, and Third World countries and was in the forefront of guerrilla activities; the Russians have supported ZAPU since before the split with ZANU. The Third Force has never been unified but remains essentially divided along ZANU-ZAPU lines; all attempts to fuse these differences have had only limited success. ZAPU is the smaller of the two with approximately one thousand fighters and operates mainly out of Tanzania, while ZANU, with between five and ten thousand guerrillas or new recruits in training, operates from camps in Mozambique and from a camp in Tanzania. The Reverend Sithole was expelled as leader of ZANU in 1976 but remained on the executive of the external wing of the ANC. Robert Mugabe emerged as the effective leader of ZANU.

At first the Third Force, now known as the Zimbabwe Independence People's Army (ZIPA) was controlled by an eighteen-man committee, nine members from ZANU and nine from ZAPU. The biggest faction of guerrillas was from ZANU and outnumber ZAPU forces by possibly as many as ten to one. A division arose between Nkomo, Sithole, and Bishop Muzorewa, who were seen as the politicians, and the High Command of ZIPA, i.e., the young leaders directly involved in the fighting. The High Command leaders included Sclomon Mutuswa (Rex) Nhongo, formerly of ZAPU but who joined ZANU forces, Albert (Nikita) Mangena, Joseph Taderera, who has a doctorate in chemistry from the University of Wisconsin, and Josiah Tongogara, who had been trained in China, fought with Frelimo forces in the 1960s, and became supreme military commander of ZANU forces. Tongogara faced charges in Zambia for involvement in the murder of Herbert Chitepo. On October 16 Mukudzei Mudzi, Kumbirai Kangai, Rugare Gumba, and Henry Hamadziripi, all members of the Supreme Council (also known as DARE) and also charged with the murder, were released. Nhongo was acting commander-in-chief until the outcome of the Tongogara case was known. Robert Mugabe, a former member of the ANC executive and general secretary of ZANU, has maintained close contact with ZIPA and appears to be one of the few political leaders now trusted by the guerrillas.

Constitutional talks between the Rhodesian government and the Nkomo faction of the ANC, which began in December 1975, broke down in March 1976. Joshua Nkomo insisted on majority rule within a year or two, while the Smith proposals would have delayed this for ten to fifteen years. On March 20 Smith called for the British Government once again to play a role in constitutional negotiations. However, he rejected subsequent British proposals for legitimizing Rhodesia's independence based on African majority rule. The British plan, announced by Foreign Secretary James Callaghan, called for African rule within two years, aid for whites who wanted to resettle, and British help in drafting an election plan to precede formal independence.

In April, in yet another effort to incorporate acceptable Africans into political positions without diminishing white control, Ian Smith increased the Rhodesian Cabinet of seventeen whites by the addition of ten Africans, four full ministers, and six deputy ministers (three appointed immediately and three more to be added at a future date). The four full ministers were all chiefs on the government payroll. The government maintained that all the ministers would be representatives of the African people; however, the African National Council maintained that they were "puppets" who had "sold out" and that their presence did not in any way alter the constitutional crisis. After the breakdown of the constitutional negotiations the Rhodesian Front Government put forward a plan to establish three regional authorities, one for the Mashona, one for the Ndebele, and a third for the whites. While recognizing that the country was integrated on an economic level, this "regionalization" plan would aim to give a measure of control of their own affairs to each of the groups involved. It was thus a modified version of the South African policy of separate development.

The Commission of Inquiry into Racial Discrimination, under the chairmanship of former Supreme Court Judge Sir Vincent Quenet, published its findings on June 14. The commission proposed significant reforms: for example, changes in the Land Tenure Act that would enable Africans to own farms in white areas and to purchase urban commercial and industrial land, the institution of a nonracial common voters' roll, and a provision to allow the Declaration of Rights to be contestable in the courts. Because of substantial pressure from white conservatives, all of the major proposals of the commission were rejected by Ian Smith in July. There was, however, agreement to open hotels, bars, restaurants, and some new categories of jobs for Africans. Smith at this point was again merely experimenting within given modes rather than attempting dynamic changes. As late as August 1976 he maintained that majority rule had been the "ultimate goal" of Rhodesian constitutions since 1923, but there could be no such thing as a timetable for transition since it could be measured only by achievement, "not by clock or calendar."

The arrival in the fall of 1975 of Soviet arms and Cuban forces in Angola led to an increased interest in Southern Africa by the United States secretary of state. In March 1976 Henry Kissinger warned Cuba against possible intervention in Rhodesia. In April, in an important policy statement issued in Lusaka, Zambia, he said that the United States was wholly committed to a rapid, just, and African solution in Rhodesia. This marked a crucial shift in United States policy from option two of National Security Study Memorandum 39. Included in his ten-point program was an endorsement of British proposals for majority rule and the transfer of political power to Africans within two years. Kissinger also said that he would ask South Africa to use its influence to promote a negotiated settlement. In addition he promised that the Ford Administration would again urge Congress to repeal the Byrd amendment. Kissinger emphasized that the United States had no plans to give military aid to the African nationalists but help would be given to neighboring countries whose economies would suffer if they enforced U.N. sanctions. American travelers were warned against entering Rhodesia because the United States Government would not be in a position to guarantee protection, and remaining U.S. businesses in Rhodesia were urged to end their operations. He also stated that educational, technical, and economic assistance would be given to an independent Zimbabwe.

While in Africa the secretary of state met with two of the five front-line presidents, Julius Nyerere of Tanzania and Kenneth Kaunda of Zambia, and also ANC leader Joshua Nkomo. Bishop Muzorewa of the ANC, however, refused to meet him. The secretary of state met with South African Prime Minister John Vorster in West Germany, June 23 and 24, and again in Zurich, Switzerland, September 4 and 5, in a continuing effort to resolve the Rhodesian and the Namibian crises. Kissinger described the U.S. involvement in these talks as an effort to avoid racial war in Southern Africa. Among the issues discussed was a plan that would provide economic compensation for whites who wanted to leave Rhodesia after a settlement, and higher economic incentives for those who chose to stay after independence. The largest part of the proposed fund, which was to be internationally raised and guaranteed, is intended to provide new capital investment to rebuild the Rhodesian economy. A similar "safety net" plan (guaranteeing white pensions and floor prices for land) had been instituted in Kenya under which 30,000 whites out of a total of 65,000 left by December 1963. The Kenyan program has cost more than $200 million and the Rhodesian scheme would cost between $1 and $2 billion. Britain, South Africa, the United States, Western nations, and large corporations doing business in the area would have to underwrite such guarantees. The idea for such a plan came originally from President Nyerere, but other Africans and some Western voices criticized the idea, seeing it in many ways as a reward for whites who had already benefited from life in Rhodesia.

In April, South Africa withdrew its 1,500 paramilitary police from Rhodesia and was now determined to stay out of the conflict between Rhodesia and the guerrillas. The thirty-four helicopters essential for antiguerrilla activities, however, were to remain on loan.

As a result of the historic meeting in Pretoria between Smith and Kissinger and the combined United States and South African pressures, Prime Minister Smith announced in September that Rhodesia would yield power to its African majority within two years. An interim government would be established composed of a Council of State consisting of two whites and two blacks, with a white serving as chairman (thus essentially giving whites a built-in veto), and a Council of Ministers. A new constitution would be written and the details would be worked out for the transition to African rule. The Council of State, according to Smith, would be supreme over the Council of Ministers, which would be predominantly African and which would have an African First Minister; however, whites would control the key ministries of Defense and of Law and Order. After consulting together on the details of the plan, the presidents of the front-line states rejected several of its terms. Indeed, it became readily apparent that Kissinger had made a tactical error by not fully informing them of crucial details such as the white control of the ministries. Furthermore, the nationalists maintained that they had never seen the agreement but had merely discussed it with the front-line presidents. Kissinger subsequently acknowledged that there was confusion because of the number of parties and delegations involved. Nonetheless, talks between Smith and the nationalists remained a possibility. The presidents, however, emphasized that guerrilla activities would continue. The British foreign secretary, Anthony Crosland, said that his government had agreed to convene a conference outside of Rhodesia, which it was hoped would lead to the establishment of a transitional government and which would be followed by a second phase that would involve the writing of a new constitution. Once a new constitution was in effect, international sanctions would be lifted. The conference was scheduled for October 25, 1976, in Geneva. The nationalists requested a two-week delay, but Britain was only willing to extend the date to October 28.

Nkomo and Mugabe formed a "patriotic front" before the Geneva meetings and agreed on a joint platform between ZANU and ZAPU. They saw
Smith as the common enemy and regarded themselves as political opponents able to unite for a common purpose; their working alliance had the
endorsement of the guerrillas. Mugabe insisted on the release of Tongogara
and of Joseph Chimurenga and Sadat Kafu Mazumba (who were awaiting
trial for the assassination of Herbert Chitepo). Sithole was invited and
subsequently appeared but as an outside figure without any real base of
support. Bishop Muzorewa had a strong and influential delegation and
appeared to have popular support in the Rhodesian urban area but no
guerrilla backing. The nationalists rejected the Kissinger package and insisted that they should deal directly with Britain, the colonial power, rather
than with Ian Smith. They were unwilling to compromise on the question
of the key ministries and considered the two-year transitional period too
long. During the talks there was a major new instance of "hot pursuit" by
Rhodesians across the Mozambique border—in response to increased guerrilla activities. A suggested nationalist formula for the transition period in
Rhodesia included a British high commissioner to head the transitional
government and control the ministries of Law and Order and Defense. In
Mozambique the transitional government had been led by a Portuguese
governor-general and Joaquim Chissano, and there were joint Frelimo-
Portuguese army commands. Britain was not eager to get involved in disputes that might develop between the movements, but it was open to the
possibility of a joint Commonwealth force.

Smith's motivation in agreeing to majority rule within two years is difficult to determine, particularly since he has so frequently stated that there
would be no majority rule in his lifetime. On one level he might have been
attempting to buy time. The rainy season in Rhodesia from October to
March has proved to be an optimal period for guerrilla activities, and in
1976 it might have been decisive. Indeed, Kissinger is said to have shown
Ian Smith three separate U.S. intelligence reports which indicated the weakness of the Rhodesian position and to have firmly stated that Rhodesia
could not look to the United States and South Africa for support. Smith
might also have gambled that divisions between the nationalists would lead
to the collapse of the talks, as had happened with the 1974 Victoria Falls

talks, or that there might be an African unwillingness to make concessions, as with Nkomo in 1975–76. Uneasy alliances between the nationalists had broken up before, and this could be yet another victory for Smith's politics of delay and division. Over the years Smith has acquired a reputation for backing out of agreements: for example, the *Tiger* talks in 1966 and the *Fearless* talks in 1968. Should the talks break down because of nationalist divisions, he would then expect support from South Africa and the United States and might even once again propose a constitutional scheme to incorporate more Africans (whom he and his government would find acceptable) into the political process.

On the other hand, Smith might at last have realized that effective power had slipped from white hands and that the time had come for some form of compromise. The balance of power in Southern Africa had shifted decisively against Rhodesia with the independence of Mozambique. Rhodesia was indeed a country at war with very little hope of ultimate victory. It was suffering from depletion of foreign exchange and from white emigration. Smith might have hoped to shape the situation sufficiently to ensure the empowerment of a moderate African regime. For whatever his purposes, he agreed to a new round of talks but insisted that the package deal with the secretary of state had to be fully adhered to. While there was some white backlash in Rhodesia (especially from conservatives to the right of the Rhodesian Front, from those who had lost members of their families or received injuries, and from last-ditchers imbued with a sense of white machismo), most whites recognized that there was a need for settlement.

South Africa continues to play a pivotal role in all negotiations. When the white redoubt ceased to have relevance with the coming of independence to Mozambique and Angola, South Africa, the richest and most powerful nation of the redoubt, was not only vulnerable but also aware of its vulnerability. Rhodesia was now almost totally dependent on South Africa for trans-shipment of its exports and imports and for military supplies, but South Africa in turn was growing increasingly disenchanted with the illegality of its neighbor. It also hoped that resolution of the problems of Rhodesia and Namibia would move world attention from the area. To this end it withdrew its paramilitary support in July 1975 and made it increasingly difficult for Rhodesian exports and imports to move through its already crowded port facilities. Rhodesians trying to emigrate to South Africa found many delays and obstacles placed in their way. South Africa was also not anxious to become involved in an unpopular and drawn-out guerrilla war in Rhodesia which ultimately could involve further confrontation with other African nations and international sanctions.

The illogicality of South Africa insisting on change in Rhodesia while continuing repressive policies internally is one of the great ironies of the Southern African situation. Obviously the euphoric days of friendship and cooperation between Rhodesia and South Africa following UDI were at an end and many white Rhodesians felt they had been sold out by South Africa. The degree to which South Africa has been able to impose itself on internal Rhodesian politics and determine the viability of the Smith regime is yet further evidence of Rhodesia's lack of sovereignty. If the guerrilla war continues, white Rhodesians will increasingly be forced from the rural areas into the cities; Salisbury, Bulawayo, and other major cities will rapidly become armed enclaves or garrison cities. Travel between them will become hazardous, and it is possible to speculate that parts of the country will come under the direct control of the guerrillas. Under these conditions white Rhodesia would probably survive only a few years, depending on the extent to which South Africa continued to exert pressure or whether in a change of policy it decided to come to Rhodesia's aid.

PROSPECTS FOR ZIMBABWE

How a militant African government would respond to whites is of course problematical. Would there be reprisals against key politicians and officials? The question of reprisals also arises in regard to the African military and police, predominantly Karanga-recruited from the Fort Victoria area, and for the well-organized network of informers. Have the police and military compromised themselves to the point where they might be tried as war criminals, or can they be absorbed into a new professional army or police force under the control of key former guerrilla leaders? Will there be a significant number of desertions or defections once settlement becomes a real possibility? To what extent will African collaborators and informers be punished?

There are several questions with reference to the restructuring of an independent Zimbabwe. Would a Marxist or socialist reordering make it impossible for the vast majority of whites to remain? Zimbabwe would undoubtedly begin a process of Africanization although the extent and intensity of this would depend on the nationalist group or alliance that gains power. A moderate government would probably propose a form of Africanization-localization, while a radical approach could go beyond Africanization of the bureaucracy to nationalization of industry, land, and business. Furthermore, the concept of private ownership might be either transformed or limited. Thus, the difference between moderate and radical perspectives is a difference between simple reform and revolutionary reordering: a mere replacement of the white establishment by an African establishment or a fundamental change in the structure of the society and in international relations. The post-independence period might be marked by the jockeying for power between rival leaders. The first government will undoubtedly consist of only those who have been in prison or exile or who fought. However, with the passing of time fragile alliances will corrode and new personalities will emerge.

The prospect for multiracial coexistence is obviously stronger under a moderate government. More white lawyers, doctors, and engineers would probably remain and the proposed compensation scheme would be protracted under these conditions. In this situation leaders of the Centre Party and of the Rhodesia Party such as Timothy Gibb and Patrick Bashford could play a significant role. It is interesting to note that none of these groups was invited to participate in the Geneva talks. But even more important would be the role of the small number of prominent white allies of Nkomo, such as former prime minister Garfield Todd, Leo Baron (now deputy chief justice of Zambia), and Dr. Claire Palley, a distinguished constitutional lawyer; at the Geneva conference Ahrn Palley, an opposition member of Parliament, was an adviser of Bishop Muzorewa. Despite the limitations placed on white parliamentary opposition groups, both by the electorate and by the Rhodesian Front government, these parties remain in existence but with limited membership.

It is essential to keep in mind that African society is far from monolithic but is composed of many elements: an African bourgeoisie, skilled and semiskilled workers, and modern and traditional farmers. The capitalist dimension of African society is relatively large if defined in terms of those persons earning over $100 per month and if farm owners are included. Such groups would presumably also back a more moderate government. Thus, Rhodesia could become a second Kenya, a country in which the white minority will lose power but not entirely disappear. The future relationships of Mozambique and Zimbabwe will also be of importance.

The possibility of a one-party state emerging in Zimbabwe, either for purposes of national solidarity or for unification of disparate elements, cannot be discounted. Indeed, the pattern in other parts of Africa indicates a relatively quick progression toward this situation. Whether such a one-party state will follow a model of democratic participation or merely become a plebiscitary party of course depends again on factors such as ideology and also, to a certain extent, ethnicity. Indeed, the emergence of a one-party state could by its very nature imply the exclusion of one ethnic group. Ethnic divisions between the Shona and the Ndebele might be reduced with the coming of independence, but there are also severe dangers of an escalation of rivalries which might on the surface appear to be ethnic but which in fact would be based on political and personality conflicts. The assassination of Herbert Chitepo in 1974 illustrates the depth of another conflict: that between rival Shona clans within ZANU. In a letter published in June 1976 Ndabaningi Sithole expressed his concern that ZANU had lost its national perspective because of kidnappings and killings. The predominance of the southeast Karanga within ZANU's High Command had alienated Manyika from the east and the Zeruru from the northeast. For Sithole the predominance of the Karanga meant that the High Command had become completely regionalized. For him, such regional division was the greatest problem that faced the new nation of Zimbabwe.

The nationalist struggle in Zimbabwe has been a protracted one, thus permitting political factions to solidify their positions. There is, therefore, a clear demarcation along ideological and regional-ethnic lines that might not easily lend itself to the concessions necessary for nation-building. In this respect the reentry of the guerrilla fighters into the civilian sphere might pose immediate problems, and in the long run military appointments for former guerrilla tacticians might open the possibility for a military coup. On a positive level accommodations along ethnic lines between different ideological perspectives and between personalities such as Nkomo and

Mugabe might all act as checks and balances. However, should the Third Force become a separate entity from ZANU and ZAPU, as it once was, and should Mugabe not successfully bridge the two elements, serious problems might arise. A settlement that excludes the Third Force or underestimates its continuing viability might ultimately lead to a violent civil war. In this case Geneva might only have provided a partial solution; the continuation of guerrilla warfare would have resolved not only the question of white capitulation, but could have permitted the emergence of the Third Force as a political entity rather than simply a military force.

The indebtedness of the movements to the Chinese and the Soviets will also have a bearing on the future of Zimbabwe, on the issue of development aid, and on possible anti-Western sentiment. The front-line countries of Mozambique, Tanzania, Zambia, Botswana, and Angola will also no doubt expect favored treatment. The United States itself can play a valuable role in guidance and aid on a technological level, in the field of education (particularly on the applied level), and in many sectors, especially in the vital transitional period when manpower shortages might arise due to rapid large-scale white withdrawal. The backing of a moderate regime by the United States and especially South Africa would obviously have wide ramifications both within Zimbabwe and for the rest of the continent. In this respect it should not be forgotten that the rate of investment is $650 million a year, mostly from foreign sources: American, British, and South African interests. Whites dominate production and over 55 percent of GDP in 1974 was derived from such areas as manufacturing, agriculture, construction, and mining. A study undertaken by the Whitsun Foundation indicated that in 1975, 6,200 white farmers produced $576 million worth of commodities, and 660,000 African farmers, $165 million. Furthermore, whites were engaged in commercial farming and employed 350,000 black workers. African farmers produced over 70 percent of the output for subsistence.

Special problems will arise in regard to urbanization following a settlement. The UDI caused relative economic stagnation, and the injection of new capital and aid will result in an urban influx which in the absence of controls will create serious dysfunction because of inadequate housing and facilities. In the immediate post-independence period opportunities will exist on the employment level, but unemployment problems will soon arise in a post-boom period, even though Rhodesia was ranked Africa's eighth richest country in a 1972 World Bank survey. These factors, coupled with inadequate urban development, might create a large alienated segment of the population, which could seriously hamper political stability.

The role of Zimbabwe in regard to South Africa, both in terms of diplomatic representation (whether or not to establish diplomatic relations) and its stance on guerrilla incursions into South Africa, will be of the greatest importance. Once again, an Nkomo government would place a different emphasis on the liberation of South Africa from that of a Third Force government. Zimbabwe and Namibia are linked to the overarching question of the resolution of the South African problem. Fronts for South African guerrillas might be opened up with the coming of independence to Zimbabwe and Namibia and with increased stability in Mozambique. The expectation is that these countries, having themselves engaged in a liberation struggle, would in turn assist the South African movements. The guerrilla incursions in conjunction with urban guerrilla activities inside South Africa will create a qualitative difference in the social and political environment of South Africa.

These projections are based on the assumption that Geneva, or some subsequent meeting, will lead to a settlement. While it is now no longer possible that Britain will grant any form of legitimacy to a white regime, it is possible that a constitutional impasse might once again take place and that a massive two- or three-year guerrilla campaign will ensue. Such prolonged guerrilla activities will inevitably lead to sustained violence and African and white bloodshed. Whatever the problems and difficulties of transition to black rule and the subsequent hazards of self-determination, it must not be forgotten that they are all infinitely superior to the control of 6.1 million Africans by a white minority regime. Ironically, if white Rhodesians had earlier opened up possibilities for meaningful African political involvment, many of these problems would have been avoided.

While in the immediate post-independence period numerous readjustments will have to be made, as in the case of Mozambique, political maturity and stability will evolve. The nation of Zimbabwe is still an abstraction, and time will be needed for articulate, indigenous and sophisticated political procedures and institutions to be developed and take root.

[2]

Mozambique

The Politics of Liberation

TONY HODGES

THE PEOPLE'S REPUBLIC of Mozambique was born on June 25, 1975,—eleven years after the *Frente de Libertaçao de Moçambique* (Frelimo) sent its first guerrilla fighters from Tanzania into the bush of the country's northernmost provinces, Cabo Delgado and Niassa, and almost five centuries after the famed Portuguese navigator Vasco da Gama dropped anchor in Mozambican waters in March 1498. The Mozambican people's final conquest of independence after years of bitter struggle sent shock waves throughout the rest of white-ruled Southern Africa—proving, as it did to Africans, that determined struggle (in Mozambique's case, against sixty thousand Portuguese troops) could in the long run put an end to the colonial subjugation of their countries.

For the first four centuries after da Gama's arrival in 1498, Portugal's presence in the area now known as Mozambique had been sporadic and limited to isolated settlements. Portugal did not start conquering the interior in a serious way until the end of the nineteenth century—in response to the territorial ambitions of its European rivals and after the demarcation of Mozambique's present borders at the Congress of Berlin in 1884-85. Most of southern Mozambique was effectively conquered by the end of the century after a series of wars against the indigenous peoples in the 1890s, but Cabo Delgado and Niassa escaped Portuguese occupation until 1908–12. Even then, African resistance did not stop, as was testified by a major rebellion in 1917 in the northwestern province of Tete.

Portuguese rule was brutal in the extreme. In the early years the African population was scarred by the horrors of slavery and slave-trading. Slavery was abolished in the second half of the nineteenth century, but its place was taken by a system of forced labor. All *indigenas* (natives) were subject to the colonial authorities' draconian labor laws, which allowed the state to impress Africans into involuntary work on behalf of settlers or the government. As the Labor Regulation of 1899 put it: "All natives of Portuguese overseas provinces are subject to the moral and legal obligation of attempting to obtain through work the means that they lack to subsist and to better their social condition. They have full liberty to choose the method of fulfilling this obligation, but if they do not fulfill it, public authority may force a fulfillment." Despite paper reforms, forced-labor practices continued at least until the 1960s.

The only Africans who were exempted from the labor laws were the so-called *assimilados* (assimilated). They were very few in number (only about five thousand in 1950) and achieved their status by proving their ability to speak and write Portuguese and to earn a relatively high income, the tokens of assimilation into Portuguese "civilization." The *assimilado* notion was based on the derogatory idea that "civilization" involved the rejection of all things African and the absorption of Portuguese culture and language. Eduardo Mondlane, Frelimo's first president, judged that: "The most that the *assimilado* system even sets out to do is to create a few 'honorary whites.' "

Mozambique was looked on by Portugal as both a source of cheap material imports and a market for its exports. All or part of Mozambique's plantation agriculture was compulsorily sold to Portugal at prices fixed below the world market rates. In the north, African farmers were forced to grow cotton for export to the detriment of the cultivation of food crops. At the same time, a highly protective tariff and foreign-exchange system was in force to ensure that Portuguese industries provided both investment and consumption goods to Mozambique. Another major objective of policy was to build up the main ports in Mozambique—Lourenço Marques (renamed Maputo in February 1976) and Beira—as key outlets for exports from the interior. Lourenço Marques became a major port for traffic from the Transvaal in South Africa and also served the mining and sugar industries of Swaziland. Beira developed as an export outlet for Southern Rhodesia, Northern Rhodesia (now Zambia), and Nyasaland (now Malawi).

But, while Lourenço Marques and Beira were built up into modern cities (and in consequence became major tourist attractions for white South Africans and Rhodesians) and white-owned export-crop plantations were encouraged by the colonial regime, almost no resources were directed to developing agricultural production and raising the standard of living in the subsistence sector, where 90 percent of the population worked. The failure to develop Mozambique and provide local employment forced many Mozambicans to migrate to South Africa and Rhodesia to work in mines and farms. The migrant labor system became a major source of foreign exchange and made Mozambique exceptionally dependent on its neighbors. For decades, almost nothing was done to provide education and medical facilities for Africans, especially those living in the countryside. In 1964–65, for example, only 636 (8 percent) of the 7,827 students in academic secondary schools were Africans. Of the 321 students at university level that year, exactly four were African. On Mozambique's accession to independence, 85 percent of the population was illiterate.

In addition, like metropolitan Portugal, Mozambique was a thoroughgoing police state until the downfall of the Salazarist regime in April 1974. There was no freedom of speech, press, or assembly. Opposition political parties and trade unions were illegal. Strikes were banned. Mozambican society was permeated with agents of the PIDE, the Salazarist secret police, and scores of oppositionists were incarcerated—and often brutally tortured —in the regime's jails. African protest and unrest were suppressed vigorously and often bloodily. Thus, about six hundred unarmed peasants were killed during a demonstration at Mueda in Cabo Delgado on June 16, 1960, according to the eye-witness account of Alberto Chipande, today Mozambique's minister of national defense. Coming at a time when the "winds of change" were already blowing strongly elsewhere in Africa, the Mueda massacre jolted Mozambique's small but growing African intelligentsia and led swiftly to the formation of Mozambique's first modern nationalist organizations.

Between 1960 and 1962 Mozambican exiles formed political parties abroad: the União Nacional Democrática de Moçambique (UDENAMO), the Mozambique African National Union (MANU), and the União Africana de Moçambique Independente (UNAMI). On June 25, 1962, these groups came together at a conference in Dar es Salaam, Tanzania, to found Frelimo, with Eduardo Mondlane (previously a professor of anthropology at Syracuse University in the United States and a United Nations official) as the movement's first president. Frelimo's long guerrilla war against the Portuguese occupiers began two years later. On September 25, 1964, Frelimo proclaimed a "general insurrection" of the Mozambican people. In fact, about two hundred and fifty guerrillas moved across the border to launch the movement's long rural guerrilla campaign. The guerrillas were increasingly successful, held down ever-larger numbers of Portuguese troops, and spread the war to Tete province, a rich farming area astride the Zambezi River, in 1968.

Rather than concede independence, the Portuguese government decided to step up its repression in a bid to crush the guerrilla movement. On February 3, 1969, the Portuguese succeeded in assassinating Mondlane with a parcel bomb in Dar es Salaam. In the wartorn north the Portuguese employed mass terror methods against African villagers, falsely believing that this would intimidate rural Africans into withdrawing support from the freedom fighters. Foreign missionaries sent word of the atrocities to the outside world, finally prompting the United Nations to appoint a Commission of Inquiry into Mozambique massacres, which revealed in December 1974 that at least one thousand were tortured or massacred during mass killings by Portuguese troops at Wiriyamu and other villages in 1971 and 1972. At the same time, hundreds of thousands of Africans from the northern provinces were forcibly evicted from their villages by Portuguese troops to remove them from contact with the guerrillas and to relocate them in *aldeamentos* (strategic hamlets).

Despite Portugal's use of sophisticated military equipment and methods of mass terror, the nationalists' tenacity and determination slowly began to give Frelimo the military edge over its Portuguese adversaries. At the end of 1973 the guerrilla war spread dramatically southward into the strategic central province of Manica e Sofala, heralding a new stage of the war in which the country's rail links with Rhodesia and Malawi came under incessant attack and the fighting reached within fifty miles of Beira, the country's second-largest city. Frelimo's offensive in Manica e Sofala had a strong psychological impact on the settler community and revealed that Portugal's plans to contain the guerrillas in the north had dismally failed. The scale of the fighting in Manica e Sofala was such by early 1974 that railway lines in the province were attacked on over thirty separate occasions in the first four months of the year. The Portuguese military position was so serious by March 1974 that Lisbon decided to airlift ten thousand more troops to the country that month to join the sixty thousand already there.

It was Portugal's string of military setbacks in Mozambique in 1973–74 that finally convinced important sections of the Portuguese establishment and military hierarchy that a political solution to the crises in Mozambique, Angola, and Guinea-Bissau (where over one hundred and fifty thousand troops had by then been committed) was urgently required. To this end, the officers of the Movimento das Forças Armadas (MFA) overthrew the Salazarist regime of Marcello Caetano in the Lisbon coup of April 25, 1974. Nevertheless, the coup did not bring an immediate Portuguese withdrawal from Mozambique. On the contrary, Portugal's new president, General António de Spínola, strove at first to call a ceasefire without conceding Frelimo's demand for independence. Vice-President Costa Gomes spelled out the government's policy on May 11, 1974, at a press conference in Lourenço Marques. A referendum, he said, would be held in which the Mozambican people would "be able to choose between one extreme of complete independence and another extreme of total integration." He said that he favored a balance between these extremes "within the great Portuguese community" and threatened that, if Frelimo did not accept the government's plans, "the army will have no choice but to go on with the fight and possibly intensify it."

But the tide of liberation was flowing too fast for Spínola's policies to stand much chance of success. "Any attempt to elude the real problem," Frelimo stated on April 28, "will only lead to new and equally avoidable sacrifices. The way to solve the problem is clear: recognition of the Mozambican people's right to independence." Rejecting Portuguese proposals for a referendum, Frelimo's president, Samora Machel, said on June 13: "You can't ask a slave if he wants to be free, particularly if the slave happens to be in full revolt."

The result of Spínola's referendum policy was the continuation of the war. A Portuguese military communique reported that forty Portuguese soldiers were killed in May and June. Troops had to be moved in force into the Manica e Sofala area, and five thousand settlers were issued guns. Continuing guerrilla attacks against railways brought repeated train derailments—and consequently mounting economic difficulties. The war spread south of Beira for the first time when traffic on the main Beira-Lourenço Marques road was ambushed on May 9. Frelimo used more and more sophisticated weaponry, including SAM-7 ground-to-air missiles, one of which hit a DC-3 transport plane carrying seven foreign military attachés in May. Yet another blow to the Portuguese war effort came on July 1, when Frelimo announced the opening of a new military front in the province of Zambézia, which was soon engulfed in war, culminating in Frelimo seizing the town of Morrumbala on July 21.

Most significant of all, perhaps, there now set in an almost total collapse of the Portuguese troops' morale. They were simply no longer willing to risk their lives in a war they knew could not be won. "A number of manifestos of left-wing groups circulate freely among soldiers here," a *New York Times* reporter wrote in May 1974; "The manifestos all demand the immediate cessation of the war and independence for Mozambique." Black troops began to desert the Portuguese armed forces, and in July a company of Portuguese troops based at Macossa drew up a manifesto supporting Frelimo signed by the entire company, including its officer and three sergeants.

While the Portuguese war effort was bordering on total collapse, the Mozambican economy was hit by a rash of strikes in the cities, as workers moved to take advantage of the liberalization that followed the April 25 coup. Most of these strikes, which started in the Beira docks in May and spread to almost all industries in the following three months, were held to win wage increases, though a few were aimed at removing racist supervisors, foremen, and managers. The Lourenço Marques docks were the scene of the most serious labor dispute when four thousand dockers walked off the job for several weeks, causing losses of twenty million escudos before

they returned to work on August 3. Up to eighty ships were held up while
waiting to unload at the strikebound quayside, and the port remained
congested for months after the strike.

Meanwhile, in the countryside Africans started seizing cattle from European farmers and invading their properties. Rural unrest reached its
height on August 10, when a semi-insurrection occurred in the area of
António Enes, near Nampula. António Enes itself was virtually sacked as
thousands of Africans, driven to revolt by low wages, scarcity of necessities,
and price rises, invaded European and Asian properties and stores. Cotton
and sisal plantations were burnt and hundreds of whites and Asians fled to
Nampula.

The nationalists' steady advances on the battlefield, the collapse of the
Portuguese troops' will to fight, the spreading rural unrest, the wave of
urban strikes, and the deepening economic crisis forced Portugal's new
government to rethink its strategy. On July 27 Spínola abandoned his
insistence on a referendum and publicly announced for the first time his
"recognition of the rights of the inhabitants of Portugal's overseas territories to self-determination, including the immediate recognition of their right
to independence." In short, Portugal's rulers had concluded that their
interests—and, indeed, those of the West in general—could only now be
defended by negotiating a smooth and stable transfer of power to Frelimo.

To this end, Machel and the Portuguese foreign minister Mário Soares
met in Lusaka to hammer out a settlement. Two days later they signed the
Lusaka Accords, which outlined a series of steps for the progressive transfer
of powers to Frelimo, culminating in formal independence on June 25, 1975.
During the interim period the country would be administered by a "transitional government" composed of nine ministers, three appointed by Portugal and six by Frelimo. An immediate ceasefire was called and a Joint
Military Commission set up, with equal numbers of Portuguese and
Frelimo representatives, to supervise its implementation.

The agreement in Lusaka was immediately challenged by right-wing
settlers in Mozambique. On September 7, the same day as the accords were
signed, a group calling itself the Free Mozambique Movement seized the
buildings of the Rádio Clube de Moçambique and other strategic installations in Lourenço Marques, appealing to Mozambicans to "remain Por-

tuguese, and to fight against all people who betray Mozambique and want to trample on the Portuguese flag." The insurgents broke their way into the Machava jail and released scores of imprisoned PIDE agents and officers.

Despite Portugal's agreement with Frelimo, Portuguese troops did little to stop the rebels' action. But Africans' response to the settlers' attempted putsch was swift and massive, despite appeals from Frelimo leaders that the suppression of the white rebels should be left to Frelimo and Portuguese troops. Lourenço Marques was paralyzed by a general strike on September 9. By the next day Africans had thrown up barricades on all the capital's access roads to prevent arms reaching the rebels. White property and stores were attacked and burned. The dramatic scale and depth of this uprising by the African populace in the capital's suburbs and shantytowns were enough to convince the white rebels to abandon their stand. Portuguese troops and police allowed them to leave their occupied buildings without a shot being fired or any arrests being made. In contrast, the Portuguese government decided to put down the black uprising by force. The Portuguese High Command met in emergency session while troops were sent into the shantytowns. Up to a hundred were killed, almost all Africans.

A little over a week later on September 20 the transitional government was sworn into office, with Joaquim Chissano, a top Frelimo leader, as the country's new prime minister, and Rear-Admiral Vitor Crespo the last Portuguese high commissioner. Frelimo's president, Samora Machel, remained outside the country until the following May. During the transitional period Portugal kept several thousand troops in Mozambique to ensure a stable transfer of power. They were progressively withdrawn, the last units leaving the country on June 24, 1975. The next day the Portuguese flag was hauled down for the last time. Direct colonial rule had finally ended and Machel became Mozambique's first president.

THE NATURE OF THE FRELIMO GOVERNMENT

"With the Proclamation of the People's Republic of Mozambique on June 25, 1975," an editorial in the Independence Day issue of Frelimo's *Mozambique Revolution* stated, "the revolutionary process in our country entered a new phase, the phase of People's Democracy, during which the lessons of the liberated zones during ten years of armed struggle will be applied at the level of the nation. We are now engaged in the task of destroying all vestiges of the colonial-capitalist State, an instrument of exploitation and oppression, and establishing a People's State which serves the interests of the working masses. This phase will be a period of intense struggle."

Two facts stand out in marked contrast to the new regime's official rhetoric. First, despite talk of "destroying all vestiges of the colonial-capitalist state," Frelimo has not tampered with capitalist property relations in Mozambique, has no major nationalization plans (barring the takeover of abandoned Portuguese firms) and envisages a major place for investment by multinational companies. Second, despite claims that Frelimo is building "People's Democratic Power," the new regime has effectively excluded the mass of the population from participation in the political life of the country and has erected an authoritarian, one-party state.

NATIONALIZATION AND LABOR POLICIES

According to Article 14 of the Constitution of the People's Republic of Mozambique, approved by the Frelimo Central Committee on June 20, 1975, "foreign capital shall be authorised to operate within the framework of the State's economic policy." Only about fifty, mainly small, Portuguese-owned firms have been nationalized since independence—and, in these cases, only because they were abandoned by owners and managers during the settler exodus that accompanied Portugal's withdrawal from the country. (The Portuguese community, which numbered some 280,000 in early 1974, was down to 80,000 by independence and perhaps only 30,000 by the end of 1976.) Among the firms taken over were small textile businesses like the Fabrica de Vestuário Eden Lda and the Indústria de Vestuário Tropical Lda, as well as the country's sixteen tea plantations and factories.

Even in these nationalized firms, however, the workers have not been directly involved in decision-making. The government's practice has been to appoint administrators from above to run these businesses, and in some cases this has led to resentment from the workers in the affected firms. A noteworthy example is what happened at the Companhia Industrial de Fundição e Laminagem (CIFEL), Mozambique's only smelting and metal-rolling business, which was set up in 1955 in Maputo and today employs four hundred workers. CIFEL was owned by the Portuguese conglomerate Champalimaud and was one of the many businesses abandoned by its owners during the 1975 settler exodus. The Mozambique government had no choice but to take over the firm, and it named two administrators to run the plant. According to the Maputo daily *Notícias*, the CIFEL workers have complained since the government takeover that the appointed administrators have been "bureaucratic" and "distant from the rank-and-file" and have maintained "unalterable and bourgeois" work methods. *Notícias* reported that the workers at CIFEL felt that the company was still a "capitalist enterprise." One worker reportedly said: "The administration has the power to make decisions and they're the bosses. Can't we who produce the wealth give our opinion on problems? Our work here is just to produce, produce, produce."

Another revealing indication of the authoritarian administrative structure set up in the nationalized industries is given by a report broadcast by Radio Maputo on October 13, 1976, of a meeting of Frelimo activist groups in Maputo, where Machel personally outlined how production targets would be set and achieved. Machel said that each sector would be given weekly, monthly, quarterly, and half-yearly targets and that each sector would be held collectively accountable for the accomplishment of its set tasks. Frelimo activist groups in factories were told to hold monthly meetings with the administrative committees of their firms and then report back to the work force, informing them of the subjects discussed with the administrators.

At the same time, Frelimo curtailed the right to strike as part of its program to impose austerity measures, raise productivity, and combat what it calls "egotism" and "colonial mentality." On September 20, 1974, in a message relayed to the inauguration ceremony of the transitional government, Machel said that "at this stage in the life of our country there is no more room for strikes." The clamp-down on strikes came in the wake of a massive strike wave that swept through Mozambican industries after the downfall of the Caetano regime. To carry through its no-strike policy, Frelimo had also to curb the activities of the rank-and-file "workers' commissions," which had sprung up after the April 1974 Lisbon coup and which played a major part in the strike wave. But, as late as October 1976, workers' go-slows and lack of cooperation seemed still to be giving Frelimo trouble. "There are workers," Machel complained in a speech broadcast on October 13, "who are still trying to resolve their problems in the way that they learned at the time of the provisional government, at the time of the so-called workers' commissions. These workers are staging silent strikes. They are deliberately causing a fall in production."

SOCIAL POLICY

The Frelimo government introduced important changes in social policy after independence. The first session of the Council of Ministers, July 9–25, 1975, adopted a series of decrees to make education, medical care, and other facilities more accessible to the majority of Mozambicans. The reforms, which took effect from August 1, were announced by Machel to a crowd of 150,000 in Maputo on July 24. They included: the nationalization of land and abolition of private rent collection; the state takeover of all private schools, including those owned by the missions; the integration of all private law practices into a state legal service; the outlawing of private funeral firms and the establishment of a state funeral organization; and the abolition of private medical practice. The school curriculum was overhauled to teach Mozambicans more about their own history and culture (instead of Portugal's, as in the past); the government declared its intention to make education and health care more accessible to the rural population, which had been virtually ignored during most of the colonial era; and in 1975 a massive literacy campaign began to tackle the country's very high illiteracy rate (85 percent). On June 14, 1976, the country's first nationwide vaccination campaign (against smallpox, tuberculosis, and measles) was launched —starting in the provinces of Niassa, Tete, and Cabo Delgado—with long-term plans to vaccinate the whole population against smallpox. In addition, the government set up a state retailing organization, the *Empresa das Lojas do Povo* (People's Shops Agency) to provide a commercial network of "people's shops" providing essential goods to the population.

An interesting part of this reform program was the adoption of a decree on February 3 that regulated rights to housing. The decree was designed to move homeless families into housing abandoned by the settlers. Rents, which were to be payable to the state, were staggered according to family income as well as size of home. But the decree was not remarkably radical. Not only was each family guaranteed possession of its own home (Article 1), but each family was granted the right to maintain an additional house or flat in the countryside or by the sea (Article 13), a measure clearly designed to defend the interests of the wealthiest sector of the community.

CREATING A ONE-PARTY STATE

On a political level Frelimo has sought since its entry into the transitional government to consolidate its political supremacy by erecting a one-party state. All opposition political groups are now illegal, and the constitution accords Frelimo the status of a state institution in its own right. All governmental bodies are subordinate to Frelimo. Thus, Article 3 of the constitution states that "the People's Republic of Mozambique will be guided by the political line defined by Frelimo, which is the leader of the State and of society. Frelimo will establish the basic political policy of the State, so as to ensure the conformity of the policy of the State with the interests of the people."

Article 37 of the constitution states that "the People's Assembly is the supreme organ of the State." By the end of 1976, however, this body still consisted entirely of appointees (the members of the Frelimo Central Committee and Executive Committee, the ministers and vice-ministers of the government, the provincial governors, military leaders chosen by Frelimo, two representatives from each province chosen by Frelimo, members of Frelimo chosen by the Central Committee, and "a maximum of ten reputable citizens chosen by the Central Committee of Frelimo"). Article 39 promises that an electoral law will eventually be drawn up, opening the way for elections to the People's Assembly within "one year from the holding of the Third Congress of Frelimo." Frelimo's Political-Military Committee announced on October 7, 1976, that the Third Congress would assemble in February 1977, so (according to the constitution) the final deadline for general elections is February 1978, a full two and a half years after independence. The elections will not be very democratic, however, because Frelimo is the only legal party.

In addition, the regime has equipped itself with a repressive apparatus to curb dissent. On October 13, 1975, the government set up the *Serviço Nacional de Segurança Popular* (SNASP—the National Service of People's Security) with sweeping powers to "detect, neutralise and combat all forms of subversion, sabotage and acts directed against the People's Power and its representatives, against the national economy or against the objectives of the People's Republic of Mozambique." Its director, who is answerable to the president, may decide whether anyone arrested should be "given over to the competent police authority, sent to court or to camps for re-education." Two weeks after SNASP's formation, on the night of October 30–31, 1975, more than three thousand people were arrested in Maputo, Beira, Nampula, Xai-Xai, and Chimoio. Many detainees have been sent to *Centros de Descolonizacao Mental* (Mental Decolonization Centers) for "re-education." The two major camps are at Inhassune, north of Maputo, and at Dondo, near Beira.

Other organizations have also been marshalled behind the regime. Among them are the Frelimo Ideological School, set up at the end of 1975 to train party cadres, and the *Organização de Juventude de Moçambique* (OJM—Mozambique Youth Organization), which was inaugurated in the Maputo area in June 1976. The mass media have also been put to use. In August 1975 Machel warned journalists that they would be "exposed" if they "serve individual interests and support deviations from the Party line." Government and party policy has been widely promoted by *jornais de povo* (people's newspapers). A coordinated media strategy was drafted at Frelimo's first National Conference of the Department of Information and Propaganda (DIP) on November 26–30, 1975. Among the proposals adopted were: the provision of radios at cheap prices; the use of *jornais de povo* in the rural areas; strict controls on the import of books, films, and records; the setting up of party bookstores; and the provision of sound relay systems in the *aldeias comunais* (communal villages) set up by the Government in a bid to raise agricultural production and to allow the diffusion of information and propaganda to the peasants.

The repressive features of the state are paralleled by undemocratic practices within Frelimo itself. The movement has held only two congresses since its founding in 1962. The last one was in 1968. In reality, this has meant that the decisions of Frelimo's forty-two-member Central Committee

—and its subordinate bodies, the Executive Committee and the Political-Military Committee—are not open to challenge through either the state or the party structures. The political line and instructions issued by the movement's top leaders are transmitted downward through Frelimo's provincial, district and locality committees. The movement's rank-and-file members are organized in *circulos* (circles) in villages, work-places, and neighborhoods.

One of Frelimo's central objectives since its accession to power has been to consolidate the movement's structures in the areas outside the wartime liberated zones of Niassa, Cabo Delgado, and Tete. In the central and southern parts of the country (and, above all, in the cities), where Portuguese repression had barred the creation of a strong party apparatus, Frelimo had to build up an organization virtually from scratch after the signing of the Lusaka Accords. In these areas Frelimo at first discouraged the formation of *circulos* and instead organized *grupos dinamizadores* (dynamization groups), with leaders appointed from above by Frelimo. The groups were designed to inculcate and spread Frelimo's political line and prepare the way for the establishment of Frelimo *circulos*. The function of the *grupos dinamizadores* was clearly revealed in a major discussion of these bodies at the first national conference of Frelimo district committees, held at Mocuba in Zambézia on February 16–21, 1975. This conference decided that "it is premature to transform the *grupos dinamizadores* into *circulos* because people's power is not yet sufficiently solidly rooted among the masses" and because "there exist in these groups reactionary and opportunist infiltrated elements," including members of "phantom organisations" (illegal anti-Frelimo parties), people "compromised with capitalism," ex-members of the PIDE, smugglers, racists, tribalists, prostitutes, and provokers of strikes. "It is necessary," the conference agreed, "to proceed to a campaign of purification in the ranks of the *grupos dinamizadores,* to discover, denounce and expel the elements which have infiltrated into them."

AN ECONOMY IN CRISIS

Portuguese colonialism left Mozambique's economy undeveloped and distorted. Very little industrialization took place under Portuguese rule and

five agricultural products (sugar, cashew nuts, tea, sisal, and cotton) traditionally accounted for over 60 percent of exports. Year after year Mozambique ran a massive trade deficit, the value of its exports usually covering
about half the country's import bill. The deficit was usually balanced by a
surplus on invisibles. These funds came from tourist revenues, charges on
the shipment of South African and Rhodesian goods through Lourenço
Marques and Beira, and the export of labor to the farms and mines of South
Africa and Rhodesia. In brief, Mozambique was "developed" as a source
of cheap raw materials for Portugal, a protected market for Portuguese
goods, and a service sector of the South African and Rhodesian economies.

Independence brought some immediate advantages to Mozambique.
Freed for the first time from the economic restrictions imposed by Portuguese colonialism, Mozambique could sell the full range of its export
crops at world-market prices instead of the artificially low prices previously
fixed by Portugal. Thus, whereas in 1973 Mozambique had been forced to
sell its sugar to Portugal at only £52 ($120) per ton, it sold its sugar in 1975
in a world market where prices fluctuated between £128 ($307) and £480
($1150) per ton. Second, Mozambique was able to boost its foreign-
exchange earnings substantially by its new-found opportunity to sell in the
open market the gold received from South Africa at the official rate in
part-payment for its migrant workers under the system known as the
Mozambique Convention. The large surplus previously reaped by Portugal
(due to the substantial rise in the free-market price of gold in the 1970s
above the official gold price) now went to Mozambique for the first time.

On the debit side, however, Mozambique—like other underdeveloped
countries—was hit hard at the time of its accession to independence by
world inflation; the quadrupling of oil prices; and, with the onset of the
world recession in 1974, a decline in commodity prices which hit export
earnings. Famines and floods in 1975–76 added further problems. All told,
industrial production was estimated to have fallen by 50 percent between
independence and mid-1976.

Above all, because very few Africans were trained for skilled jobs in the
colonial era, Mozambique was hit by the exodus of almost all the country's
technicians, civil servants, skilled workers, experts, administrators, and
farmers, a flight accompanied in many cases by deliberate acts of economic

sabotage. At one abandoned firm, Monteiro and Company, which employs seven thousand workers and is now run by a government-appointed administrative committee, the company's Portuguese managers stopped paying wages before their departure, embezzled funds needed for regular operating expenses, smuggled out currency, failed to renew vital contracts, and plundered the firm's equipment. Once back in Portugal, they received 31 million escudos in Portuguese bank accounts between January 1975 and March 1976.

It was a similar story in the rural areas, where Portuguese farmers abandoned numerous plantations and often tried to take valuable agricultural equipment with them out of the country. On their own initiative many farm laborers tried to keep these abandoned estates in operation.

Sugar production fell from 285,581 tons in the 1974–75 crop to an estimated 253,600 tons in 1975–76. At the same time, Mozambique was hit by the huge fall in world sugar prices from over $800 per ton during the previous world commodity boom to around $240 per ton in October 1976. Sisal production fell steadily: from 21,000 tons in 1973 to 19,000 tons in 1974 and 15,000 tons in 1975. All the country's tea estates, which cover some 15,750 hectares in Zambézia, were abandoned by their owners. The resulting dislocations brought production down by 25 percent (4,495 tons) to 13,143 tons in 1975. Cotton production declined as well by as much as 40 percent, according to some estimates, from the 1974 output of 180,000 tons. Reports coming in from cashew nut processing factories in the second half of 1976 indicated that output of this commodity (in which Mozambique has been the world leader) had dropped too.

Since these five agricultural commodities earned Mozambique over 60 percent of its export revenues in 1973, the huge fall in agricultural production sent export earnings tumbling to about $125 million per year, according to a United Nations mission that visited Mozambique after the country's decision to apply sanctions against Rhodesia in March 1976. Export revenues had been over $140 million in 1974.

On the other hand, imports of subsistence foods increased because of the departure of white cash-crop farmers and widespread flooding in the southern province of Gaza in February 1976. Annual food imports were estimated in 1976 to include about 40,000 tons of rice (which Mozambique used to export), 90,000 tons of maize, and 120,000 tons of wheat. Even if the value of total imports remained at the same level in 1976 as in 1974 (a little over $400 million)—which, given world inflation, would imply a substantial drop in the volume of imports—the trade deficit would have widened to at least $275 million.

As noted above, Mozambique's trade deficits have traditionally been offset by a surplus on invisibles. In 1974, for example, the current invisibles surplus of 3.9 billion escudos almost exactly offset the trade deficit of 4 billion escudos. In 1976, however, not only was the trade deficit expected to have widened, but earnings from invisibles were thought to have fallen too. The U.N. mission estimated that the current account deficit would reach an annual $175 to $200 million. Tourist revenues, previously earned almost exclusively from wealthy white South Africans and Rhodesians, completely dried up from 1974 onward. Earnings from the export of mine labor to South Africa, after rising considerably in 1975, fell back in 1976, partly because of the deepening recession in the South African economy, which pushed black unemployment in South Africa to 1.5 million. The number of Mozambican migrant workers in South Africa's mines fell from about 127,000 in November 1975 to an estimated 75,000 in August 1976. Recruitment slumped from nearly 2,000 a week in 1975 to under 400 per week in the second quarter of 1976. In the second place, foreign-exchange earnings per miner fell. This was because the market price of gold slipped downward from a high of $195.50 an ounce on the London gold market at the end of 1974 to less than $120 an ounce in October 1976, thereby sharply narrowing Mozambique's foreign-exchange earnings from the sale of the gold bars it receives at the rate of $35 an ounce as part-payment for its miners under the Mozambique Convention.

Earnings from the handling of South African freight (which over recent years have brought in up to 30 percent of total foreign exchange earnings) fell too, primarily because of a decline in port productivity following the departure of skilled Portuguese administrators, experts, and stevedores. In the early months of 1976 freight volumes moving from South Africa to Maputo (which handled 18 percent of South Africa's exports and imports in 1975) were reported to have fallen from 25,000 tons a day to 18,000 tons.

In addition, Mozambique suffered considerable losses because of the government's decision in March 1976 to close its border with Rhodesia. Worst hit were Mozambique's railways and ports, which used to handle the bulk of Rhodesia's exports and imports as well as shipments from several other countries that had to be carried via Rhodesia's railway system. According to the U.N., lost port and railway revenues would cost Mozambique between $57 and $75 million over the first year of the border closure. All told, the U.N. estimated, the border closure would lose Mozambique between $108 and $134 million in annual foreign-exchange earnings. The U.N. forecast that ten thousand Mozambicans would lose their jobs and that additional costs would be incurred in emergency development projects made necessary by the border closure and in the building-up of stocks, previously lower because of access to Rhodesian stocks. The U.N. put the total cost of the border closure at $139 to $165 million in the first year; $108 to $134 million in the second; and $106 to $132 million per year thereafter.

With a current account deficit reaching an estimated $175 to $200 million in the year following the application of sanctions against Rhodesia, Mozambique faced a difficult future. By October 1976 an international appeal for aid launched by the U.N. had brought promises of assistance totaling about $100 million, but most of it was in the form of loans that would add to Mozambique's long-term external debt. The capital account was unlikely to make any contribution toward financing the current account deficit in the absence of a big increase in international aid, since private capital outflows increased following a government decision to grant special transfer facilities to expatriate personnel working under government contracts.

OPPOSITION TO FRELIMO

Frelimo came to power in 1974–75 on a crest of popularity, credited by the great majority of the population as the movement that had led the long, bitter struggle for national independence. But the new Mozambican regime could not be said to be a strong one. Indeed, Frelimo's construction of an authoritarian, one-party regime was an indication of the political dangers it knew it faced.

The depth of the regime's economic difficulties prompted Frelimo to launch a tough austerity program and drive for increased productivity. In

August 1976, for example, Finance Minister Salomão Munguambe announced that government spending would fall from 12.8 billion escudos in 1975 to 9.3 billion escudos in 1976. The government has held out little prospect of an improvement of living standards and has urged workers to work harder.

This program appears to have been met with widespread ill-feeling by Mozambicans, especially those in the cities who had engaged in the 1974 strike wave and expected independence to bring improvements in their standard of living. The soldiers of the FPLM (People's Forces for the Liberation of Mozambique) also appear to have resented the regime's austerity drive. Above all, workers' hostility to government policies, as the CIFEL example suggests, seems to have flowed partly from resentment at the way in which these policies have been imposed from above without their own democratic involvement in decision-making.

Though Frelimo was successful, by and large, in halting the massive strike wave that swept Mozambique after the April 1974 Lisbon coup, Frelimo representatives had to travel to Moatize in Tete in February 1975 to persuade striking coal-miners to return to work. In the same month a report submitted by the Frelimo branch in Maputo noted that "the people in Maputo had supported the formation of groups of activists to curb the infiltration of rightists, as well as leftist opportunists and direct militants" and decried the "presence of agitators among the working class." On September 25, 1975, Machel complained that "in a bid to hinder the realisation of the people's aspirations, the enemy resorted to disorganising production, by instigating disinterest in work and, when possible, even by paralysing work through counterrevolutionary strikes."

The government austerity program aroused considerable discontent in the FPLM, forcing the government to summon a meeting of 350 FPLM cadres on December 10–13, 1975, which, with Machel himself present, warned against "enemy infiltration" into the armed forces and ordered all FPLM units to spend at least twelve hours a week studying Frelimo's political line and engaging in self-criticism sessions. After the meeting, several hundred FPLM soldiers were arrested, an inquiry was opened, and some of those detained were accused of subversion. A few days later, on December 17, four hundred soldiers in an FPLM detachment at Machava, on the outskirts of Maputo, staged an ill-prepared rebellion. After seizing control of a number of installations in the Machava area, the rebels tried to march to the center of Maputo. By the next morning they had been routed by troops loyal to the government. Limited to the capital, the rebellion at no point posed a serious challenge to the government; and its rapid crushing undoubtedly helped the regime consolidate its power in the country. Nevertheless, the rebellion showed the depth of discontent among FPLM troops, some of them hardened veterans of the liberation war.

At the end of 1976 the Frelimo regime was still meeting opposition from urban workers to its austerity and production drives. A special meeting of Frelimo activist groups was held in Maputo in October to discuss the problem, and Machel's speech to the meeting was broadcast to the nation on October 13 by Radio Maputo. "We have heard the case," Machel said, "of a clothing factory, where from 60 shirts a day they increased production to 150. What they wanted was an increase in wages, and they told the management: We will increase production only if you pay us more." Machel went on to complain that "in other firms which already have an administrative commission the workers demand that the profits should be divided among them" and that "there have also been other cases, where after a technician has fled the workers go to the management and say: Now his wages should be divided among us. We have remained here to do his work." Describing such notions as "ideological diarrhoea," Machel implored: "Increase production; increase productivity—this must be our task. Demonstrations have never been organized to increase production. We must stage demonstrations to increase production, to increase productivity. This is our task."

Machel also accused some workers of "anti-white racism." "There are people," Machel said, "who do not accept the authority of bosses, just because they are white. Isn't that so? Ideological diarrhoea; ideological confusion. . . ."

Rightist opposition to the Frelimo government came initially from reactionary settler groups like the Free Mozambique Movement and the *Dragoes da Morte* (Dragons of Death). Right-wing groups were believed responsible, for example, for attacks against railway trains on February 19 and March 29, 1975. The latter caused eighty-one deaths and £700,000

($1,680,000) worth of damage. In September 1975 pencil-bombs were discovered in Maputo.

Several white opponents of the transition to independence were deported, both during the transitional government's term of office and after independence. In October 1975, to cite just one example, Frelimo deported Rogério de Canha e Sa, an ex-governor of Vila Pery district, after he had expressed a hostile attitude to black rule in the country. Other settler opponents of Frelimo were detained. They were believed to number about two hundred in the early months of 1976. In June, however, they were all released and deported after discussions in Rome between Mozambique's foreign minister, Joaquim Chissano, and the Portuguese foreign minister, Melo Antunes.

The Frelimo regime has also kept on guard against supporters of the so-called "phantom parties," small African anti-Frelimo groups, which were banned after Frelimo's entry into the transitional government. The better-known of these very small groups had included the *Comité Revolucionário de Moçambique* (Coremo—Mozambique Revolutionary Committee), led by Paulo José Gumane, and the *Grupo Unido de Moçambique* (Gumo —United Group of Mozambique), which had been founded in 1973 by Joana Simião. In Gumo's manifesto published on May 3, 1974, it had advocated autonomy for Mozambique within a Lisbon-based federation, the continued presence of Portuguese troops in Mozambique, and a firm stand by Portugal against Frelimo guerrillas. In June–July 1974, however, Frelimo supporters took over the leadership of Gumo, expelled Simião (charging that she was a PIDE agent), and finally dissolved the group. Simião then set up another small group on August 13: the *Frente Comum de Moçambique* (Frecomo—Common Front of Mozambique). Her allies this time were two ex-leaders of Frelimo, Lázaro Kavandame and Uria Simango (a past vice-president of Frelimo), who had both been expelled from the Front in 1969 at the time of Machel's elevation to the presidency following Mondlane's assassination. On August 24 Frecomo fused with four other anti-Frelimo groups, including Coremo, to form the *Partido de Coligação Nacional* (PCN—National Coalition Party). The PCN called for a referendum on the country's future (in line with Spinolist policy) and sought to prevent Portugal from hammering out a deal with Frelimo over the PCN's head. When Portugal reached a negotiated settlement with

Frelimo in Lusaka in September 1974, the PCN was driven by its own factional interests to align itself with the Free Mozambique Movement and support the abortive settler putsch. In so doing, it totally discredited itself among the African population.

Several hundred supporters of the PCN were imprisoned by the transitional government. They included Paulo Gumane, Joana Simião, Uria Simango, and Lázaro Kavandame. Two hundred and thirty-nine of these prisoners were presented to the press by Frelimo on March 16, 1975, and three hundred and sixty were displayed to the press on April 21, 1975. Kavandame, however, reportedly escaped from detention and, early in 1976, set up an underground opposition group called the Cabo Delgado Front. Its aim is supposedly to "liberate" the province of Cabo Delgado, an area populated by the Makonde ethnic group. There is no evidence to suggest that the group has posed a serious threat to Frelimo, though it is true that reference to its existence has been made by the Mozambique authorities. In February 1976 Radio Maputo reported that a political commissar at Montepuez had been dismissed for "supporting enemy reactionaries of the Cabo Delgado Front."

On July 25, 1976, another underground group was allegedly formed: the United Democratic Front of Mozambique (Fumo). Under the leadership of Dr. Domingos Arouca, a lawyer who once supported Frelimo, Fumo adopted a program at its founding meeting at Mocuba. This document proposed the reintegration of Mozambique into Portugal as a federal republic, a pro-Western policy supporting free enterprise, and respect for "the ethnic and tribal realities." As with the Cabo Delgado Front, there is no evidence that this group exists as a serious force.

A torrent of anti-Frelimo propaganda has also been broadcast into Mozambique by the Rhodesian regime's "Voice of Free Africa" (dubbed "Radio Kizumba" or "Radio Hyena" by Frelimo). In addition, Frelimo has faced repeated border incursions by Rhodesian troops and aircraft, carrying out "hot-pursuit" operations against Zimbabwean nationalists based in Mozambique.

Finally, while no clear-cut political divisions have emerged (at least in public) within Frelimo, since independence the movement's leadership has felt it necessary to launch repeated purges in the party and the *grupos dinamizadores.* This has been part of Frelimo's drive to consolidate its structures in the country, impose its unpopular austerity and productivity drives, and build a disciplined, monolithic party. The swift succession of purges indicates that criticism and expressions of discontent have continued to present problems for the regime.

Among those purged by Frelimo has been Pedro Juma, a long-standing Frelimo leader, who was accused of corruption and dismissed from his post as governor of Maputo on August 11, 1975. At Frelimo's eighth Central Committee meeting on February 21–28, 1976, five top leaders were expelled and sent for "re-education" by the "popular masses." They included three Central Committee members (Mateus Anibal Malichocho, Xavier Baptista Sulila, and Joaquim Maquival), the director of Frelimo's health services (Leonardo Daniel Cumbe), and the director of the Frelimo Ideological School (Gideon Ndobe). Further purges took place later in the year. Radio Maputo reported on September 2, for example, that Tomé Eduardo, the governor of Sofala, had told a meeting in Beira that infiltration by "reactionary agents" had been noted in both Frelimo and the FPLM. The governor of Tete said that "confusion among the people" had been observed. On September 12 the radio reported that officials of the Frelimo activist group in the Directorate of Agriculture and Forestry in Chimoio, the capital of Manica, had been purged. And two days later the radio announced that the governor of Sofala had issued the slogan "Launch a purge in the ranks of the activist groups, government, and FPLM" at a top-level meeting in Dondo, which discussed the problems of "infiltration" by opponents of Frelimo and ordered several officials dismissed.

Not too much should be made of these overt signs of opposition. Frelimo is still not wholly in control of a country that stretches from Tanzania in the north to South Africa in the south, but it is determined to become so. Moreover, its leaders have a clear view of how they wish Mozambique to develop. Their programs are too ambitious to be realized as quickly as they plan, and there are and will continue to be evidences of discontent and necessary adjustments. To people released from the rigors of colonial demands it is not palatable to be dragooned into efforts that seem scarcely less arduous. Yet Frelimo has not fought so long to give up its aims easily. What we may expect is a substantial period of internal stress caused as much by the natural difficulties in the way of turning Mozambique into a more self-sufficient country as by any resistance to its efforts. Much will depend too, at least in the short run, on the course of the liberation struggle in the rest of Southern Africa and Mozambique's role therein.

NONALIGNMENT

The Frelimo regime has adopted a general stance of nonalignment in its international dealings. It has refused to allow any foreign powers to set up military bases on its territory, and it has declared its support for the demilitarization of the Indian Ocean. As Article 24 of the constitution affirms: "The People's Republic of Mozambique defends the principle of turning the Indian Ocean into a non-nuclear zone of peace." The point was repeated by Foreign Minister Chissano in a speech to the United Nations General Assembly on October 6, 1975: "We are of the view that the Indian Ocean should constitute a denuclearised zone, free of military and naval bases and fleets."

Nonalignment denotes for Frelimo (like other Third World nationalist regimes) a policy of seeking wide-ranging international relations, with a view to extending the country's range of potential trading partners and sources of economic aid. In other words, freed from the special trading and other constraints imposed under colonial rule, Mozambique's new rulers are trying to increase their room for economic maneuver by diversifying the country's international connections. Thus, in general, the Mozambican government has tried to cement friendly relations and get assistance from any country willing to cooperate—from the Soviet bloc, China, Arab oil-producers, and the major capitalist countries. In so doing, it has succeeded in establishing bases for cooperation with numerous Western governments that denied Frelimo support during the war for independence and gave valuable support to the Portuguese. The collapse of Portugal's African empire rendered obsolete the premises of the United States' Southern Africa policy, codified in *Tar Baby,* Option Two of National Security Study Memorandum 39 (NSSM 39), adopted by the Nixon administration in February 1970—which had projected a strategy of "selective relaxation of our stance towards the white regimes" (including both Rhodesia and the Portuguese colonies) on the grounds that "the whites are here to stay and the only way that change can come about is through them."

The shift in the balance of power in Southern Africa convinced the United States and the other Western powers that the preservation of stability in Southern Africa required a rapid solution to the potentially explosive crisis in Rhodesia, if possible by engineering an orderly transfer of power to a "moderate" black government. This required a strong push as well to forge a new, cooperative relationship with the regime in Maputo. Frelimo, in line with its policy of nonalignment, was, broadly-speaking, willing to reciprocate.

Even before independence, a British minister, Judith Hart (then minister for overseas development), held talks with Frelimo leaders in Dar es Salaam in May and promised substantial aid to Mozambique after independence. The Commonwealth summit conference, held that month in Jamaica, floated plans for a Commonwealth assistance program if Mozambique applied sanctions against Rhodesia. When Mozambique did close the Rhodesian border in March 1976, the Commonwealth launched its aid program and the British government sent David Ennals, the minister of state for foreign affairs, to Maputo in April to announce loans to Mozambique totaling $30 million.

Though the United States was not invited to Mozambique's independence celebration in June 1975, the U.S. assistant secretary of state for Africa, Donald Easum, had met Machel as early as October 1974 and announced that the United States was "looking forward to a cooperative relationship with the new Mozambique." On September 23, 1975, the American secretary of state, Henry Kissinger, met Chissano in New York and signed a joint communique establishing diplomatic relations. In particular Kissinger saw that the United States needed to cultivate close ties with Frelimo as part of the American effort in 1976 to further a negotiated settlement of the Rhodesian crisis. To this end Kissinger offered $12.5 million of aid for Mozambique in a major speech in Lusaka on April 27, 1976, that outlined American policies in Southern Africa. Though the aid package roused conservative opposition in the United States Senate, the Ford administration finally signed an aid agreement in Maputo on September 29 that totaled over $9 million.

Another Western power, Sweden—which had given Frelimo some backing during its war against Portugal—acted to cement its ties with Mozambique's new rulers and angled for business openings in the country. In March 1976 the Swedish minister of development paid a ten-day visit to Mozambique. During the visit the Swedish delegation signed an agreement to provide $45 million over three years to build a dam on the Sabie River. Sweden also agreed to build a power station at Quelimane. In April 1976 Swedish technicians visited timber plantations in the Chimoio region with a view to developing a pulp and paper factory and also visited various sites with mineral deposits.

While welcoming these overtures from the capitalist world, the Frelimo government has also found it in its interests to maintain cordial relations with China and the Soviet Union, the two countries that gave Frelimo its greatest military aid during the liberation war. Again, it has done so as a nonaligned, Third World nationalist regime, not as a "satellite" of the U.S.S.R. or China. Though Frelimo ritualistically describes the Soviet Union as the "liberated zone of humanity," Chissano pointedly stated at a Soviet embassy reception in Maputo in October 1975 that outside help during the liberation war did not give any country the right to dictate policy to Mozambique. Mozambique's new rulers have sought economic aid from both China and the Soviet Union. Not surprisingly, they have therefore steered clear of embroilment in the Sino-Soviet conflict.

On February 25, 1975, Machel led a Frelimo delegation to Peking to start a seventeen-day tour of China and North Korea. Both countries promised aid, China announcing that it would provide a massive $57 million interest-free loan. During the Angolan civil war, Sino-Mozambican relations were not broken, even though China was strongly hostile to the Soviet-aided People's Movement for the Liberation of Angola (MPLA), with which Frelimo had enjoyed close relations since the early sixties through their joint membership in the Conference of Nationalist Organisations of the Portuguese Colonies (CONCP).

The Soviet Union, however, did follow up China's Angolan debacle by redoubling its assistance to the Frelimo government. A series of meetings in Moscow in 1976 culminated in May when Machel and Soviet leaders signed agreements covering aid in commerce, education, sea transport, fishing, air transport, and public health.

As a natural corollary of its nonaligned policy and its membership in the OAU, the Frelimo government has also tried to forge close ties with neighboring African countries, in particular with Tanzania and Zambia. President Julius Nyerere of Tanzania was the first head of state to pay an official visit to Mozambique after independence, arriving on August 30 for a week-long tour of the country. At the end of his visit, on September 7, Mozambique and Tanzania signed a series of agreements providing for a special economic and diplomatic relationship between the two countries. A permanent commission with eight ministers from each state was set up to examine ways of making their economies more complementary. Tanzania and Mozambique produce two-thirds of the world's cashew nuts, and it was decided that the commission should formulate plans for a joint marketing policy. The agreements also allowed each country to represent the other at a diplomatic level and to issue passports and visas for each other. Of particular interest was a clause instructing the commission to "take into account the possibility that other countries might wish to cooperate in mutually advantageous undertakings"—a hint that Mozambique and Tanzania might form a new regional African economic community, perhaps with Zambia and Swaziland.

Frelimo's close political ties with Tanzania's ruling party were underscored by Machel in a speech he gave in Dar es Salaam in May 1975. "Our ideology is the same," he said. "We have the same principles and the same orientation. We have followed the same policies against colonialism, imperialism and exploitation. Therefore, there will be no frontier between us."

Though there are obstacles to Tanzanian–Mozambican cooperation (language barriers and a lack of direct road and telecommunications links), both countries' governments proceeded with the plans outlined in September 1975. On April 3, 1976, Marcelino dos Santos, the minister for development and economic planning, led a thirty-two-member delegation to Dar es Salaam to participate in the first session of the commission set up the previous September. The meeting finished its work on April 9 with a communique announcing that plans had been made "to take steps aimed at strengthening and consolidating the fraternal bonds formed between the two peoples during the years of the people's war for the liberation of

Mozambique." Four subcommissions were set up, dealing with trade, industry, and finance; diplomatic and consular affairs; education and culture; and communications, transport, and public works. One key decision of the meeting was that a "Unity Bridge" would be built over the Rovuma River to provide a direct road link between the two countries.

Meanwhile, there have been increasing signs that this type of cooperation is being widened in scope to include Zambia. On April 11, 1976, for example, it was announced that, following a joint defense and security meeting in Maputo, the governments of Zambia, Mozambique, and Tanzania had agreed to set up a joint institute for the training of their defense and police forces. On April 20 Zambia's President Kenneth Kaunda flew to Mozambique for a five-day state visit (after announcing that Zambia would send a fifty-one-strong medical team to Mozambique and donate 100,000 bags of maize for relief to flood victims in southern Mozambique). At the end of the visit Kaunda and Machel signed the Maputo Agreement, setting up a Joint Permanent Cooperation Committee and reaffirming solidarity between Frelimo and Zambia's ruling United National Independence Party (UNIP). Cooperation between the two countries, a communique stressed, would be extended to Tanzania. The Maputo Agreement included a commitment to build a direct rail link between Mozambique and Zambia, linking Zambia's industries with the Moatize-Beira railway. In another move clearly designed to forge closer economic ties between the two countries, a paved road was built between Katete in Zambia's eastern province and Bene in Tete during 1976.

MOZAMBIQUE AND THE CRISIS IN SOUTHERN AFRICA

The Mozambican people's victory (like that of the Angolans a little later) had a profound impact on the remaining white-ruled countries of Southern Africa, above all because it provided an inspiring example to blacks in Zimbabwe, Namibia, and South Africa of what a determined struggle against white rule could achieve. In South Africa the Mozambican events gave added impetus to the growing black consciousness movement and its most promising organizations: the Black People's Convention (BPC), the South African Students' Organization (SASO), and the South African Students' Movement (SASM). Tsietsi Mashinini, president of the Soweto Students' Representative Council (SRC) and a leader of the Soweto uprising of June 1976, put it this way in an interview in October 1976: the victories of the freedom fighters in Mozambique and Angola "brought political awareness of the potential black people carried in their hands."

In fact, the Lusaka Accords prompted the BPC and SASO to call a pro-Frelimo rally in Durban on September 25, 1974. It was banned by the government and the demonstrators were violently dispersed by the police. Over thirty black leaders, including Zethulele Cindi, the secretary-general of the BPC, were arrested under the Terrorism Act. "What stands out," the London *Times* commented after this incident, "is that the South African government hopes to silence any response to the Frelimo triumph in Mozambique. This amounts to an admission of its realization that the advent of a black government in Mozambique after a successful military campaign against white rule is bound to stir deep feelings in its black population. Silenced or not, they are bound to ask 'is our turn coming?' "

The black victory in Mozambique posed still greater dangers to the white settler regime in Rhodesia. Besides rousing the militancy of Zimbabweans, Mozambique's accession to independence raised the prospect that sooner or later the Ian Smith government would lose its trade routes through Beira and Maputo (on which Rhodesia had previously relied for the transit of over 80 percent of its exports and imports). In addition the possibility now arose that Mozambique's new government would allow the Zimbabwean nationalists to set up bases on its territory and help infiltrate guerrilla units across Rhodesia's eastern border. The Salisbury government knew that this would merely be an extension of the assistance given by Frelimo since 1971 to ZANLA (the Zimbabwe National Liberation Army), ZANU's military wing, which had been launching guerrilla drives into northeastern Rhodesia from Frelimo's liberated zones in Tete.

On a broader level the collapse of Portugal's African empire undermined a central tenet of the Pretoria government's strategy for the whole Southern African region: the reliance it had placed on a *cordon sanitaire* of white-ruled buffer states north of its border. South Africa adjusted its strategy and decided to seek a rapprochement with the new Frelimo rulers in Mozambique.

THE SOUTH AFRICAN GOVERNMENT REACTION

A spate of important speeches by leading members of the South African government in the last few months of 1974 sketched out the essentials of Pretoria's new policy toward Frelimo. While the Lusaka negotiations between Frelimo and Portugal were still in progress, the South African Prime Minister, John Vorster, in a speech on September 6 to the South African Parliament said his government had received "assurances" from Portugal that South African interests would not be harmed by the transition to Frelimo rule. "On the matters on which assurances were sought," he said, "positive answers were given."

The South African government, he said nine days later, wished Frelimo well. "Whoever takes over in Mozambique has a tough task ahead of him. It will require exceptional leadership. They have my sympathy and I wish them well." He went on to say that "a black government in Mozambique holds no fear for us whatever. We are surrounded by black governments as it is, and we ourselves are in the process of creating some more by leading our black homelands to independence."

At the same time, however, Vorster was careful to warn Frelimo that South Africa would hit back at Mozambique if the newly independent country allowed its territory to be used by guerrillas of the South African liberation movements as a "springboard" against the Pretoria regime. "I would like to think that that would not happen," he said in a September 15, 1975, interview. "But if it does, it will naturally lead to a head-on collision between ourselves and Mozambique."

It soon became clear that Vorster's optimism and talk of "assurances" were well-grounded. While Machel promised on September 20 that Mozambique would become a "revolutionary base against imperialism and colonialism in Africa," Chissano assured Pretoria that the new government was prepared to coexist with its powerful white-ruled neighbor. "We do not pretend to be the saviours of the world," he told a press conference in the capital on September 17. "We will not be saviours or the reformers of South Africa. That belongs to the people of South Africa." A month later, in an interview with the Mozambican weekly *Tempo,* Chissano explained that

Mozambique would become a "revolutionary base" in ideas alone and would not interfere in the international affairs of other countries.

DEPENDENCE ON SOUTH AFRICA

The Pretoria regime exploited Mozambique's chronic economic dependence on South Africa to extract the required "assurances" from the Frelimo leaders. Stressing Mozambique's stake in the maintenance of good relations with South Africa, Dr. Nicholaas Diederichs, then South Africa's finance minister and currently its president, made the point in November 1974:

> I need only mention the harbour at Lourenço Marques, the bulk of whose traffic derives from trade between South Africa and other countries, the tourist trade—mainly South African—of Lourenço Marques and other coastal resorts, the job opportunities provided in South African mines and industries for many thousands of Mozambique workers, and, finally, the Cabora Bassa hydroelectric scheme, which would not be remotely viable without the sale of power to the Republic [of South Africa].

A brief examination of the factors noted by Diederichs reveals the powerful leverage that Pretoria knew it could use to pressure Frelimo into cooperation on a political level.

South Africa's right to recruit labor in Mozambique (in return for the use of the port of Maputo) derives from the Mozambique Convention, signed with Lisbon at the beginning of the century. Under the Convention, Mozambicans could be recruited for twelve to eighteen months. For the first six months they were paid their full wages, but for the remainder of their employment they were paid only 40 percent, the rest being banked monthly with the South African Reserve Bank. Every quarter, the South African Reserve Bank used to inform Portugal's Banco Nacional Ultramarino (BNU) of the total in the "mines" account, and payment was then made to Portugal in gold bars calculated at the official gold price of $35 per ounce (from 1933 onward the rate was not changed when the official gold price went up to $38 per ounce in 1971 and $42.22 per ounce in 1973). The gold bars were traditionally transferred from Mozambique by the BNU to Lisbon, which made payments to Mozambique in local currency in order to pay the miners on their return from South Africa.

Before Mozambique won its independence, Portugal was able to sell on the free market the bullion it received under the Mozambique Convention. In this way Portugal could make a handsome windfall profit, because the market price of gold soared in the early seventies far above the official rate (despite the two upward revaluations) to reach an all-time high of $195.50 per ounce on the London gold market at the end of 1974.

As we have seen above, Frelimo's benefits from the system set up by the Mozambique Convention began to wane in 1976—because of the downward slide in the market price of gold and the reduction in the number of Mozambican migrant workers in South Africa's gold mines. In consequence, Mozambique's estimated earnings from the export of mine labor fell to around $100 million in 1976. Nevertheless, this would still be nearly one fifth of the total value of 1974 foreign currency receipts. South Africa has exploited this dependence to the full in its drive to keep Frelimo wedded to a collaborative course.

Migration of Mozambican Miners to South Africa

	1971	1972	1973	1974	1975
Departed	79,700	80,940	79,446	90,179	102,725
Returned	88,488	83,366	71,309	76,378	83,456

According to the Economist Intelligence Unit, the relatively high market price of gold and the increase in employment of Mozambican miners in South Africa stood to earn Mozambique $175 million of foreign exchange in 1975, the equivalent of a staggering one third of the country's entire foreign exchange earnings of $525 million in 1974. This in itself is a striking indication of the Frelimo regime's vested interest in the preservation of "normal" relations with South Africa.

Nevertheless, during 1976 Frelimo's benefits from the system set up by the Mozambique Convention began to wane. First, the market price of gold drifted downward, falling below $120 per ounce in the second half of the year, thus narrowing Mozambique's profits from its gold sales. Second, South African mine labor recruitment from Mozambique decreased sharply from nearly 2,000 per week in 1975 to under 400 per week in the second quarter of 1976. By August, employment of Mozambican miners was down to 75,000. The reasons were several: the fall in the gold price led to a fall in production and employment and the threat of closures in less-efficient mines; and, with 1.5 million black South Africans out of work due to the deep recession in the South African economy, the mining industry reduced its dependence on foreign labor. In consequence, Mozambique's estimated earnings from the export of mine labor fell to around $100 million in 1976.

Mozambique's other major source of foreign exchange earnings on its current invisibles account is its shipment of South African exports and imports via the port of Maputo. Maputo's port, whose modern development began with the construction of the Transvaal railway in 1886, is one of the largest in Africa. In 1975 it handled 18 percent of South Africa's exports and imports and shipped about 25,000 tons of South African exports per day. Moreover, foreign exchange earnings from transport trade facilities (primarily, though not entirely, from the shipment of South African imports and exports) have averaged about 30 percent of the country's total foreign exchange earnings in recent years.

In the early months of 1976 the freight volume moving from South Africa to Maputo slumped to around 18,000 tons a day, when port productivity fell following an exodus of the port's Portuguese administrators and skilled workers. But the South African regime, as part of its campaign to keep on good terms with Frelimo, reaffirmed its long-term plans to route a large part of South African trade through Maputo (despite the construction in South Africa itself of a major new port at Richard's Bay). It put pressure on South African exporters to ship cargo through Mozambique and has also sent skilled workers by air to Maputo to maintain the port's efficiency.

The third main factor impelling Frelimo's leaders to maintain friendly relations with the Pretoria regime is the giant Cabora Bassa hydroelectric scheme, built in Mozambique's Tete province by a Portuguese-led electrical consortium, Zambco, to provide electricity to South Africa under the terms of a 1969 contract with the Electricity Supply Commission of South Africa (ESCOM). Vorster, telling South African members of Parliament on August 30, 1974, that Mozambique could not survive economically without cooperating with South Africa, noted that Cabora Bassa (the fourth largest hydroelectric scheme in the world) would become a "white elephant" if the electricity was not sold to South Africa.

Work on the Cabora Bassa dam, sited on the Zambezi River near Songo, began in 1969 and was completed at the end of 1974. The first hydroelectric generators had been installed and tested by the beginning of 1975. And a second power station was planned on the north bank of the Zambezi to take Cabora Bassa's eventual total capacity to 4,000 MW.

Under the 1969 contract, ESCOM was pledged to buy an initial 680 MW, rising to 1,470 MW in 1979, at 0.3 cents a unit for twenty years. There is no alternative market to South Africa that could make the project viable. So, on March 15, 1976, Mozambique and Portugal signed an agreement for electricity sales to South Africa. Under the March 15 agreement a new consortium, the *Companhia Hidroelectrica de Cabora Bassa* (HCB), was set up. Led by the Portuguese government, HCB includes all those who have invested in the project, but Mozambique is not expected to take a controlling share until the project's £500 ($1200) million debt has been whittled away over the next fifteen to twenty years through the sale of electricity to South Africa.

Power was scheduled to start flowing along the twin 850-mile powerlines to South Africa's Apollo station (and then into the South African grid) in September 1975, but commencement of electricity supplies was suddenly postponed early in the month. A year later regular transmissions to South Africa had still not started. The reason was not political; only the simple fact that, at 0.3 cents a unit, the electricity would be so cheap that sales would be scarcely sufficient to cover interest payments on HCB's debts, let alone repay the principal. So regular transmissions were held up while HCB pushed for a renegotiation of the 1969 contract.

Another consideration for Mozambique's new rulers is South Africa's emergence as the country's main and most convenient source of imports. South Africa displaced Portugal as Mozambique's leading supplier for the first time in 1973. That year 20.3 percent of Mozambique's imports came from South Africa. Imports from South Africa totaled 2.3 billion escudos (compared to 2.2 billion escudos of imports from Portugal), almost double Mozambique's imports from South Africa in 1972 (1.3 billion escudos). South African exports to Mozambique include machinery, spare parts, iron and steel, fertilizer, and wheat. Like other black-ruled countries in southern and central Africa (Lesotho, Swaziland, Botswana, Zambia, Zaïre, and Malawi), Mozambique finds South Africa to be the closest and cheapest marketplace for the purchase of a wide range of manufactured goods.

Dependent, therefore, to such a degree on South Africa, the Frelimo government in Mozambique has charted a pragmatic, collaborative course toward the South African regime. As Vorster put it in Parliament on November 5, 1974:

> We have asked that certain agreements between Mozambique and our country be honoured because it was in South Africa's interest that the ports of Lourenço Marques and Beira remain open and the railways carry traffic. It is also in South Africa's interest that the Mozambique labour agreement be honoured and the Cabora Bassa power scheme be successfully completed. I am glad to be able to tell you that in spite of certain difficulties these agreements will be reasonably honoured.

Evidences of Mozambique's political and diplomatic stance toward Pretoria have been manifold. In February 1975, for example, Oliver Tambo, the leader of the African National Congress of South Africa, said that there was "a gap between what Frelimo will do for us and what we would like them to do." Radio Lisbon, on May 31, 1975, reported Machel as explaining that "South Africa is going to change its policy and there will be no aggression. It is necessary for men of all colours and races to walk, live and work together. This is a struggle in itself and there is no need for weapons. With political work, much political work, our country will become an example." Shortly before independence the South African consulate-general in Maputo was officially closed, but it soon reopened under the guise of a trade mission. South African technicians continued to work at Cabora Bassa, and, even before South African Railways' top-level visit to Maputo in July 1976, SAR officials had continued to work in their offices at Maputo port. In April 1976 one top Frelimo leader, Manuel Bandeira (the Mozambican minister of agriculture), entered a South African hospital for medical treatment.

There have been occasional incidents on the South African–Mozambican border, but they have all involved Frelimo attempts to prevent Portuguese expatriates crossing illegally into South Africa. On each occasion both South Africa and Frelimo authorities have been eager to reaffirm their desire for friendly relations. Thus, in March 1976, after seventeen Frelimo soldiers had been detained at Nelspruit after being caught chasing a group of Portuguese across the border, the South African minister of police, J. T. Kruger, said that "I want to give the assurance that I know what I am talking about. . . . There is no reason to think Frelimo will not respect our border once the fence has been repaired." On April 8 Kruger announced that the seventeen Mozambican soldiers had been released after Mozambique had given assurances that the border would not be violated again.

MOZAMBIQUE'S IMPACT ON RHODESIA

In tune with its collaborative stance toward South Africa, Machel's government (like the other front-line governments of Tanzania, Zambia, and Botswana) played a prominent part in the détente diplomacy over Rhodesia's future in 1975. Mozambique never dissociated itself from the Dar es Salaam Declaration, adopted by the OAU Liberation Committee in April 1975 (and endorsed by the OAU's 12th Ordinary Summit in Uganda in July 1975), which in essence endorsed the so-called Lusaka strategy: the bid launched at the end of 1974 in Lusaka by the front-line states and the reorganized African National Council (ANC) of Zimbabwe to reach a negotiated settlement of the Rhodesian crisis with the Smith regime. Both during the transitional government's term of office and during the first weeks of independence Frelimo did not support guerrilla incursions into Rhodesia from Mozambican territory. Furthermore, in April 1975 the Mozambican authorities arrested the secretary-general of ZANU, Robert Mugabe, and placed him under house detention. Following the assassination of ZANU's chairman, Herbert Chitepo, in Zambia on March 18, 1975, Frelimo arrested the ZANLU chief of staff, Josiah Tongogara—the man widely regarded as the mastermind of the ZANLA offensive in northeastern Rhodesia—and sent him to Zambia. There, along with other leading members of the ZANU Supreme Council and the ZANU High Command, he was detained under suspicion of involvement in the Chitepo affair, until released to participate in the Geneva Conference, October–December 1976.

The Rhodesian regime's dogged refusal to make even minimal concessions to the Zimbabwean nationalists (despite the urging of South Africa)
finally forced the front-line black states to endorse a new wave of guerrilla
attacks against the Smith regime. Mozambique and Tanzania switched
course earlier than Zambia, the turning point in Frelimo policy coming
shortly after the fiasco of the August 1975 summit meeting of Smith,
Vorster, Kaunda, and the Zimbabwean nationalists at Victoria Falls on the
Rhodesian–Zambian border. This failure convinced Frelimo's leaders that
the settler regime in Rhodesia would never concede a transfer of power to
the Zimbabwean nationalists without an intensification of military and
economic pressures.

By February 1976, there were an estimated ten thousand Zimbabwean
guerrillas training in camps in Mozambique. Instructors from the Tanzanian People's Defense Force arrived in Mozambique to help train the
rapidly swelling number of recruits, and Soviet arms arrived at the Mozambican ports of Nacala and Beira. By February fighting was reported to have
spread from the long-standing northeastern zone to the east and southeast
of Rhodesia, indicating that Mozambique was now allowing guerrillas to
cross into Rhodesia along the entire length of its border.

Mozambique coordinated its Rhodesia policy closely with the other
front-line states. A summit meeting held in the northern Mozambique city
of Quelimane in February 1976 and attended by presidents Machel,
Kaunda, Nyerere, and Seretse Khama agreed on a common policy to step
up the guerrilla war against the Smith regime. Though Mozambique, like
the other front-line states, endorsed this new wave of guerrilla actions,
Frelimo had not abandoned hopes of securing a negotiated settlement of the
Zimbabwean crisis—as Mozambique's support for the British-sponsored
Geneva conference in October–December 1976 underscored. In fact,
Frelimo was keen to see an orderly transfer of power to a black government
in Zimbabwe—very much on the model of its own transition to power after
the September 1974 accords with Portugal. The relaunching of the guerrilla
offensive in early 1976 was designed simply to force the Smith regime into
serious negotiations on the transfer of power to a black government.

At the same time, Mozambique, like the other front-line states, sought
to keep the "armed struggle" under tight rein through its control over the

guerrilla camps and the supply of arms and funds to the Zimbabwean nationalists. In line with a decision of the OAU summit conference in July 1976, all OAU funds for the Zimbabwean liberation struggle were channeled through the OAU Liberation Committee and Mozambique's Bank for Solidarity. In addition, Frelimo and Tanzanian soldiers effectively ran the guerrilla camps and were responsible for the supply of arms and much of the training. Finally, Mozambique and the other front-line states promoted the leadership team associated with the Zimbabwe People's Army (ZIPA), the so-called "third force," over other factions in the Zimbabwean nationalist movement. Leaders of the other factions complained of "interference" by Mozambique in the internal affairs of the Zimbabwean movement and charged that Frelimo refused to let them visit the guerrilla camps.

At the Quelimane meeting, the four front-line presidents also agreed that the Mozambican government should apply United Nations sanctions against Rhodesia and close the Mozambique-Rhodesia border. Mozambique's first serious threat to apply sanctions had been given the previous October by Chissano in an address to the United Nations General Assembly. There, Chissano had appealed "to all members of the United Nations to apply a complete and total boycott against Rhodesia" and said that "Frelimo and the People's Republic of Mozambique are ready to assume all responsibility in conformity with their international duty."

The border closure came on March 3, 1976. Machel announced:

> To support the liberation struggle of the Zimbabwe people in accordance with the decisions of the U.N. and the OAU . . . with effect from today, 3rd March 1976, the Mozambique People's Republic closes all its frontiers with the British colony of Southern Rhodesia; prohibits any form of communications with the territory dominated by the racist regime; bans the passage through its territory and air space of any traffic of persons and goods originating from or bound for Southern Rhodesia. The PRM fully applies the sanctions against the British colony of Southern Rhodesia. The PRM confiscates all assets belonging to the illegal regime, to firms with headquarters in the territory of the British colony of Southern Rhodesia and to citizens living in our territory who recognize the illegal regime.

The immediate effect of the border closure was to bar Rhodesian access to the ports of Beira and Maputo, the ports that had traditionally handled over 80 percent of Rhodesia's foreign trade, and to throw the Smith regime into precarious reliance on its two remaining rail links with the outside world, the railway through Botswana to Mafeking in South Africa and the railway from Rutenga to the South African border at Beitbridge. In addition, the expropriation of Rhodesian assets in Mozambique lost Rhodesia one sixth of its rolling stock (2,300 railway wagons worth $46 million). In short, Smith was now totally dependent on the good graces of the South African government for Rhodesia's economic survival. Moreover, along with the escalation of the guerrilla war, both the United States and South Africa redoubled their pressures on the Smith regime to agree to a negotiated settlement with the nationalists.

What were the repercussions on Mozambique of these policies? In the first place, Mozambique's support for the Zimbabwean guerrillas brought repeated Rhodesian raids across the Mozambican border. This had been a common occurrence at the time of ZANLA's use of Frelimo's liberated zones in Tete before Portugal's withdrawal from Mozambique; in 1971, for example, Rhodesian troops were involved in a massacre (later to receive wide publicity) in the village of Mucumbura in Tete.

A series of Rhodesian attacks over the border were made in February, June, and July of 1976. The constant state of tension along the border forced the Mozambique government to start arming a "people's militia" in the border regions. At the same time Mozambique had to cope with an influx of refugees, many of them young children and old people, who fled the fighting in eastern Rhodesia. Their numbers were estimated to be twenty-five thousand by October 1976. It was against one of Mozambique's refugee camps that the Rhodesian security forces launched a particularly bloody raid on August 8. The camp (at Nhazonia, some twenty-five miles from the border) was run under the auspices of the United Nations High Commission for Refugees (UNHCR) and, according to Prince Saddruddin, the UNHCR's high commissioner, over six hundred of the camp's eight thousand refugees were slaughtered in the raid. The Rhodesian government claimed that its troops had attacked a guerrilla camp, killing three hundred "terrorists," but international condemnation was strong.

Though Mozambique's economic ties to Rhodesia were small by comparison to its chronic dependence on South Africa, the economic ramifications of the border closure were not unimportant for Mozambique. A United Nations mission report, published by the Economic and Social Council on April 30, gave a detailed picture of the costs of the border closure. Under normal circumstances Mozambique's ports and railways could expect to handle some 4 million tons of transit traffic passing through Rhodesia. Since 1972, however, the level had fallen to about 2.3 million tons in 1975, partly because Zambia closed its border with Rhodesia in 1973, thereby halting Zambian copper shipments via Rhodesia to Beira; and, after Portugal's decision to withdraw from Mozambique, because Rhodesia started diverting some of its traffic to South African routes in anticipation of an eventual border closure by Frelimo.

The United Nations mission estimated the reduction in foreign-exchange earnings by the railways and ports as a result of the application of sanctions at between $57 and $74 million per year. In addition, $5 to $10 million per year was lost by related services (clearing, bonding, forwarding, insurance). Nearly $1 million was lost in airport taxes and landing fees for Rhodesian aircraft, and annual tourism earnings of $4.5 to $5.5 million were lost. The United Nations mission also estimated that Mozambique lost $22 to $25 million in annual remittances from Mozambican migrant workers in Rhodesia (believed to number roughly 80,000). The total annual loss of foreign-exchange earnings on Mozambique's current invisibles account was between $89.5 and $115.5 million. In addition, the loss of export markets in Rhodesia, the U.N. mission calculated, would cost Mozambique about $16 million per year over the first eighteen months to two years of sanction. The mission therefore estimated that Mozambique's current account deficit would suffer to the tune of between $108 and $134 million per year as a direct result of sanctions, leaving a forecast total current account deficit of around $175 to $200 million in 1976.

The mission further estimated that development projects made necessary by the border closure (the provision of alternatives to roads and facilities cut off by the closure of the frontier) would cost $31 million and the building-up of stocks (particularly of food), previously lower because of access to Rhodesian stocks, would cost $6 million. The mission calculated that 10,000 Mozambicans would lose their jobs, 5,000 in ports and railways and 1,000 in related transit agencies and organizations.

Mozambique knew that it could count on international aid to compensate for at least some of its losses. Aid totaling some $100 million, primarily from the capitalist countries, had been pledged by October 1976 in response to the U.N.'s March 17 emergency appeal. However, much of this was in the form of loans which will add to Mozambique's long-term external debt, raising the prospect of a heavy burden of future debt-service payments. Much of the aid pledged was also not immediately available. So, it would seem improbable that foreign aid will compensate fully for the costs of the border closure, let alone offset Mozambique's estimated annual current account deficit of $175 to $200 million. There seems little doubt that the government in Maputo wants a settlement of the Zimbabwean crisis and a reopening of the border as fast as possible.

No African country is sacrificing so much to secure majority rule in Southern Africa as is Mozambique. At a time when its own economy is still far from reorganized, it has deliberately taken upon itself further dislocations through its active role in the Zimbabwean struggle. Until that issue is settled, Mozambique's internal situation will continue to be rent with difficulties. What Frelimo's leaders hoped would be short-range programs have inevitably been turned into long-range ones. Goals are delayed. Yet Frelimo's ultimate objectives remain, and in time its leaders hope to begin to move systematically toward realizing them.

[3]

South Africa

Battleground of Rival Nationalisms

GWENDOLEN M. CARTER

SOUTH AFRICA ENTERED a new era of black-white confrontation in June 1976, when thousands of African high school students in Soweto, who were demonstrating against teaching in Afrikaans, exploded into violence after police shot and killed a teenager. Unlike earlier clashes that led to tragedy, like the mass shootings at Sharpeville in March 1960, this one was not ended by the regime's use of force even though many were killed and the government imprisoned hundreds of others involved in violence and also most of the articulate leaders of black protest throughout the country. On the contrary, demonstrations and riots spread from area to area affecting black universities as well as townships. In September 1976 they erupted in white urban areas, notably in Cape Town, where African and Coloured youth combined in a visible demonstration of the effectiveness of the new spirit of black consciousness.

What was behind this outburst? What would be its effect? Would African and black nationalism, so long suppressed by discriminatory laws and force, finally achieve fundamental change within the strongest, richest, and most developed state in Africa? Or would the dominant white Afrikaner nationalism that had controlled the government for over a quarter of a century maintain, and even reinforce, the controls so carefully built up through the legally enforced paraphernalia of apartheid?

Coming as it did at a time when the whole of Southern Africa appeared to be in flux, black urban violence in South Africa had a worldwide impact. Was it derivative of the success of liberation movements in Mozambique and Angola that now form the governments of independent states? Was it stimulated by the historic African nationalist movement, the African National Congress (ANC), as the latter's leaders outside the country claim? Or did it mark the emergence of a new and potent force, fully urbanized black youth, whose frustrations at the narrow and arbitrarily drawn limits imposed on them and their families by apartheid were finally being vented through destruction of government property in the townships but later perhaps the white cities themselves? Was it a combination of all these and other factors?

And on the other side, how would white Afrikaner nationalism respond over time? Initially through force in its long-established pattern of repression. Unbelieving that black youth could act by itself, authorities looked for outside agitators, black or white, warned of the menace of communism, and refused to respond to calls for far-reaching change made not only by white moderates and the English-language press but equally cogently by much of the Afrikaans press and even some of their own Nationalist supporters. The Nationalist Party meeting in September 1976 that celebrated Prime Minister B. J. Vorster's ten years in office forcefully reaffirmed the basic government policy that Africans have political rights only in the fragmented and underdeveloped Bantustans (or homelands) on the periphery of the country despite the scorn of urban black youth for the concept. Yet the proposal of a cabinet council with Coloured and Asian representatives meeting to discuss policy issues with white government officials, although unacceptable to those seeking direct parliamentary representation, did suggest some hard thinking at high levels as to how to afford some representation in the central system without yielding ultimate white power.

Was it too late for such expedients? Did the demands of enraged black youth to share power—demands often made earlier by African nationalists but always denied—have potency absent in the past, partly because their base within the country had changed, but more particularly because its international environment had done so? Or would the Nationalist government use its undoubted military and economic power to silence opposition and even criticism at home even while it was urging the constitutional transfer of political power to the black majority in Rhodesia and not preventing a similar process in Namibia? And even if this latter policy ensured moderate black governments on both frontiers, as the South African government hoped it would, could Afrikanerdom indefinitely hold down the black majority at home, not only in the face of the blacks' pressures for change, but also those of the outside world?

South Africa has long been buttressed by substantial and mutually rewarding Western investment, much of it from Great Britain, but a growing percentage from the United States, Japan, West Germany, and France. By 1974 the value of American private investment in South Africa was estimated at $1.46 billion, more than 20 percent higher than two years before, and representing 16 percent of all the private foreign investment in that country (the British share is 58 percent). The four hundred and eighty American firms reported by the South African *Financial Mail* in August 1975 included some of the largest and wealthiest companies in the United States: twelve of the fifteen top-ranking concerns according to the *Fortune* list of 1971, fifty-five of the top one hundred, and one hundred and thirty-six of the top five hundred. Forty-five percent of the total U.S. private investment in South Africa is in manufacturing, to which American technology contributes as much as its capital.

The attractiveness of investment in South Africa lies not only in its phenomenally rich mineral resources, its three-tier economy with an iron and steel industry competitive with those in the rest of the world, and a wide range of manufactures, but also in its controlled and generally docile labor force mostly paid at minimum wage levels and without effective bargaining facilities. Sporadic strikes and walkouts in recent years plus adverse foreign publicity over low wage rates and poor conditions of work have done something, though not much, to improve conditions. But two substantial three-day strikes in the key Johannesburg area stimulated by black youth and, despite official reports to the contrary, probably willingly participated in by at least township workers, have given pause to some American and other Western investors. So, too, Congressional concern at the size and scope of American investment in South Africa. Should disorders and workers' discontent surface frequently and on a large scale, the attractiveness of participating in the South African economy would be far less. Whether or not African and Coloured labor share all the political objectives of black youth, there can be little doubt of their own awareness of the need for effective organization to improve their positions within the economy, and for leverage to bring this about.

Behind what is presently going on in South Africa lies more than a century of open protest against the steadily increasing political and economic restrictions and discrimination imposed on blacks by the dominant white minority. The process of formulating and organizing these protests helped to forge an African nationalism that transcends ethnic divisions and social and economic circumstances. Recently it has been broadened to black nationalism, that is, including Coloured and Asian, without undercutting the force of Africanism. From the first, however, African nationalism has been confronted, as is black nationalism today, by a powerful white Afrikaner nationalism imbued with a sense of its own superiority. Long an important political force, Afrikanerdom has been since 1948 in virtually undisputed control of the instruments of government and has used its stringent apartheid policies to contribute to the country's phenomenal economic growth.

At the heart of the present situation in South Africa lies the clash between these two nationalisms, the one protecting the privileged economic and social position of whites within the country by every means at the disposal of a determined government and people, the other demanding the rights and potential power belonging to the majority. Unless we understand how these nationalisms developed and were fired in adversity, we cannot appreciate the intensity of feeling that animates them both. History has been a powerful force in shaping both nationalisms, and the interactions between black and white over the centuries form a major factor in determining their reactions to the present crisis.

THE FIRST CLASHES BETWEEN WHITE AND BLACK

The long history of the black-white relations in Southern Africa dates back to 1652, when the Dutch East India Company established a way station to the East at the tip of the African continent. The Dutch settlers, who landed near what is now Cape Town, were a purposeful and independent group whose elitist Calvinism filled them with a sense of mission to dominate the heathen and to build their own characteristic society in the new land.

Spreading out beyond the established confines of the settlement, they soon clashed with indigenous peoples for control of the land. The San, or Bushmen, were driven from their hunting grounds and in the long run virtually exterminated; the cattle-raising Khoikhoi, or Hottentots, fought the white encroachments but ultimately became little more than hangers-on and servants. In the meantime, slaves had been brought from the East Indies and Africa itself despite an imaginative proposal that the settlement should depend on white labor. Particularly in the early days, when there were few white women in the settlement, miscegenation was common. From the intermingling of slave, Bushman, Hottentot, and white blood came the varied peoples known as Coloured, one of the population groups of modern South Africa. From the experience of slave-owning and of conquest came the expectation of domination over peoples of color that still marks much of Afrikanerdom, and indeed most of the white population of South Africa.

More effective adversaries than those in the Western Cape met the whites who spread east along the coast in their search for new land. Well-organized Nguni tribes that had been seeping south and west for centuries blocked the white advance along the line of the Great Fish River, which today forms the western borders of the Transkei and Ciskei. The first of a long series of frontier wars erupted in 1791. Ultimately, however, the African tribes were also crushed and scattered, their members turned into farm labor or squatters or driven into the limited areas once labeled "reserves" and now "homelands." Later, the same process of conquest by arms took place in Natal. But the spirit of African resistance was not quenched.

DUTCH (AFRIKANERS) VERSUS BRITISH

The Dutch settlers also experienced the bitterness of conquest and the search for new homes. In 1795, when the Dutch were allies of France in the Napoleonic Wars, the English occupied the Cape; in 1815 they annexed it. The influence of British missionaries and the liberalizing trends in England itself led to a new status for Hottentots and Africans at the Cape: in 1834 slavery was abolished. British mores and commercialism reshaped the character of local society. The cumulative effect of what they viewed as interference with their chosen way of life resulted in a long slow movement of many Dutch (later called Boers, or farmers, and ultimately Afrikaners) away from the Western Cape in what became known as the Great Trek.

Some trekkers crossed the mountains with their ox-wagons and cattle and spread into the fertile lands of Natal. There they clashed with Zulus and suffered a massacre that they avenged at Blood River in 1838, a victory still commemorated by modern Afrikanerdom. But their efforts to create a separate state were foiled by British annexation of Natal in 1845. This largely English-speaking colony was subsequently to complicate the racial composition of South Africa by bringing indentured Hindu Indians to Natal to work in the sugar plantations. Though intended to return, most stayed and were joined by Moslem merchants and others over the years. Their descendants form the fifth strand of the country's complex racial structure.

Though frustrated in Natal, the Boer trekkers were successful to the north in establishing two republics, the Orange Free State and the South African Republic (Transvaal). In both republics all-white male electorates affirmed the doctrine of "no equality of black and white in church or state."

The Boer republics might have been left alone had it not been for the discovery of great sources of wealth under their soil. Diamonds found at Kimberly in 1867 led to gerrymandering the border in 1871 to include that area within the English-controlled Cape. As British imperial interests in Southern Africa ebbed and expanded, the Transvaal was annexed in 1877 but returned to Boer control after a British army was defeated at Majuba Hill in 1881. But the discovery of gold in 1886 in the Witwatersrand reef in the center of the Transvaal spelled the end of isolation.

THE IMPACT OF MODERN CAPITALISM

British and European entrepreneurs and capital flooded into the area to establish the elaborate underground equipment necessary to exploit the gold veins that lay deep in the earth, while thousands of Africans were recruited to provide the necessary hand labor. The nascent capitalism that had been an inevitable feature of Southern Africa since the earliest white settlement was transformed into a major, some would say *the* major, molding influence in what was to become South Africa. It thus became a part of worldwide industrial and commercial capitalism.

Before that time, despite the disruption of tribal organization, there were Africans who continued to produce not only for their own needs but also for sale. Some did well in adopting new crops and techniques. Although their relations with Afrikaners were often marked by roughness, there was little of the calculated racial discrimination that stamped many of their later interactions. As long as the struggle was primarily for land, it was possible to accommodate both black and white on what was fairly easily available. Now the emphasis turned to labor. The ever-increasing demand for cheap manpower to service the mines and all the associated aspects of the economy led to the imposition of taxes and other measures that steadily squeezed out self-sufficient peasant economies to reduce their competition and to force Africans into the wage system. To the basic tensions between the black majority and the dominant white minority was added an ever-widening gap between African and, to a lesser degree, Coloured and Asian labor, and white capitalists.

The Afrikaner regime in the Transvaal resisted the impact of mining and finance capitalism by denying *uitlanders* (foreigners) the vote. In 1896 an abortive coup known as the Jameson Raid sought to overthrow the Transvaal's administration and provide the new economic interests with political power. Both Cecil Rhodes, Prime Minister of the Cape, and the British Government were implicated in the raid. The angry recriminations that followed led inexorably to the Anglo-Boer War, 1899–1902.

Despite the mobilizing of troops from all over the British Empire, including the Cape and Natal, the war was long drawn out because of the skill of Boer tactics and fighting. The herding of Afrikaner women and children from their farms into camps in which many of them died of disease added further bitterness to their final defeat.

SOUTH AFRICAN INDEPENDENCE: A WHITE-CONTROLLED STATE

A generous peace coupled with the promise of self-government and independence under a South African drafted constitution helped to overbridge the hostility caused by the war. Moderate whites from all parts of the country joined in shaping what was to become the Union of South Africa in 1910, an independent Dominion like Canada and Australia within the British Commonwealth of Nations. But the political and economic price of such reconciliation was paid by the Africans.

In the Cape, Africans had possessed the vote since 1853 on the same qualified franchise (economic and educational qualifications) as whites and Coloured; in seven border constituencies in the Eastern Cape they exercised a strong political influence on the election of candidates. Cape liberals sought to expand these franchise provisions to the other provinces but without success. The most they could achieve was to entrench their own voting provisions in the new constitution by requiring a special procedure for their amendment (also extended to the equality of English and Dutch, subsequently Afrikaans). Moreover, the constitution provided that only whites could be elected to Parliament.

Africans had not been silent while whites designed the structure for an independent South Africa. Their nascent political organizations dating from 1882 had been reinforced by African political journalism, which began two years later with a widely read newspaper, *Imvo Zabantsundu* (Native Opinion), edited by an articulate and sophisticated African, John Tengo Jabavu. Opposition by educated Africans to discriminatory measures was paralleled by their claim to share the status and rights of "civilized British subjects." On the eve of South African independence, the National Native Convention protested the exclusion of Africans from Parliament. In 1912, three years later, the South African Native (subsequently African) National Congress was formed under the leadership of four extremely able British-

and American-trained African lawyers. Until banned in 1960 following the Sharpeville massacre, the African National Congress remained the chief standard-bearer and articulate voice of African nationalism.

There was much against which to protest. Late nineteenth-century laws stimulated by pressure from mine owners were specifically designed to push Africans off the land to work in white-controlled mines, commerce, and agriculture. So were the Native Labour Regulation Act of 1911, the Natives Land Act of 1913 (which ejected squatters from white farmlands), the manipulation of the pass laws and influx control, and a succession of other governmental efforts to stimulate a flow of cheap labor for white use. There were also other factors forcing Africans and other blacks into the wage economy: growing population pressures, cheap food from abroad as ports and the growing railway network increasingly tied South Africa into the economy of the West, local crop diseases and periodic droughts, price fluctuations abroad, and the late nineteenth-century worldwide trade depression. Not only blacks but whites suffered their dislocating impacts.

AFRIKANERS STRUGGLE FOR POWER AND
THE AFRICAN RESPONSE

In the aftermath of World War I, Afrikanerdom confronted a new and in effect its greatest crisis. An increasing number of relatively unskilled Afrikaners were forced off their farms by persistent drought. As they flooded into the cities, they found that the English-speaking occupied the top positions in industry, commerce, and mining while Africans and Coloured held the unskilled jobs. In the 1920s Afrikanerdom faced the world's worst poor-white problem with some 60 percent of its people in or near disaster. Only radical measures by government seemed capable of meeting their needs.

Whites were clearly in control in the new Union of South Africa, but which whites? Originally and ever since, the Prime Minister has been an Afrikaner. But Afrikaners at large felt that the English-speaking were entrenched both politically and economically, and too greatly influenced by British imperial interests. In 1912 General Barry Hertzog broke away from the cabinet dominated by General Louis Botha and General Jan Christiaan

Smuts, which was dedicated to uniting the English-speaking and Afrikaners. Hertzog campaigned through his National Party for a separate Afrikaner nationalism capable of working on equal terms with the English-speaking, and ultimately of capitalizing on the Afrikaners' majority position within the white community. World War I saw an abortive rebellion by some Afrikaners against South Africa's participation in the struggle. In 1919 the Broederbond was formed to promote Afrikaner advance; three years later it became a secret society dedicated to the ultimate establishment of a *boere republiek,* that is, one controlled by Afrikaners. The Broederbond has remained one of the most potent influences on Afrikaner politics and education ever since.

In 1922 radical white miners on the Rand struck against an economy proposal by gold-mine owners to allow Africans to assume some semiskilled jobs. In bloody fighting the strike was put down by the government under General Smuts, who had succeeded Botha on the latter's death. Though temporarily defeated, white labor in the end was victorious. In 1924 Smuts was turned out of office by Hertzog at the head of a coalition of his National Party and the largely English-speaking Labour Party. The ultimate result was the enactment of what was known as "the civilised labour policy" that carved out areas of the economy reserved for whites.

As increasing numbers of Afrikaners became urbanized, the National Party, the political organ of Afrikaner nationalism, acquired its second major pillar of electoral support. Traditionally the Afrikaner farmers of the *platteland* (countryside) and the *dorps* (villages) had provided its base. Now they were joined by the growing mass of Afrikaner urban workers whose employment and living centers brought them directly into contact with Africans. White labor's real and imagined fears of African competition joined with the capitalists' objective of a controlled black labor force to stimulate the growing, intricate pattern of restrictions on all blacks, but particularly on the majority Africans.

Besides protecting white labor against African competition and providing it with an assured economic status, the Hertzog government was determined to eliminate the African vote from affecting electoral results in Cape Province, the one place within South Africa where Africans shared voting rolls with whites. Failing to achieve this result through his own political resources and confronting the crisis of the depression, Hertzog joined with Smuts in 1934 to form a new political party, named the United Party, to institute economic and political changes. Once again the Africans were sacrificed.

Africans were, and are, as well aware as whites that the franchise is the key to political power. Rural and urban Africans protested the threat to the Cape African vote. Under a new umbrella organization, the All African Convention, more that four hundred delegates meeting in Bloemfontein in mid-December 1935 drafted a comprehensive charter of African grievances and urged that the African franchise be extended, not reduced. Their protests were in vain, and, by a constitutional amendment passed by the necessary two-thirds majority, Cape Africans were taken off the common roll. After 1936 Cape Africans could qualify for a direct vote only on a separate roll to elect three whites to the House of Assembly to represent their interests, and indirectly with all other Africans through a cumbersome procedure for four white senators. In 1959 even this small degree of representation was abolished.

Although the Africans were defeated on the issue of the Cape African vote, their ferment in the late 1930s and 1940s resulted in a new spirit of unity that transcended area and ethnicity and brough rural and urban Africans closer together. Earlier there had been sporadic anti-pass demonstrations and strikes, but the African leadership had depended largely on the conservative tactics of verbal and written protests and appeals. Now new forms of pressure like mass action and boycotts were discussed. The time would come when these means of pressure would be used by Africans, and still later in conjunction with Asians and/or Coloured.

Afrikanerdom was no less in ferment. Dr. Daniel F. Malan broke from Hertzog over the latter's decision to unite with Smuts and formed his own "purified" National Party, which preached a more extreme Afrikaner nationalism. Moreover, the thirties saw a withdrawal of Afrikaners from community organizations. Afrikaner students seceded from the countrywide student organization to form a separate one of their own in a move that was to be reflected at the end of the sixties by the black student withdrawal into SASO (South African Student Organisation) from the largely English-speaking National Union of South African Students

(NUSAS). Afrikaner Boy Scouts seceded from the world body. In 1938 a country-wide commemoration of the Great Trek was turned into an exclusively Afrikaner pageant. Out of it sprang the Ossewa Brandwag (ox-wagon guard), whose militaristic organization competed with Malan's party during World War II for the allegiance of Afrikanerdom. Although decisively defeated in the election of July 1943 by Smuts' United Party, Malan demonstrated effectively at that time that his party had the major political support of Afrikanerdom. On May 26, 1948, the Nationalists, with the support of the small Afrikaner Party, achieved a majority in the House of Assembly and Dr. D. F. Malan became prime minister.

While rival groups were competing within Afrikanerdom for dominance, new leaders and programs were arising within the African National Congress. In 1943 the Youth League was officially inaugurated with members like Anton Lembede, A. P. Mda, Nelson Mandela, Oliver Tambo, and Walter Sisulu, whose names were to become household words. Nelson Mandela, imprisoned since 1961, is still the most widely acclaimed leader of black South Africans. Also in 1943 the African National Congress issued its most important document since 1919, AFRICANS' CLAIMS IN SOUTH AFRICA, which not only emphasized African opposition to racial discrimination but also appeared to endorse universal franchise without qualifications. The Youth League set itself the task of generating a spirit of self-reliance and militant nationalism among the African masses to achieve these goals.

In its Programme of Action, adopted in December 1949, the African National Congress, spurred by the Youth League, specifically set forth tactics of direct action—boycotts, strikes, and civil disobedience—that could be used in the "struggle for national liberation." In 1946 some fifty thousand African gold mine workers on the Witwatersrand had staged a walkout protest against low wages and discriminatory conditions at the call of the African Mine Workers' Union led by John B. Marks, long a member of both the Communist Party and the African National Congress. In the same year the Natal Indian Congress had begun a passive resistance campaign in Durban against restrictions on Indian land ownership and occupation. In 1952, stimulated by these examples of protest and despite the harsh official response, the African National Congress was to call its own passive resistance campaign against "unjust laws." Most of the laws specified had been passed by the new Afrikaner Nationalist government, moving swiftly to systematize controls on the black population and enforce a more rigid racial separation.

AFRIKANERDOM SHAPES RACE RELATIONS

In 1948, when Malan's Afrikaner Nationalists came into office, whites were startled to learn that the number of Africans who had moved perforce off the overcrowded and undeveloped lands in the reserves to white farms and into urban townships, was greater than the numbers still remaining within the reserves. Moreover, white dependence on black labor for the country's growing industrialization and secondary industries had led, as the government's Fagan Commission disclosed in that year, to "a settled, permanent Native population" in the urban areas. To Afrikanerdom this was a new crisis.

Malan's National Party had campaigned on a platform of apartheid (racial apartness) without specifying how it was to be achieved. Once in power with its overwhelming Afrikaner support, the National Party has successfully increased its parliamentary majority at almost every election from then to the present. This majority has been used not only to push through progressively restrictive programs of racial segregation in white areas that have affected all black groups—African, Coloured, and Asians —but ultimately, and most significantly, their corollary of separate territorial development for Africans. The keynotes of the latter program were the denial of African rights in white areas, an emphasis on the ethnic diversity among Africans which African nationalism had long sought to overbridge, and the development of the scattered pockets of African reserves into Bantustans, or homelands, to which all Africans, regardless of domicile, experience, or desire, were said to belong.

The Nationalists began quickly to build up the intricate structure of legally enforced apartheid, the impact of which has been progressively extended. Their first real target was the Coloured, whom Hertzog had earlier called "an appendage to the whites" because of their long and close association. The Prohibition of Mixed Marriages Act, 1949, and the 1950 amendment to the 1927 Immorality Act struck at Coloured-white marital and extramarital relations. The Representation of Voters Bill, introduced in 1951, aimed at and ultimately, after a long constitutional struggle, succeeded in 1956 in removing the Coloured from the common roll in Cape Province, as the Africans had been removed in 1936. All three measures have remained sources of intense bitterness for the Coloured, and the government's own Theron Commission recommended in mid-1976 that they be rescinded. Nonetheless, despite other current efforts to conciliate the Coloured and considerable white sympathy for sharing the vote with them, the government immediately rejected these proposals.

Two other early and far-reaching pieces of legislation laid the cornerstones of the urban segregation policy: the Population Registration Act and the Group Areas Act, aimed at restricting each population group to defined places in or near urban areas as far as ownership, occupancy, and trading were concerned.

Traditionally, and still, Africans outside the homelands are closely controlled in their movements and living places by influx control, must at all times carry a pass (a document including information on ethnic origin, birthplace, age, employment, etc.) under penalty of summary arrest, and must secure official permission to accept or change jobs. Indians have been prohibited from living in the Orange Free State since 1891 and have long been subject to varying restrictions on property rights, occupancy, and trading in the Transvaal and Natal. The ultimate goal of the Group Areas Act was to extend restrictions in order to establish residential "racial purity" by shifting groups from one place to another. In the process Coloured and Asians have been moved out of long-established communities in Cape Town and Johannesburg to far less desirable sites, Africans have lost their limited urban freehold areas, a few whites have had to move, and all blacks are threatened with impermanence.

Insistent pressure, formalized in 1967 into far-reaching regulations, has forced Africans not born or long domiciled or employed in urban areas to return to the rural areas, notably the Bantustans, and be turned into migratory labor. Migratory workers, following the pattern long established by the mines, are forced to oscillate between rural areas and workplaces, sent to particular jobs by labor officials in the homelands, and forced to return to their rural bases at the end of specified periods of service, commonly a year.

Three other basic laws that were aimed particularly at Africans were the Bantu (the Nationalist term for "African") Authorities' Act of 1951, the Bantu Education Act, and the Native Labour (Settlement of Disputes) Act, the last two passed in 1953. The first of these laws was designed to reestablish the authority of government-appointed chiefs, and it made provision for the lowest tier of what was to become the structure of the ethnic homelands. The second, and at the time most bitterly opposed of the laws, moved African education from provincial to central government control, reduced the role of churches and other voluntary bodies in the educational process, and threatened to make education a handmaiden of apartheid by training Africans only for inferior roles in South African society. Subsequently, African higher education was also brought under central government control, and thereafter with rare exceptions the small number of Africans, Coloured, and Asians who moved on to university training were forced to do so by correspondence or to attend segregated institutions with predominantly Afrikaner staffs and principals.

The legislation affecting African labor that was passed in 1953 did little to change the highly discriminatory conditions from which it suffered and remains essentially in force today. Though far outnumbering all other industrial and commercial workers, Africans have always been formally excluded from the definition of "employee" in the Industrial Conciliation Act, and thus from any direct participation in the industrial councils through which employers and registered trade unions work out their differences. Nor can they participate directly in negotiations over wages. The closest they come to having an influence on their wages and conditions of work is through the mediation of a white official of the Bantu Labour Board, which rarely affects the outcome of such negotiations. Moreover, although African trade unions (contrary to the common view) are not illegal, have existed in the past, and do so at the present, they have never had any assured rights. The government presently endorses works councils on a firm-to-firm basis, thereby giving management the predominant influence. In addition, until the spring of 1973, when there were persistent African walkouts in Natal, the ban on strikes by Africans imposed in 1942 continued to exist. When a modification of the strike ban was instituted in 1973, it was so hedged with restrictions as to be more significant in theory than practice.

AFRICAN PRESSURES FOR CHANGE—AND THEIR DEFEAT

As the apartheid net tightened, Africans girded themselves for nation-wide protest. In January 1952 leaders of the African National Congress demanded both the abolition of "differentiating laws" and direct representation in Parliament and provincial and municipal councils as "an inherent right." If their grievances were not remedied, they declared, their intention was to launch a passive resistance campaign. In reply the prime minister's private secretary maintained that a claim of inherent right by Africans was "self-contradictory" since the differences between Africans and whites "were permanent and not man-made." To remove restrictions on "the possible gradual development of a completely mixed community," he declared, "is not a genuine offer of cooperation, but an attempt to embark on the first steps toward supplanting European rule in the course of time" that would lead to "disaster." The words have a contemporary ring.

On April 6, 1952, white South Africa celebrated the tercentenary of Jan Van Riebeeck's arrival at the Cape in 1652. Africans boycotted many of the celebrations and at one counter mass rally, Professor Z. K. Matthews of Fort Hare College, who was president of the Cape ANC, declared that "only the African people themselves will ever rid themselves" of "political subjugation, economic exploitation and social degradation." June 26, 1952, was selected as the date to begin the passive resistance campaign. Despite government bannings and subsequent arrest of some leading black leaders, the Defiance Campaign started on time. Batches of volunteers in one town after another courted arrest by open violations of apartheid regulations such as entering African locations without permits, or sitting on benches marked "for whites only," or using white entrances to post offices. Although the number of volunteers varied from month to month, more than eight thousand had been arrested by December 1952, most of them in the Eastern parts of Cape Province, and the second largest number in the Transvaal. The membership of the ANC swelled to one hundred thousand, the nucleus of a mass movement; defiers became future leaders; and the campaign began to enter the reserves.

But already there had been nationwide arrests of ANC and South African

Indian Congress leaders, the latter lending moral and financial support. More serious for the continuation of the campaign were sporadic and unconnected outbreaks of violence in East London and Port Elizabeth in which a few whites and many more Africans were killed. White sentiment flared and as soon as Parliament reassembled in January 1953, the government introduced the Public Safety and Criminal Laws Amendment bills. The former made provision for proclaiming a state of emergency and was used in 1960 after the Sharpeville shootings. The latter instituted heavy penalties, including lashes, for supporting a campaign of passive resistance or soliciting or accepting help for such a campaign. It was a decisive step toward the ever-increasing coercive measures taken in response to open black protests.

Shifting from disobedience to demonstration and from an African to a multiracial popular front, the Congress Alliance, that is, the ANC and its allied Indian, Coloured, and white organizations, held a massive Congress of the People at Kliptown near Johannesburg at which the Freedom Charter was adopted by voice vote of the three thousand persons present. Prepared through hundreds of small open discussions that formulated popular demands, the Freedom Charter opens with the words:

> We, the people of South Africa, declare for all our country and the world to know:
> that South Africa belongs to all who live in it, black and white, and that no Government can justly claim authority unless it is based on the will of all the people. . . .

It demanded that "every man and every woman" have the right to vote, that the people share the country's wealth under public ownership, that land be redivided among those who worked it, that education be "free, compulsory, universal and equal for all children," that there be houses, security, and comfort for all, and that South Africa be "a fully independent state which respects the rights and sovereignty of all nations." It ended with the words: "These freedoms we will fight for, side by side, throughout our lives, until we have won our liberty."

The government's answer was to arrest one hundred and fifty-six leaders of the Congress Alliance in December 1956 and put them on trial for high treason. In a case stretching over four years all the accused were progressively discharged or finally held to be not guilty of the government's charge of intending to overthrow it by force. While the trial was continuing, the ANC split between those who upheld the multiracial sentiments of the Freedom Charter and those who identified more with the Pan-Africanism sweeping the continent as country after country was moving to independence under African control. The latter group, under Robert Sobukwe, broke away in 1959 to form the Pan-Africanist Congress (PAC). It was the PAC that organized the demonstrations against carrying passes on March 21, 1960. When police fired on an unarmed crowd at Sharpeville in the Transvaal, killing seventy-two Africans and wounding some one hundred and eighty-six, including women and children, a new watershed was created in South African history.

The government panicked, declared a state of emergency, outlawed the ANC and PAC, arrested and detained some nineteen hundred people, including for the first time members of the predominantly white Liberal Party, which stood for a universal franchise under its leader, the internationally known author Alan Paton, and imprisoned thousands of so-called African "idlers." Urgent appeals from inside South Africa for consultation with Africans were disregarded by the government. International censure of the wanton killings was followed by an outflow of foreign capital. Only very gradually and with the aid of American capital did the situation return to a semblance of normality, at least for whites.

Despite the banning of their organizations, Africans made one last effort to construct a wide public front for public protest. Though its preparations were handicapped by internal dissension, the All-In Conference, with more than a thousand Africans in attendance, met in Pietermaritzburg in Natal in March 1961. But raids and arrests frustrated its call for a three-day work boycott. It was the last effort to organize a mass public demonstration. With all channels of peaceful protest barred to them, Africans turned to violence. Even then, sporadic targets for sabotage by the ANC's Umkhonto We Sizwe (Spear of the Nation) meticulously avoided taking human life.

The few terrorist acts in 1962 of the PAC-inspired Poqo spurred the government's counteractions, which systematically destroyed virtually all effective African leadership and organization in the country, except the

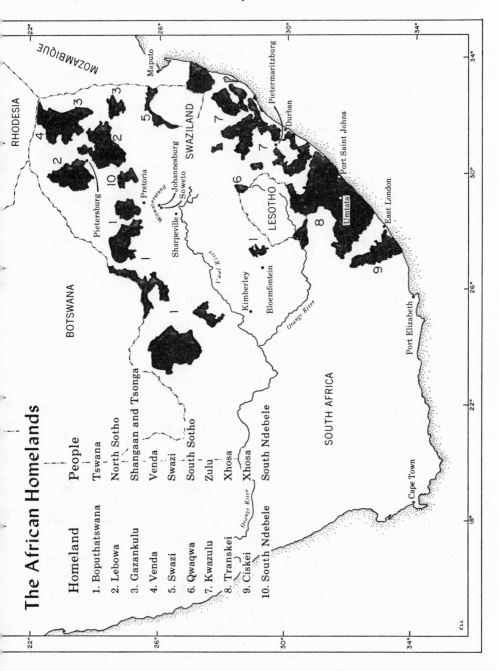

The African Homelands

Homeland	People
1. Boputhatswana	Tswana
2. Lebowa	North Sotho
3. Gazankulu	Shangaan and Tsonga
4. Venda	Venda
5. Swazi	Swazi
6. Qwaqwa	South Sotho
7. Kwazulu	Zulu
8. Transkei	Xhosa
9. Ciskei	Xhosa
10. South Ndebele	South Ndebele

underground headquarters at Rivonia, a suburb of Johannesburg. With its capture in June 1963, leaders still at liberty in the country and valuable files fell into police hands. Nelson Mandela (already in prison but tried again), Walter Sisulu, and other black and also white associates were sentenced in the 1964 Rivonia trial, the former leaders to life imprisonment on Robben Island off Cape Town. Sobukwe was already on Robben Island and, although subsequently released, has remained under restrictions. The politically organized internal African struggle for rights was crushed. The ANC exile leadership under Oliver Tambo and Duma Nokwe and that of the PAC under Potlako Leballo and others sought what external support they could, but their contacts with persons within the country were tenuous, and their possibilities of organizing infiltration were frustrated by the distance between independent African-controlled countries and South Africa. Only after the independence of Mozambique, in June 1975, did a major African-controlled independent state share a boundary with South Africa.

THE BANTUSTAN (HOMELAND) PROGRAM: THE AFRIKANER ANSWER TO THE RACIAL SITUATION IN SOUTH AFRICA

What had happened from 1960 to 1962 confirmed the government in its determination to push ahead with what it now termed "its answer to the racial problem in South Africa": separate territorial development. As the subject of many Afrikaner *volks* conferences in the thirties, forties, and fifties, the Afrikaners' own history seemed to many of them to support the belief that a true nation evolves from ethnic exclusiveness. Neither Prime Minister Malan nor his successor, Prime Minister J. G. Strijdom, believed, however, that a far-reaching program of territorial separation of Africans could be implemented in practice when Africans already formed so substantial a proportion of the urban working force. The next prime minister, H. F. Verwoerd, and his secretary of native administration and development, Dr. W. M. Eiselen, were convinced, on the contrary, that such a program was feasible. They pointed to the High Commission territories, Swaziland, Basutoland (subsequently Lesotho), and Bechuanaland (subsequently Botswana), as prototypes of Bantu homelands. Even the possibility of ultimate independence for the ethnic units they envisaged did not disturb them since, as was said of Basutoland, which was embedded within South African territory: "It can become politically independent [as indeed it did in 1966] but it will always be economically dependent on South Africa."

The government had pushed through the so-called Promotion of Bantu Self-Government Act in 1959, which removed from Parliament the white representatives who were selected by Africans. Thereby it cut the last official link Africans had to the country's process of lawmaking. The same statute made provision for what the government called the Africans' appropriate form of representation. Territorial authorities were to be set up—and ultimately were—in nine "national units," or ethnic entities for different tribes, although by that time no substantial rural area was occupied exclusively by a single ethnic group. The national units were to be formed—and by government fiat have been—of scattered patches of land around the periphery of the country that had long been reserved for African occupancy (see map). The rationale for the program set forth in the preamble of the Act was that "the Bantu peoples of the Union of South Africa do not constitute a homogeneous people, but form separate national units on the basis of language and culture."

This view and program were the antithesis of African nationalism. As such, they were bitterly opposed by nationally-minded Africans both then and now for denying African rights in a country built through the efforts of all its people, black and white. Moreover, they saw, and see, the Bantustan program as the capstone of apartheid since it promised to entrench inequality through balkanizing South Africa. The 87 percent of the land that was richly endowed with minerals and that included all the industrially developed areas was to be left, and it remains in the exclusive domain of the white minority, which comprises about 17 percent of the population. The Africans, who total more than 70 percent of all South Africa's people, were to be, and are restricted as far as rights are concerned, to a bare 13 percent of the land, nearly all of which lacks major exploitable resources, is largely undeveloped, and is seriously overpopulated in relation to carrying capacity.

The government's own Tomlinson Commission, which undertook an exhaustive examination of possibilities for the socioeconomic development of the reserves, reported in 1956 that no more than half the existing population of those areas could grow enough food on them to support themselves. It recommended that the other half of the population of the reserves be removed from agriculture and involved in a massive program to develop local commerce and manufacturing and create the necessary fifty thousand new jobs annually for the next twenty-five years. The magnitude of such a task was underlined by the commission's own statement that "as far as industries are concerned, the Bantu Areas are in fact a desert."

The government promptly rejected these major recommendations and the necessary financing of the equivalent of $70 million a year for the next five years and a total of $291 million for the coming decade. In their place it established a Bantu Areas Investment Corporation with limited funds to stimulate industrial development in the reserves. It also launched the border industries program in 1956, under which some white-owned industries were induced to relocate on the borders of reserve territories through a combination of lower minimum wage and other requirements, and restrictions on their further expansion in urban areas. These measures were quite inadequate to cope with the basic problem of developing peripheral areas confronted with the overwhelming attraction of highly developed industrial and commercial centers. The government's hope, however, was that the political inducements of the Bantustan program would outweigh economic considerations, would provide Africans with an acceptable alternative to the objectives of African nationalism, and would fend off growing foreign criticism of apartheid's legally enforced inequality and discrimination. The government was to have more success, at least temporarily, in all these respects than might have been expected.

Some Africans, indeed, notably some leading figures in the Transkei, found the offer of partial self-government in a homeland attractive. They saw little chance of influence and development within white-controlled South Africa. Moreover, the Transkei had special features and a history that made Bantustan, or homeland, status appear more reasonable than for other areas. It already possessed a substantial and by far the most consolidated area of any of the projected Bantustans. Some 60 percent of all Transkeians had homes within its boundaries, whereas less than 50 percent of the ethnic groups in other proposed homeland areas were domiciled within them. In addition, the Transkei, along with the Ciskei, had had the long political experience of the Eastern Cape. Until qualified Transkeians, like other Cape Africans, were removed from the common roll in 1936, they had voted with whites for parliamentary representatives. No less important, Transkeians had had their own local representation from 1903 on through the quasi-political General Council of the Transkeian Territory.

In 1955 a committee of the General Council, which previously had maintained an active interest in national as well as local affairs, was persuaded to accept the Bantu authorities system, the base of what became the Bantustan, or homeland, system. The Transkei Constitution Act of May 29, 1963, made provision for an all-African Legislative Assembly consisting of sixty-four appointed chiefs and forty-five elected members. The election for these members was conducted on the basis of adult suffrage open to all Transkeian Africans inside or outside the territory, the first time Africans had voted in South Africa without being restricted by property and educational qualifications. Only twelve of those elected supported the separate territorial development program; thirty-three envisaged the Transkei's limited self-government as a means of working on behalf of rights for all Africans in a multi- or nonracial South Africa.

When the Transkei's first government was chosen on December 6, 1963, however, the votes of the chiefs determined that the post of chief minister went to Chief Kaiser Matanzima, a forceful exponent of separate development who foresaw more opportunities for his own ambitions and black nationalism within that territory than elsewhere in the country. As other Bantustans were set up and acquired limited degrees of self-government, the Transkeian government remained in the van, constantly pushing for more control over its local affairs and securing more economic support from the South African government.

Homeland leaders differed among themselves in their degree of enthusiasm for separate development. The most vigorous critic of the system has been Chief Gatsha Buthelezi of Kwa-Zulu, the fragmented ethnic unit for what is the most populous ethnic group in South Africa, numbering well over four million. Buthelezi has always made it clear that he only accepted the separate development program for that area under strong central government pressure and accepted his own position as chief executive councillor because of his responsibility for his people as an hereditary chief and a traditional adviser to the paramount chief. Along with some of the other homeland leaders, notably Dr. Cedric Phatudi of Lebowa and Professor Hudson Ntsanwisi of Gazankulu, he also justified his government-established position as a platform for pressing for advances for Africans throughout the country.

In line with its philosophy that the Bantustans provided the only legitimate sources of political authority for Africans, the central government afforded their leaders a considerable degree of access to government officials, including from 1974 on, meetings with the prime minister. At these sessions homeland leaders challenged a wide range of apartheid restrictions, and in public meetings outside, the restrictions, were criticized particularly by Buthelezi in words that would have resulted in imprisonment if voiced by other Africans. Since the government wished to treat the homeland leaders as the representatives of *all* Africans, they were able to bring up issues affecting urban Africans, like long-desired freehold tenure, home ownership, and civic rights. But many urban Africans, particularly the young, were bitter that they were ignored and bypassed in this way. Much of this bitterness was extended to the homeland leaders, who were widely accused of conniving with apartheid.

Homeland leaders had apparently forged a common front, when meeting in Umtata in the Transkei in the fall of 1973, to act in unison in dealing with the white government. By the time they met again a year later, the united front of homeland leaders was at an end. The Transkei Legislative Assembly, whose second and third elections had both returned a substantial majority of elected members supportive of Chief Matanzima, had requested the South African government to grant the territory independence. Continued frustration at the lack of response by the central government to appeals to reduce apartheid restrictions contributed to this decision. More significant, however, appear to have been the large-scale financial support accorded the Transkeian government and even more the ceding of Port St. Johns, a pleasant, previously white watering place on the Pondoland coast of the Indian Ocean, which has provided the Transkei with the one and only outlet to the sea of any of the homelands.

That there was substantial opposition within the Transkei to accepting independence, but that Chief Matanzima was prepared to be ruthless in crushing it, became clear on the eve of the fourth and last preindependence election in September 1976. The most vigorous opponents of independence within the Legislative Assembly, including several whose reelection was not in doubt, were placed in detention on charges of associating with the ANC and conspiring to create violence at the time of independence. The final electoral returns indicate that Matanzima's party would have secured the majority among the seventy-five elected members in any case, but with much of the opposition in custody, it won an overwhelming majority among them as well as among the seventy-five chiefs who make up the rest of the current Transkeian Legislative Assembly.

TRANSKEI INDEPENDENCE AND THE CITIZENSHIP ISSUE

On October 26, 1976, the South African government formally granted the Transkei independence. This first political structural change in South Africa since the Act of Union, 1910, marks a new watershed in the country's history. To most nationalist Afrikaners it signified the striking success of the program of separate territorial development, which had been designed to establish racial peace throughout the country. But well before the cession of independence, the sharp division over citizenship between the South African and Transkeian governments highlighted a basic flaw in the government's homeland policy that seems likely to cause the program to acerbate black-white race relations rather than improve them. The persistent black demonstrations and riots in and from urban black townships since Soweto erupted in June 1976 provided further evidence that the failure to respond to the demand of urban Africans for acceptance of their permanence within the so-called white areas may nullify whatever potential advantages for continued white control the homeland policy might have provided.

The ultimate objective of the South African government in pushing the homelands to independence is to turn all Africans in the country into foreigners who would occupy the same status within South Africa as do the citizens of Lesotho, Swaziland, Botswana, or any other country from which migratory labor comes to work in the mines or other enterprises. By this means, the population ratio of whites to blacks within South Africa would be decisively changed to the great advantage of the former. Indeed, whites could eventually become the majority group within the country, with only the Coloured and Asians sharing their South African citizenship.

The government's Homelands Citizenship Act of 1970 declared that all Africans, other than foreign migrants, who are living in "white" South Africa should secure certificates of citizenship from their homeland governments. By mid-1975 only 1.4 million out of 18 million Africans had opted for ethnic citizenship. The Republic's Status of the Transkei Act, 1976, pushed the central government's basic postulate to the fore. It declared in effect that all Xhosa or Sotho speakers who were not citizens of another homeland automatically became Transkeian citizens at the moment of independence and ceased to be South African citizens. The constitution adopted by the Transkeian Legislative Assembly sharply contradicted this proposition. After stating that "every person" born in the former Transkeian territories "may become a citizen of the Transkei," it specifically declared that South African citizens, that is, the million or more Transkeians outside the territory, who may desire Transkeian citizenship must make formal application for it. The fundamental difference between the two acts is clear: the South African government is attempting to divest itself automatically of formal responsibility for Transkeians in the so-called white areas, whether urban or rural, by cancelling their citizenship; the Transkei government, supported by all other homeland leaders and spokesmen for urban blacks, insists that no African shall be forced against his or her will to give up South African citizenship rights.

The issue is crucial for both sides. For the Transkei and the homeland governments to agree to the South African government's attempt to force Africans outside their territories to give up their existing citizenship rights would irrevocably divide them from urban Africans. For the South African government to accept the African instead of its own policy on citizenship would be to abandon the basic tenet of separate development.

Directly facing this impasse, Dr. J. H. Moolman, Director of the Africa Institute of Pretoria and a distinguished establishment figure within Afrikanerdom, told the members of the outspokenly nationalistic "junior Broederbond," the Rapportryers, in April 1976, that separate development is both unacceptable and indefensible, "against the grain of the world-wide tendency," and inevitably "rejected by the thinking world." In place of separate development, he declared, "the solution we are looking for is a formula, or serious formulae, for peaceful, honest coexistence between blacks and whites." The government has not yet conceded the point.

Before Transkei independence Chief Lucas Mangope had given notice that Bophuthatswana, despite its fragmented state, would seek independence although no date was set. On the eve of Transkeian independence the other homeland leaders maintained that they would not seek independence for their territories and mutually agreed not to attend the independence ceremonies. Three of these leaders, those from Kwa-Zulu, Gazankulu, and Lebowa, have been particularly emphatic that they will not consider abandoning their peoples' right to share in the resources and political life of South Africa as a whole.

Transkeian independence received a hostile international reaction. The Organization of African Unity and the 1976 United Nations General Assembly (with the United States alone abstaining) unanimously affirmed their determination not to recognize Transkeian independence. In an unusual move aimed at forestalling possible administrative action, a majority in the U.S. House of Representatives opposed recognition of the Transkei. The EEC (the European Economic Community) also voted against recognition. Except for a Peruvian general, no foreign representative came to the independence celebrations from outside South Africa.

Nonrecognition of Transkei independence is primarily a protest against South African apartheid and reflects the view that, by accepting independence, Matanzima is conniving with apartheid. His action is also criticized for dividing the African front and starting the process of fragmenting South Africa. Transkei leaders maintain that their territory was once an independent black state forced by the British into the Union of South Africa, but this view only confirms fears that it will be difficult, if not impossible, to reestablish the unity of South Africa.

Matanzima's own justification for his action is that it enables several million Africans to free themselves from the discrimination of "the unjust society." Rigorous restrictions on meetings, speech, and organizations continue to exist, however, within the Transkei. He says also that the Transkei will follow "its declared policy of non-racialism," and that it is "fundamentally irrelevant" whether Transkei "freedom was obtained earlier than, or simultaneously with, the rest of the oppressed people of South Africa."

What will be relevant is whether or not Transkei leaders use independence in the interests of aiding the struggle for political rights of blacks who reject the homeland concept, as well as those who accept it.

How Transkeian leaders use its independence vis-à-vis South Africa is likely to have considerable influence on external, and even internal, attitudes toward the territory. Because South Africa wishes to demonstrate the success of its homeland policy, it is unlikely to attempt to curb outspoken criticism of apartheid by Transkeian leaders or prevent them from welcoming outspoken critics of the apartheid regime. Lesotho's economic dependence on the Republic has failed to limit either of these evidences of independence despite earlier expectations that it would do so; the Transkei is likely to attempt to do still more to demonstrate its freedom from South African control. On the other hand, the aversion and indeed fear of ANC and PAC activities within the Transkei make it unlikely that its territory can be used as a base for such overtly political organizations.

Some African states may sooner or later find themselves forced to deal with the Transkei, either because of geographical proximity, e.g., Lesotho, or because of South African pressure. That government will attempt, and probably successfully, to force the BLS countries (Botswana, Lesotho, and Swaziland), which are members with South Africa in a common customs union (see Chapter 6), to admit the Transkei as a member despite the countries' resistance to such a move. Ivory Coast, Gabon, and Malawi have long had close relations with South Africa. But the OAU as a whole is unlikely to change its stand. Nor are those in the urban townships and the growing body of white opinion which recognizes that the homeland program has never afforded a genuine alternative to a mixed society within the boundaries of South Africa and that statistics reinforce the claims of African nationalism.

THE LACK OF VIABILITY OF THE HOMELANDS

The homelands presently consist of one hundred and ten separate pieces of land (the Transkei still consists of three) scattered around the periphery of South Africa (see map). Government plans in 1975 for further consolidation would eventually bring the number to thirty-six (the Transkei would end up with two) with Kwa-Zulu, for example, being reduced from forty-eight to ten separate pieces of land, each divided by white-owned farms requiring special papers for transit, and Bophuthatswana from nineteen to six. The "final" settlement is based on the 1936 Native Land and Trust Act, which promised to increase African-held land from 7 percent to 13 percent of the country's land area. The density of population per kilometer in the nine homelands in 1972 ranged between twenty-three in Bophuthatswana and sixty-seven in Kwa-Zulu with an average density of forty-six, compared to eighteen for the whole of South Africa, and thirteen for "white" South Africa (see Table 1). Not surprisingly, homeland leaders do not accept the limits on the land allocated to their territories.

Within these fragmented areas are domiciled some 45 percent of the African population, rather more than seven million in 1970, and substantially more at the present time, both because of the high birthrate in these territories, and because of the forcible resettlement of some 1.6 million Africans uprooted from so-called black spots in white areas to whom at least another half million are to be added by government fiat. Since agricul-

TABLE 1:   Area, Population, and Density
of Population of the Homelands

	Area km^2	Total population present in homeland	Density per km^2
Transkei (Xhosa)	36,850	1,726,900	47
Ciskei (Xhosa)	9,310	525,960	56
BophuthaTswana (Tswana)	37,670	876,980	23
Lebowa (North Sotho)	21,480	1,086,380	51
Gazankulu (Shangana)	6,700	268,780	40
Venda (Vhavenda)	6,060	268,700	44
Swazi (Swazi)	2,120	117,460	56
Kwa-Zulu (Zulu)	31,550	2,106,040	67
Basuto-Qwaqwa (South Sotho)	460	25,960	56
	152,200	7,003,160	46
South Africa	1,223,315	21,402,470	18
"White South Africa"	1,071,115	14,363,360	13

ture is mainly carried on in traditional fashion and exploitable resources are virtually lacking (partly at least due to redrawing of boundaries to include these resources within white areas), a high proportion ranging between 35 percent and 55 percent of all males between the ages of twenty-five and sixty-four are forced into migratory labor to earn what is needed to support themselves and their families (see Table 2). It should be noted that the Transkei has one of the highest proportions of males forced into migratory labor, nearly a quarter of a million in 1972.

Despite the government's stimulation of border industries and growth points within the homelands, at least a third of the 100,000 *new* work-seekers a year from the homelands are similarly forced into migratory labor to the industrial and commercial centers in "white" South Africa. Another third of these new work-seekers secure government jobs within the home-lands, largely due to the substantial funding provided by the central govern-

TABLE 2:　Absence of Black Population from Homelands 1970

Nation	Total	Percentage of inhabitants 15-64 years in homeland		Number of men temporarily absent
		Men	Women	
Xhosa-Transkei	54.9	35.3	62.9	224,500
Xhosa-Ciskei	55.9	38.1	56.1	37,200
Tswana	35.5	24.4	32.8	37,600
North Sotho	56.0	35.0	59.5	91,200
Shangaan	35.5	18.4	40.7	38,700
Venda	67.2	40.1	76.1	30,200
Swazi	17.2	12.5	16.4	5,000
Zulu	51.3	36.7	53.2	164,300
South Sotho	1.8	1.2	1.9	2,500

Source: Lombard, J. A. and Van der Merwe, P. J. Central problems of the economic development of the Bantu Homelands. *Finance and Trade Review*, June 1972, Table 3.

ment, amounting to between a half and four fifths of their annual budgets. (The South African government will provide 80 percent of the Transkei's budget for its first year of independence.) Any reduction in this funding is likely to throw still more old and new work-seekers into the migratory labor pool that sends them to the industrial and commercial centers within "white" South Africa, from which the homeland policy is supposed to remove them.

The compulsion on homeland Africans to engage in the oscillating migratory labor system results not only from the lack of work opportunities within those areas but also from the drastic restriction imposed under Section 10 (1) (d) of the Urban Areas Act, which provides that any African entering a proscribed (in effect, an urban or semiurban) area to work after April 1, 1968, is permitted to stay only one year at a time and must then return to his original domicile to await another call or job. While in the urban area, he must live in a unisex hostel where he shares a room with other migrants. Migrants must secure their first job through a labor bureau in their homeland which allocates them in response to existing needs in the white areas and the migrant's preference. Thereafter, reemployment is generally at the same kind of job. Under the "call-in" system, the worker may be reemployed by the same mine or factory or firm after the compulsory return to the homeland. If not, he must await another opportunity for employment.

In general, the system limits opportunities for training and advancement, particularly since there are so many unemployed work-seekers always waiting in the homelands. The effect on the urban wage structure of so controlled a labor system is to keep it low. The government strongly favors the oscillating migratory labor and would prefer that all Africans be ultimately pressed into it and thereby undercut the supply of skilled labor from which South African industry is seriously suffering, despite the fact that some five million Africans are already more or less permanently living in urban or peri-urban townships near white town and cities.

The social problems created by the oscillating migratory labor policy are vast. In the cities, where migrants live in close proximity to other males, there is rampant homosexuality, and, not surprisingly, migrants also cause a high percentage of illegitimate children in the African townships. In the homelands there is a dispiriting apathy among the women and children whose husbands and fathers are unemployed, awaiting jobs, or away for successive periods of service in the urban areas. When they return, there is a compulsion to procreate, which accounts for the abnormally high birthrate that resulted in almost half of all rural Africans being under fifteen years of age in 1970. Moreover, health standards in the rural areas are poor, with comparatively few hospitals and clinics. Buthelezi once aptly characterized the homelands as "rural slums," far from the glowing picture presented by the government's propaganda.

The government's effort to decentralize industries and encourage economic development within the homelands can be well justified if the political connotation is removed. More land and genuine consolidation of their territories, for which all homeland leaders call, could stimulate improved agriculture and cattle raising and labor-intensive enterprises like shoemaking; thereby these areas could support a higher proportion of their populations. What is obviously necessary, however, is to permit the African population greater mobility within the country by gradually eliminating the rigid provisions of influx control. But this is only likely to happen as part of a comprehensive redirection of government policy.

THE PROBLEMS OF URBAN AFRICANS

Some nine million Africans, nearly twice the total white population, live in the so-called white areas, many of them far away from the homelands. Nearly four million Africans work on white farms. The majority, however, comprising more than five million, are in urban townships lying on the edges of towns and cities throughout the country. Except for Pretoria, where the number of white government workers swells the total white population, and Cape Town, where the Coloured are more numerous, Africans outnumber whites in virtually all urban areas. While the white population of Johannesburg is less than half a million, Soweto, which lies about fifteen miles outside it, houses well over a million Africans, making it the fifth largest city in Africa south of the Sahara.

African townships, and in some areas also Coloured or Asian settlements, serve largely as dormitories for the workers who commute to their weekday jobs in white households, places of business, factories, and the like. A quarter of a million commute by train, bus, or other means from Soweto alone. The mines and complexes like ISCOR, the state-financed iron and steel corporation, and SASOL, which produces oil from coal, have their own compounds where largely migratory African labor is housed, often near the townships. The four largely urban centers of industrial concentration within the country—the Southern Transvaal, the Western Cape, Durban-Pinetown, and Port Elizabeth-Uitenhage—have a compulsive attraction for labor. Of these four areas, the Southern Transvaal, and particularly within it the PWV (Pretoria-Witwatersrand-Vereeniging) triangle with its spreading gold mine complex, heavy industry, and the commercial capital of Johannesburg, has accumulated the greatest concentration of black labor.

Only Africans who meet specific provisions can remain within a prescribed area like Soweto for more than seventy-two hours. These provisions are: (1) continuous residence since birth in that particular area; or (2) continuous employment with the same employer for at least ten years, or lawful residence for at least fifteen years; or (3) the wife or unmarried daughter or son under sixteen of anyone qualifying under (1) or (2); or (4) labor bureau permission to be in the area.

Those in category (1) qualify under Section 10 (1) (a) of the Urban Areas Act and are the best off. They have relative permanence of residence unless they are designated "idle" or "undesirable," in which case they too can be expelled. A university survey in 1969 found that 92.9 percent of those between eighteen and twenty-five and nearly 50 percent of all adults surveyed had been born in Soweto. The percentages are surely higher now. Category (2), qualifying under Section 10 (1) (b), provides approximately the same security except that the right of residence is lost if a fine of more than R100 or imprisonment for more than six months is incurred. Persons acquiring this status must have entered the prescribed area before April 1, 1968, and continue to work for the same employer.

Despite these restrictions the African urban population has grown steadily and continues to do so. What is distinctive is that such a high proportion of the teenagers and those in their twenties have known no other conditions. It is the completely urbanized youth that have demonstrated and rioted so persistently since June 1976. They have experienced discrimination and humiliation of their parents all their lives. Moreover, they are better educated then earlier generations, and thus more sensitive to the deprivation they suffer compared with the conditions of the whites. Most Soweto dwellings are featureless four-room "matchboxes" without electricity or water, though there is also the middle-class suburb of Dube that has some fine houses. What is most galling to the residents are the lack of opportunities ahead; the tyranny of the police, black and white; and the pervading sense of government domination. They have absorbed black consciousness out of the conditions under which they must live.

Nationalist policy since 1948 has aimed not only to bring the African urban population around Johannesburg into one more or less consolidated area, the South Western Township (abbreviated to Soweto), which covers about eighty-five square kilometers, but also to extinguish all freehold rights to land. The Nationalist justification for the policy is that the urban African population, despite its long-settled character and significant role in the "white" economy, is only in the area as long as its members are needed by the whites. On this reasoning, the right of permanent residence in Soweto would be tantamount to denying the basic criterion of separate development. (Afrikaners also have a long-held belief that ownership of land is related to citizenship.) Only in growth centers like Babelegi, a part of Bophuthatswana and so designated homeland territory, are such rights permitted. The proposal that Soweto be declared a homeland that Chief Buthelezi transmitted on behalf of the mayor of Soweto at the Bantustan leaders' meeting with the prime minister in January 1975 met with a blank refusal.

In addition to freehold rights to land, the most pressing demands of Soweto's population are adequate housing, expanding trading rights, better transport facilities, more police protection particularly on the trains, and self-government.

There is a serious lack of housing in Soweto, characteristic also of other African townships. Nearly fifteen thousand duly qualified families were on the Soweto waiting list for houses at the start of 1973, while some two thousand additional houses are needed annually for newly married couples. The average number of people to a house is 5.8. (Widows and divorcees cannot lease homes but only sublease.) Serious deterioration in some areas threatens to bring back slum conditions.

After 1968 Africans were prohibited from building their own houses on thirty-year leasehold land, and if those houses they had already erected were sold or the owner died, they had to be turned over to the West Rand Administration Board, which is directly responsibile to the central government. In the late spring of 1975 these provisions were modified to permit home ownership again on thirty-year leasehold land, but this concession was quickly nullified by restricting ownership to those possessing homeland citizenship, which few Soweto residents were willing to adopt for fear it would further imperil their urban residence. Following the outbreak of disturbances in Soweto in June 1976, however, the government announced that this restriction was removed, though preference is still accorded persons from the Transkei or with homeland citizenship. Subsequently residents have been encouraged to buy their homes by moderate prices and relatively easy loan provisions, underwritten by some employers. (Official regulations, however, were long delayed.) The thirty-year limit on leasing the land on which homes stand is also said to have been made more flexible. It seems doubtful though that these concessions have diminished the basic pressures for change and more likely that the fact that the concessions were made as the result of disorders encourages further use of violence to secure other advances.

African traders in Soweto have long been allowed to deal only in "daily essentials" or "necessaries," although there have been slight modifications of these restrictions recently. Goods such as clothing must be bought ouside of Soweto, that is, from white or Indian shops. African traders were not allowed to build their own premises after 1968 and could only operate in premises leased from local authority. In general each trader is limited to one business in an urban area.

Although voluntary contributions to the Johannesburg *Star*'s TEACH program had helped to ease the shortage of school buildings, there were far from enough classrooms for the primary level before the disorders and obviously still more serious shortages now. (Almost all TEACH program schools were left untouched when government schools were burnt.) Insistence on "home" language instruction in lower grades has been particularly complicated for Soweto, where there is much ethnic intermarriage and despite government efforts residence does not follow linguistic lines. Homeland leaders asked the government to follow the language provisions for schools adopted in their own territories, in several cases English at an earlier level than permitted in the urban areas, but this request has still not been granted. The government did withdraw its provision for teaching higher levels in Afrikaans as well as English after the June demonstrations. The prevailing shortage in secondary school facilities continues, especially since Orlando High School was badly damaged by fire during the disorders. Still more serious is the government's policy of building only post-Standard Six schools in the homelands. Soweto has no boarding school or teacher training institute. Education for Africans is neither free nor compulsory, and lack of opportunities for those with educational qualifications contributes to the high drop-out rate. Improved educational facilities at all levels are high on the list of current demands.

Soweto, like other black townships throughout the country, has no effective self-government. In 1968 the old advisory boards for the townships were replaced by an Urban Bantu Council composed of forty-one elected members chosen by the eight ethnic groups in Soweto. This council, which has no legislative or executive powers, has operated since July 1, 1973, as best it can under the controlling white West Rand Administration Board, whose members are appointed by the government. Such boards, which now exist throughout the country, are supposed to meet their expenses through the African rents and rates in the respective areas they control. The influence of Urban Bantu Councils has thus been largely restricted to exhorting the residents and pleading with the administration. The Soweto council proved ineffectual and indeed helpless during the disorders.

While worldwide attention has inevitably been focused on the spreading demonstrations and disorders in urban townships throughout South Africa since June 1976, the way for them had already been prepared by black university students, black adults, and black workers during the years before. Indeed the characteristic features of black consciousness and protest were already widely accepted.

THE REEMERGENCE OF AFRICAN PROTEST

In the period following the Sharpeville shootings in 1960, the failure of the All-In Conference, the disruption of sporadic efforts to create change through planned violence, and the Rivonia trial and sentencing to life imprisonment on Robben Island of outstanding African nationalist leaders, most notably Nelson Mandela and Walter Sisulu, organized African protest had sunk to its lowest level. The combination of police surveillance, aided by African informants in the townships, legally permitted periods of continuous detention for suspected witnesses as well as those associated with banned organizations, and calculated brutality hidden from publicity except when cases came to trial shaped a period of black quiescence through fear and despair.

Throughout most of the sixties such vocal opposition to discrimination as there was in South Africa came through the liberal white spokesmen of interracial organizations like NUSAS (National Union of South Africa Students), the Liberal and Progressive parties, Defense and Aid with its efforts on behalf of the dependents of political prisoners, and from 1967 on the University Christian Movement (UCM). The black members of these organizations kept in the background, under suspicion from the government because of their membership and avoiding the kinds of actions that had resulted in sending so many of their fellows to prison and Robben Island. Inevitably the white leaders of these organizations came to be regarded as the spokesmen for all dissent, and all too often *pro forma* protest took the place of hard-headed planning.

The breakout from this syndrome of dependence came first from black university students on their segregated campuses. In a move comparable to the withdrawal of Afrikaner university students from NUSAS in the 1930s, the black students organized themselves in 1969 into what they called the South African Students Organization (SASO). Shortly after, they broke away entirely from predominantly white NUSAS. In two ways SASO was distinctive: it sought to unite Africans, Asians, and Coloured within its organization not simply to associate their separate movements in a common front as had the Congress Movement; and in addition its leaders made a calculated effort to instill a new black consciousness by deliberately and openly separating themselves from the liberal whites who had long supported African claims. In some ways they were echoing the Africanism of the Pan-Africanist Congress but with the larger aim of uniting blacks as a whole, all of whom shared a common experience of discrimination. Moreover, in their view, dependence or even formal relations with whites and the associated philosophy of multiracialism diverted blacks from the essential awareness that fundamental change in South Africa could come only through their own purely black efforts; whites, no matter how sympathetic, inevitably form part of the discriminatory system that blacks must ultimately transform. Their opposition to and attacks on the Bantustans and their leaders were no less outspoken, for they saw the homeland concept as a Trojan horse to undermine the black resolve to secure rights in an undivided South Africa.

It was not without reason that this new organization arose on the black university campuses. The government itself had prepared the ground for this seed by isolating almost all black students on ethnic campuses, Xhosas and Zulus at Fort Hare and Ngoye respectively, other Africans at the University of the North at Turfloop, Coloured at Bellville in the Cape, and Asians at Durban-Westville; even the black medical school was effectively separated from the white medical students at Durban University (it is now to be moved to Ga-Rankuwa in Bophuthatswana). The physical separation of the black campuses from each other was another incentive to the formation of SASO. So too was the earlier history of division between nationalist groups in South Africa and its reflection in the various student movements that surfaced surreptitiously in the sixties. The organizers of SASO saw themselves as unifiers by putting forward the objective of a black organization of blacks for blacks.

Tactics came first and ideology later. African leaders of independent Africa, African achievements in the sixties, and West Indian and African writers were strong influences: Fanon, Senghor, Sekou Toure, Nyerere. The American black power movement and the writings of black American leaders had their impact, but in the context of what SASO leaders looked on as the inevitability of a common society in the United States. They saw black consciousness as the universal. Their ultimate goal was to achieve not merely a better economic status or a modicum of political rights but a drastically different type of society to be shaped by blacks themselves in terms of their own inner motivation.

Following close on the formation of SASO came the Black People's Convention (BPC), sometimes spoken of as the adult reflection of SASO but with a wider, more specifically political thrust. The BPC, like SASO, opposes on principle ethnically exclusive political organizations and activism as antithetical to the united black front. This outspoken stand has made it difficult for the BPC to enlist much support from Indians, who have tended to emphasize their own distinctive historical and cultural traditions. The Coloured have also remained somewhat aloof. On the other hand, Indian and Coloured students joined the African demonstrations against their educational system and staffing that led to the closing of their colleges in 1973. Moreover, as already noted, Coloured youth joined with Africans in Cape Town demonstrations in white sections of that city in September 1976.

What is apparent from the history of SASO, BPC, and various other reflections of growing black consciousness is that government-enforced segregation provided the seedbed within which such attitudes germinated, and thereafter gave rise to a new strategy of confrontation across the color line. The government reacted through expulsions, bannings, and from September 1974 on with detentions and imprisonment of leading members of SASO and BPC avowedly because of the proposed pro-Frelimo rally at Curries Fountain Stadium in Durban to express solidarity with the people of Mozambique in achieving independence in June of 1975. Thus, the black-white confrontation was reinforced. That it now goes deep into the consciousness of urbanized youth has been demonstrated by the extended series of demonstrations and outbreaks of violence since June 1976.

Less overtly organized but at least initially more effective than black organizations in securing change have been the sporadic strikes by black workers that have marked employer-employee relations from 1973 on. By that time, of the more than six million Africans in the work force, at least two million were engaged in mining, construction, manufacturing, commerce, finance, and transport. Although approximately one sixth of all African workers are affected by the bargaining processes provided under the Industrial Conciliation Act of 1956 and the Wage Act of 1957, in none of them do the workers have a direct voice. Their interests are supposedly looked after by a white official from the Bantu Labour Board who, not surprisingly, almost invariably favors the interests of white workers and employers.

Due to government harassment and restrictions, African trade union membership, which totaled some 150,000 in 1945 and 60,000 in 1961, had dwindled by 1967 to approximately 16,000 in thirteen unions. Although illegal after 1946, strikes did occur during the 1960s but probably affected fewer workers and achieved even less than during the 1950s.

At the end of 1971 thirteen thousand Ovambo workers in Namibia (South West Africa) went out on a long and partially successful strike that received international publicity. From January to March 1973 workers struck approximately one hundred and fifty firms in Natal seeking higher wages. What was unique about this situation as far as South Africa was concerned was that the strikes took place one after another without any apparent organization. The absence of negotiating machinery vastly complicated efforts to arrive at their resolutions. Unlike earlier strikes, force was not used against the strikers, and by and large they achieved their purpose of gaining appreciable wage increases. More far-reaching effects were the overseas publicity on below-subsistence wages paid by foreign as well as South African firms, the establishment of negotiating machinery by many firms, commonly in the form of liaison or works committees with varying degrees of workers' participation, and a new awareness of the latent power in the hands of African labor. When two three-day strikes kept most Soweto workers at home in September 1976, this awareness was reinforced.

The South African apartheid system cuts across what might otherwise be the solidarity of labor vis-à-vis employers and has long put white labor on the same side as white employers. Although forced into contact and joint activity by the workplace, there is implicit black-white confrontation. Though there is now more mobility in both jobs and wages within industry, it can only take place with the agreement of white labor, much of which is drawn from Afrikanerdom. White labor, fearful of effective competition, uses its influence with both employers and government to protect its highly privileged conditions. Political authority, economic and financial policies, and labor relations form tightly knit sources of power for the white minority. They are often used alternatively and pragmatically by the government. They form the backbone of the system of Afrikaner domination in South Africa.

CAN CHANGE COME? CAN IT BE AVOIDED?

American policy toward Southern Africa under both presidents Nixon and Ford rested until April 1974 on the assumption that change would come only through the whites who dominated the country. Suddenly confronted with the reality of African liberatory power, first exemplified in Mozambique and Angola, and currently in Rhodesia (Zimbabwe) and Namibia, the U.S. government necessarily changed its policy assumptions at least as far as those territories are concerned. Throughout the West there is constant questioning as to what is going to happen in South Africa, where African and indeed black urban violence spread like a slow-burning forest fire, appearing occasionally where least expected, though still mainly centered in Soweto. Is it the whites or the blacks, the Afrikaners or the Africans who are going to determine what happens in the next few years as South Africa's protective buttressing of white-controlled areas is gradually stripped away? Is it ultimately to be peaceful change, or conflict and an armed struggle?

So far, the South African government has continued to maintain that separate territorial development is the only answer to African aspirations that it will permit. It has achieved the success of launching the Transkei on its path of independence; it appears that Bophuthatswana will also follow. There can be little doubt that no matter how troublesome the Transkei may be in its attempts to convince the African countries that it is genuinely independent, it will continue to receive economic and financial support in good measure from the South African government in the effort to persuade other homelands to accept independence. Despite the affirmations of homeland leaders, Mangope of Bophuthatswana abstaining, that they will *not* accept independence, the pressures will continue. Even Chief Gatsha Buthelezi, the most forceful opponent of homeland independence, has had to struggle to secure support for this position within Inkatha, the Zulus' own organization which Buthelezi maintains could become a national one for all Africans. Inducements to follow the Transkei and Bophuthatswana may be difficult to refuse if counterpressures from blacks subside.

Nonetheless, there is open criticism even within Afrikaner ranks of the government's continued determination to base its policies for Africans only upon separate development. There are also pressures from blacks, including homeland leaders, and from the white parliamentary opposition to reconsider and change the tightly centralized political structure of South Africa. What are the chances that this might be done?

Afrikanerdom is a tightly knit community whose interlocking organizations reaching into every sphere of life are unified and powered by the National Party's political control. The right-wing breakaway from that party of the HNP (Herstigte Nasionale Party) in 1969 to oppose Prime Minister John Vorster's "outward-looking policy" of cultivating relations with African-ruled states almost created a crisis within Afrikanerdom. The overwhelming desire for unity continues to provide the HNP with more influence on national policy than its failure to secure seats in Parliament would seem to warrant. Afrikaner political dominance is directed to protecting not only the white power position within South Africa but also the particular interests of Afrikaners. There are basic differences, therefore, between an Afrikaner Nationalist government and a white government even without any black input. The sharp refusal of the Vorster government to consider restoring the Coloured to the common roll is one obvious indication of this fact.

Both of the white opposition parties, the United Party and the Progressive Reform Party, have put forward plans for federal arrangements that would decentralize the exercise of political power. Chief Gatsha Buthelezi also proposed a type of federal system in his Hoernlé lecture in January 1974. The common feature of such plans is to separate predominantly black and predominantly white areas and provide for substantial self-government for each. The Nationalists maintain that separate development could produce this result by a confederation including independent homelands with white South Africa. This approach, like the others, founders on two obstacles: no plan takes into account the position and power of urban Africans, or indeed urban blacks as a whole, and all of the plans end up with whites in a dominant position at the central pinnacle of the structure.

A more far-reaching idea, said to have been floated by the powerful Bureau of State Security (BOSS), which is headed by General Hendrik van den Bergh, who is believed to be Prime Minister Vorster's closest adviser, proposes a Swiss-style cantonal system under a multiracial or confederal central authority. The cantons would be semi-autonomous and include some black, some white, and some mixed. Under this system, blacks and whites would share a common citizenship and, it is hoped, a common national interest. They would control their own police and internal security; the federal government would control defense and foreign affairs. Presumably the federal government would be put into power either by an indirect system of cantonal voting or by universal franchise.

While such a plan seeks to subdivide political decisions in such a way that no one group has dominance over the others, it says nothing specific about the economy. Presumably the process of decentralization of resources and commercial and industrial development, which is the healthiest part of the homeland program, would be continued. Nonetheless, there can be little doubt that the southern Transvaal, in particular the Pretoria-Witwaters-rand-Vereeniging area, will remain the keystone of any future economic and thus political framework for the country. It would have to be under the federal government, therefore making the selection of its members of crucial importance.

If one turns away from proposals for structural change in the political system of South Africa to consider what the present Nationalist government might concede in the face of continued unrest and violence in the urban townships, the possibilities seem far narrower than the needs. Urban townships might be provided with their own elected administrators and given sufficient self-government to handle the most urgent of their problems. A vigorous program of building houses might be launched, entertainment facilities built (there is only one cinema in Soweto at present), and transport facilities improved. The students place a high priority on a more open, high-quality, and self-governing educational system extending from primary levels through the university, at least in Soweto. (They also press for a nonracial university system throughout the country.)

But beyond such improved conditions, not only for Soweto but in all African townships, what could make the most decisive difference would be to provide Africans with freehold tenure of land, and formally to assure urban Africans their permanence of residence. These latter provisions go to the heart of the doctrine of separate development, and to concede them officially would be to accept the inevitability of a mixed society within South Africa.

For African labor the key step would be to include Africans as "employees" within the structure of collective bargaining under the Industrial Conciliation Act. The official recognition of African trade unions or of Africans as members of mixed trade unions could begin to transform industrial relations, although entrenched white labor interests would almost inevitably remain the dominant factor in employer-employee bargaining. Direct African participation in bargaining for wages would be the natural parallel to inclusion under the Industrial Conciliation Act. For Africans to take advantage of these new opportunities, however, would require a substantial program of industrial training and a great deal more mobility within enterprises, including removal of the unofficial but pervasive bar on blacks holding jobs in which they can give orders to whites.

Yet, important as these changes would be—and it is far from certain that any, let alone all, will be considered—they do not answer the basic demand for black political rights and thus shared power. Economic and financial changes may temporarily blunt the edge of black anger but not for the long run. So the crucial question remains: what political changes that satisfy blacks will be accepted by whites?

Strong as South Africa appears, it is a state that is riddled with contradictions. This has always been the case but it is increasingly so. Every step taken by the white supremacy system to relieve the pressures and tensions within its boundaries creates another contradiction. Curbing the influx of labor into urban areas adds to the population pressures in the homelands at a time when it is government policy to develop them into viable systems. Greater dependence on migratory labor means increasing the flow of relatively unskilled workers at a time when the imperatives of rapid growth to support the system demand more skilled manpower. Providing the homelands with their own political institutions as alternatives to a voice in white institutions creates its own challenge from a black-power base—whether from the independent Transkei or from the outspoken criticism of Chief Gatsha Buthelezi, Professor Hudson Ntsanwisi, or Dr. Cedric Phatudi— which may increasingly merge with the challenges from the black urban townships.

These contradictions that all relate in one way or another to the homeland policy set up, in turn, contradictions within Afrikanerdom. Earlier the tension between *verkramptes* and *verligtes* revolved around the "outward-looking policy"; today it revolves increasingly around the validity of the homeland program as *the* answer to South Africa's race policies. On another, even more important level the interview with a BOSS official reported in *Newsweek,* October 25, 1976, indicates a divergence in the basic interpretation of the practical realities within South Africa between that powerful organization and the Afrikaner Nationalist government.

If the homeland program is not *the* answer on which Afrikanerdom has pinned its faith, what then? The whole structure of apartheid is undermined at a vital point. Three years ago the then minister of Bantu affairs, Mr. P. Janson, said publicly that the urban African was there to stay, thus voicing a fundamental contradiction of the basic postulate of apartheid. The government may try to continue the fiction that urban Africans are citizens of the homelands whether they have ties to them or not. But the recognition that they are permanently living within "white" South Africa is a vital and disrupting new factor in Afrikaner thinking, however much other public figures like Treurnicht, deputy minister of Bantu administration, may try to dispel it.

Urban demonstrations and disorders bring another significant force into the South African scene. By breaking the surface image of stability in South Africa, they set up tensions within the country and also have an impact on foreign opinion, including that of investors. A major part of the attractiveness of South African investment for investors abroad has been the stability of the country and the availability of a docile labor force. Now the situation is leading investors to question both postulates. Moreover, with the fall in price of South Africa's basic commodity, gold, its standing in the international money market has sharply declined. Facing the need to raise the equivalent of over a thousand million dollars, the peristatal corporations began to experience greater difficulty in raising the capital from the Eurodollar market, where, immediately after the Soweto riots in 1976, the South African rating was as low as that of Argentina. The necessary loans and special deals were then sought in the United States.

Thus there are two new features to the South African situation that demand rethinking and attempts to evolve new kinds of policies. In the first place, and most important, the homeland program has proved inadequate in coping with the basic issue of the majority Africans, and in particular their increasing and indispensable role in the urban areas. In the second place, the new instability marked by township violence spilling over into white urban areas intensifies internal tensions and undermines international confidence.

There are two polar possibilities in this situation. One is that Afrikanerdom will retire into the *laager* (stockade) to attempt to hold on by force to its privileged position of power, even if it means, as it undoubtedly would, a sharp decline in white standards of living, not to mention those of blacks. The other possibility is that Prime Minister Vorster will once again display the pragmatism that led him to the "outward-looking policy" and accept in fact, as well as in words, the inevitability of the permanence of urban blacks, thereby acknowledging the basic fallacy of separate development. The Organization of African Unity still considers South Africa an African state but one with the obligations to dismantle its apartheid system. Will Afrikanerdom accept the challenge? Or will South Africa remain the battleground, and an ever more dangerous one, of Afrikaner and African nationalism?

WHAT SHOULD BE WESTERN POLICY IN THIS PERIOD OF CRISIS?

What should the West do officially to urge the South African government to respond to the forces within that country that have increasingly laid bare the inadequacies of its black policies? Secretary Kissinger has spoken both of urging "justice" within South Africa and of ultimate majority rule. What immediate and long-range possibilities do Western policy-makers envisage for an evolving program of extended rights and representation for black South Africans? Or is the West content at this time to attempt to defuse what are seen as the most immediately explosive situations in Southern Africa—those in Rhodesia and Namibia—and leave aside the most crucial of them all: South Africa.

In approaching the former situations, Kissinger was careful to consult first with the front-line African presidents and also with at least some of the nationalist leaders of Zimbabwe. Although he saw a few blacks while in

South Africa who were prepared to speak openly and cogently of black frustration and demands, those conversations would have had far more meaning both inside and outside South Africa had they included the most trusted representative of Soweto's black youth, Manas Buthelezi, chairman of the Black Parents' Association, and above all, Nelson Mandela, still the most widely acknowledged leader of black South Africa despite his many years of prison on Robben Island. Unless American and other Western officials are willing to deal directly with those trusted by the majority blacks, they will inevitably continue to be stamped with the reputation of conniving with, if not supporting, the apartheid regime.

It is not for the West to determine what steps should be taken at this time, or subsequently to answer the legitimate demands of the South African black majority. It is its responsibility to try to open channels of communication with the majority that have long been kept closed by the South African government, and to identify itself openly with the ultimate objective of majority rule in South Africa as elsewhere in Southern Africa. In this situation it is the United States that should take the lead to urge the equivalent of the national convention within South Africa for which so many have been calling. It seems safe to assume that Britain and other Western European countries would lend their support to any such initiatives with the South African government, as the United States is lending its support to the British in the Rhodesian negotiations for transfer of power in Zimbabwe to majority rule. The United States has important connections with South Africa and should not be hesitant in using them for such a purpose. This may well be a long-term process; it is time that it began.

The Africans have tried for many decades to find ways to capitalize on their numbers within South Africa and throughout the continent. They are no longer prepared to depend on peaceful methods to urge basic changes within the apartheid structure. Decisions on the future character of South Africa press ever more urgently upon the whites, and particularly on the governing Afrikaners. The answer they give may well mean the difference between war and peace in the state that has more to contribute to the African continent than has any other single country, but that still stands as its greatest affront.

[4]

Angola

Division or Unity?

JOHN MARCUM

PORTUGAL'S LAST governor-general folded his flag and sailed out of Luanda the day before Angola's independence on November 11, 1975. During the preceding year and a half that followed the army coup of April 1974, Portuguese authority had dissipated. Having failed historically to associate Africans with the construction of a territory-wide administration or to allow Africans to organize and politicize within territory-wide associations, the Portuguese tried to compensate for centuries of neglect by creating a broad-scoped transitional government. It included all three of Angola's ethnically based liberation movements.

Lisbon's war-weary troops wanted to go home. They had no stomach for enforcing a rational "political solution." And they proved unwilling to oversee the dissolution and merger of three liberation armies into a common national army. As its authority evaporated, Lisbon was unable to conduct the Angolan elections that it had scheduled to set up a politically legitimate national government.

Moving into the power vacuum, Angola's nationalist movements, spurred on by their external backers, sought power via a "military solution." The result was escalating violence that thrust Portugal's petroleum-rich colony into civil war even before it had achieved statehood. And the world's great powers fanned the flames in a frenetic contest for privileged political and economic relations.

Lisbon had never devolved substantial political power on the resident European population, which numbered some 335,000 by 1974, many of them peasants sent from Portugal after World War II to relieve population pressures at home. Thus Angola's economically privileged but relatively unskilled and ill-organized whites were in no position to seize power. Instead, as intra-African violence mounted, the white population fled en masse to an uncertain fate in the political and economic chaos of postwar Portugal.

Although the goal of a unified Angolan state received widespread rhetorical support within the forums of the United Nations and the Organization of African Unity, neither of these collectivities was organized to impose a peaceful resolution of incipient civil war and ethnic balkanization. Instead, outside powers, great and small, forsook multilateral peacekeeping action for the risks of self-seeking unilateral intervention: troops from Zaïre, military trainers from China, arms from the Soviet Union, covert funds from the United States, a commando column from South Africa, and, finally and decisively, an expeditionary force from Cuba. Angola emerged as a single state from the human tragedy of civil war that might have stalemated and left the country divided into three ethnic states (Bakongo, Mbundu, Ovimbundu) and the Cabinda enclave. But it had been unified by military conquest not by political consolidation.

Would continuing dependence on Cuban troops and technicians render Angola a dependent of Havana? Did mutual defense provisions in the subsequent Angolan-Soviet accord of October 1976 signal that Moscow was intent upon acquiring naval facilities and a launch pad from which to expand its influence throughout the Southern African region? Or was Cuban intervention which provided a fortuitous opportunity to humble Yankee "imperialists" essentially a selfless action of solidarity on the part of a small, Third World country? Would the new rulers of Angola be able to reconcile the ethnic bailiwicks of those whom it had defeated in the struggle for power? Would the oil wealth of Cabinda, soon to pour some $700 million into the Angolan economy each year, enable the government to launch a successful program of economic reconstruction and development along socialist lines? Or would revolutionary "solidarity" draw Angola into a mounting confrontation with South Africa along the extensive southern boundary with Namibia (South West Africa)? Could the Carter administration establish constructive relations based on mutuality of interests with a regime that had come to power despite American efforts to block it?

COLONIAL BACKGROUND TO 1961

Portuguese penetration into Angola dates back almost five centuries to 1483. Early diplomatic relations with the Congo Kingdom of the north were followed by a slow, spasmodic conquest that finally extended Portuguese authority over the interior in the nineteenth century. Depopulated and demoralized by a slave trade and related internal wars that ravaged it up until the middle of the past century, Angola became for Portugal a private preserve of raw materials and cheap labor.

The avowed goal of the *Estado Novo* of António Salazar (premier of Portugal, 1932–68) was to assimilate Angola into the Portuguese nation. For example, from 1951 Angola and other African possessions were considered "provinces," integral parts of Portugal. Yet as of 1950, only half of one percent of the African population had become *assimilados* (about 30,000), while over 99 percent remained *indigenas*, or unassimilated, "uncivilized" persons without political or civil rights. One reason for this situation was that it cost about $50 plus bribes to local administrators for those few who had the educational and other prerequisites for becoming *assimilados*, whereas a relatively well-paid African schoolteacher could earn only $17 per month. Therefore, the privileged status with its accompanying right to vote for Salazar government slates lacked appeal. Dr. Salazar himself recognized the snail's pace of assimilation when he said in 1961: "A law recognizing citizenship takes minutes to draft and can be made right away; a citizen that is a man fully and consciously integrated into a civilized political society takes centuries to achieve."

Reforms following upon the outbreak of fighting in 1961 were timid. Absolute power remained vested in a governor-general appointed in Lisbon, reinforced by secret police (PIDE) and ultimately some sixty thousand troops. Severe literacy and financial qualifications continued to restrict the franchise for indigenous inhabitants, few of whom had the opportunity to learn to read and write Portuguese. No legal opposition was allowed.

After the Second World War, Angola emerged as an important economic asset for Portugal. In 1959 annual coffee exports rose to nearly fifty million dollars, diamonds to over twenty, and newly discovered oil and iron reserves plus an influx of West German and other Western capital promised increasing revenue in foreign currency. Portugal's total exports paid for less than one half its imports; in 1959 Portugal's deficit in its balance of payments was about $150 million. This deficit was made up with a $45 million balance of payments surplus of exports over imports from "overseas provinces." The coffee, sisal, and cotton plantations, diamond mines, and other wealth of Angola, all owned by Europeans, were rendered profitable by African labor. For the latter there was still the economy of the *palmatorio,* a wooden mallet used to punish unsatisfactory workers. In a report on Angolan refugees in August 1961, two respected British observers wrote:

> The system of Contract Labour is one of the chief grievances of the African people in Angola. It is some indication of race relationships in Angola that about half a million Africans are held "in contract" and forced to work for the Portuguese government and Portuguese traders. African men are conscripted for periods of up to eighteen months of Contract Labour; women are forced to do work mending roads, and children from eight years of age upwards are known to have been employed in the copper mines and the coffee plantations. Labourers are frequently ill-treated. For years there has been a constant stream of Africans moving across to the Congo to escape Contract Labour. Some Contract Labourers have run away from their work but if they are caught they are severely beaten.

Commenting on a relatively mild report on labor conditions in Angola made by a commission of the International Labor Organization, which conducted its survey under Portuguese surveillance and without any means of protecting African informants from reprisals, a former missionary in Angola, the Reverend Malcolm McVeigh, pointed out that "idleness" remained an offense. Moreover, obligations to work, either for the state or for private employers on the latters' terms, still defined the economic relationship of African to European. Referring to reforms in the labor code, the United Nations Committee on Portuguese Territories concluded: "Since vagabondage is punishable under the Portuguese Civil Code, the Committee considers that whether or not the new legislation brings an improvement in the daily lives of the indigenous inhabitants will depend to a great extent on how the laws are interpreted and applied." Meanwhile, Europeans continued to earn approximately three times the wages of Africans for doing the same work.

Perhaps it was in the educational field that the Portuguese colonial record compared most unfavorably with those of more advanced colonial powers. As of 1956 approximately one percent of the African school-age population was attending school; in neighboring Northern Rhodesia (subsequently Zambia) the figure for 1958 was 11 percent; and whereas the Northern Rhodesian government was spending approximately four dollars per capita for education in 1959, the Portuguese government was spending but one tenth of one cent per capita in 1956 ($476). There were few secondary schools, populated mostly by Europeans and *mestiços,* a middle caste enjoying near-European privileges. There were no universities. Of the handful of Angolan students permitted to study in Portuguese universities, many fled Portugal after the outbreak of the Angolan war placed them under mounting pressures from the police.

This stagnant educational policy that prevented the emergence of a strong educated elite also facilitated political repression. Whereas in the unsettling wake of the Second World War, the comparatively permissive colonial administrations of Britain, France, and Belgium begrudgingly allowed socially aware Africans to organize, politicize, and gradually to acquire a measure of political power, the Portuguese remained contrastingly and implacably hostile to an organized expression of African cultural, let alone political, dissent. Coerced political docility, or silence, was the responsibility of local officials and police, supplemented by PIDE, which was introduced into Angola in 1957, by networks of police informers, and finally (1959–60) by progressively augmented European military forces. The Salazar government was thus able systematically to root out and destroy groups and individuals suspected of nationalist activity or sympathies.

As a consequence, surviving nationalist groups suffered common insecurity and shared common characteristics. Their leadership ranks were thin, coming from the politically aware portion of a tiny educated elite. Moreover, these groups were handicapped by travel restrictions, police harassment, and general penury. Their range of action, life-spans, and political vision were limited. Localized, they remained parochial. Most were unable fully to surmount the bounds of primary ethnic (or regional) relationships (e.g., Bakongo) or of class ties (e.g., the multiracial intelligentsia of Luanda).

Clandestinity also left its mark. Decimated by infiltrators and corroded by the insecurities and tensions of underground politics, nationalists became exceedingly distrustful. Furthermore, when they sought refuge abroad, they immediately confronted a new situation that was no less suffused with insecurity and frustration. The debilitating condition of clandestinity gave way to the equally debilitating condition of exile.

Foreign refuge enabled some nationalists to avoid arrest and/or to regroup, seek international assistance, and then mount a new challenge to Portuguese rule form outside. Indeed, some left the country precisely in order to enter into political action. It was possible to organize among compatriots—émigrés and laborers—living and working within the more permissive political context of neighboring countries, for example the Bakongos residing in Zaïre.

Increasingly then, after 1957, displaced nationalist leaders and young militants congregated and reorganized abroad. Following the outbreak of the Angolan conflict in early 1961, they concentrated on building movements capable of effecting the politicization and military liberation of their homelands through action launched from exile. Their failure to attain this goal until 1974, and then only indirectly, was in part attributable to chronic frustration and fragmentation induced by long years of political repression, underground existence, and exile.

THE DYNAMICS OF CHANGE

The liberation movements of Portuguese Africa served as powerful catalysts of social, economic, and eventually political change. At the outset of the northern Angolan uprising, it was generally anticipated by rebels and international observers alike that limited violence synchronized with diplomatic pressure at the United Nations would suffice to force Portugal to make a chain of concessions that would lead inexorably toward independence. But if such Bourguibist strategy had worked against the French in Tunisia and similarly if nationalist rhetoric, riot, and mutiny had stampeded the Belgians out of the Congo, armed uprising appeared only to steel Lisbon's resolve to hold on to its anachronistic empire. The Salazar government refused to step onto the slippery path of reform. It continued to deny Africans the right to political self-determination and clung instead to the principle of inalienable Portuguese sovereignty. Without its colonies, Portugal, it was felt, would shrink into a country of little political consequence and limited economic potential.

After an initial phase of fluidity (1961–63), the Angolan conflict stalemated at a rather low level of insurgency. Elsewhere, profiting from the Angolan experience which demonstrated the need for political mobilization of peasants and politico-military training of cadres *before* launching an insurrection, nationalists from Guinea-Bissau and Mozambique rather more methodically planned and phased into guerrilla operations by 1963 and 1964 respectively.

This chain of insurgency brought change to both Portugal and Africa. Portugal's armed forces more than doubled in size, consumed more and more of the government budget (by 1974, 45 to 50 percent), grew politically powerful, and, like the French army during the Indochinese and Algerian wars, developed an insatiable need for ever more material and psychological support. In official budgetary terms military expenditure rose from 35.6 percent in 1961 to 40.7 percent in 1969, whereas expenditure on socioeconomic development dropped from 22 percent in 1960 to 14 percent in 1968. Emigration from Portugal soared, reaching an annual rate of some 170,000 in 1971, including a large outflow of young men of draft age. In 1972, *The Economist* (London) calculated that 1.5 million Portuguese had found employment abroad, compared with a labor force of only 3.1 million in Portugal itself. The results—manpower shortages, inflationary pressures, and stagnancy in the rural-agricultural sector—were only partially offset by industrial expansion (including light-arms manufacturing) and a growing tourist trade (West European and Americans).

In the African territories change was even more noticeable. Administrative and legal reforms such as liberalization of labor codes and abolition of the legal distinction between *assimilados* and *indigenas* constituted perhaps its least significant aspect. Africans were left as disenfranchised, voiceless, and politically impotent as ever. The real change came in education and economic development. Insurgency and international criticism jarred the Portuguese into a belated recognition that any possibility for converting the legal fiction of assimilation into a sociopolitical reality would require a massive program of general and civic education. Between 1960–61 and 1968–69, primary-school enrollment in Angola rose from 105,781 to 366,658 (including Europeans). Foreign Minister Rui Patricio claimed that in the decade 1962–72 school enrollment at all levels in Angola rose from 150,000 to 600,000. The nuclei of universities were created in Angola and Mozambique. Special programs were established to train rural elementary teachers (*monitores*), and army personnel began teaching in African bush schools. There was a decisive break with the lethargy of former years. Indeed, the elementary-school syllabus in Angola was sufficiently modernized to become superior to its antiquated equivalent in metropolitan Portugal.

Portugal's staying power was obviously dependent on increased economic capacity to finance both the overseas military effort and new educational programs. By 1964 financial pressures had reached the point where Lisbon felt compelled to reverse its long-standing policy of excluding or severely restricting the flow of foreign capital into its overseas territories. Traditional policy had been to screen the colonies from undue contact with foreigners, their ideas, press, and economic institutions. Except for what was viewed as the nefarious influence of Protestant missions assured of entry by the Congress of Berlin (1884), external influence was in fact kept minimal.

The right-wing Salazar government shared with Marxist-influenced African liberation movements a fear that because of economic weakness in capital and technology, an open door to foreign investors would result in replacing inefficient Portuguese monopoly enterprise with that of giant corporations based in the United States and Western Europe. Indeed, Portuguese and African nationalists shared a concern over the vulnerability of the African territories to the "neocolonial" effects of penetration by and dependency on powerful, self-interested American or multinational corporations. Premier Salazar went so far as to suggest that economic ambitions motivated the United States misguidedly to join the Soviet Union in attempts to undermine Portuguese authority in Africa.

By 1964, however, economic necessity and the counsel of Europe-oriented economists who argued for breaking out of economic isolation brought a major policy reversal. Investment laws were altered so as to become congenial to foreign capital, and *The New York Times'* annual economic review for 1965 correctly predicted a massive inflow into Angola of American, West European, and South African capital. The open-door policy brought investments in capital-intensive extractive enterprise: for example, Gulf Oil in Cabindan petroleum and Krupp in Angolan iron. And South African capital assumed a new and central importance not only in such massive projects as the hydroelectric dam on the Cunene River on the Namibian border, but in local industry as well.

By 1970 Portugal was no longer perched securely atop an economically hobbled colonial elephant. Disjunctive and irreversible changes were creating new and contradictory dynamics. On the one hand, African social and political awareness of relative deprivations developed along with educational and economic change. On the other hand, the 335,000 Portuguese in Angola, who were increasingly linked into South African security and finance, were intent upon maintaining their ever more prosperous ascendancy, both political and economic.

NATIONALIST STRATEGY AND PORTUGUESE RESILIENCE

In general, the strategy of the African liberation movements was to rely on a combination of unconventional warfare and international diplomatic pressure to wear down Portuguese resolve. The goal was an Evian-type settlement such as was won by the Algerians after an eight-year war against France. At the outset, however, African nationalists (and many outside observers) misjudged Portuguese psychology and underestimated the willingness or ability of the Salazar government to commit scarce resources to a protracted defense of its colonial heritage. The intensity of this determination to stay (Lisbon openly disdained other colonial powers for capitulating to the demands of African nationalism) was evident in the size of the expeditionary forces sent to Africa—of Portugal's total armed forces of 218,000 in 1972, something in excess of 130,000 were in Africa.

In the face of this resolve, the liberation movements made some effort at developing a common, interterritorial strategy but relied mainly on developing separate guerrilla campaigns based on timetables and tactics suited to local conditions and capabilities. The Popular Movement for the Liberation of Angola (MPLA), the Mozambique Liberation Front (Frelimo) and the African Independence Party of Guinea and Cape Verde (PAIGC) cooperated within the loose framework of an association known as the Conference of Nationalist Organizations of the Portuguese Colonies (CONCP). But their collaboration was limited to joint lobbying and propaganda work and exchanges of military information. The diffuse nature of guerrilla warfare and geographic separation militated against three-territory action so synchronized as to place maximum strains on the Portuguese.

With air- and sea-craft obtained from the North Atlantic Treaty Organization (NATO) powers, Portugal was able to shift its forces rapidly from one pressure point to another. In early 1971 the Nixon administration authorized the direct sale of Boeing 707's to the Portuguese government, known to want them for use as military transports, despite the American pledge to maintain an "embargo on all arms" for use in Portugal's colonial wars. And a report by a research unit of the U.N. Secretariat subsequently noted that "the increased use of aircraft for transport of troops is reported to have gone a long way towards solving one of Portugal's major military problems."

Meanwhile, the African strategy of attritional warfare came up against a formidable economic obstacle to success. A Midwestern newspaper put the matter this way: "One optimistic supposition has been that, in time, the poorest of the West European countries would tire of the cost—in money and manpower—of supporting these rearguard colonial wars. But that thesis is tenable only if the price of holding on to the territories is greater than the return." The *Kansas City Star* (May 1, 1970) correctly judged that "major oil revenues"—which reached some $61 million in 1972—resulting from a Gulf Oil investment of $150 to $250 million in Cabinda would alter this cost-benefit equation "radically." As a result, African nationalists and those who supported their cause, suggested the *Star*, "will not have to find another peg than economics to hang their hopes on."

Higher Portuguese casualty rates in Guinea-Bissau and Mozambique represented such a peg. In all three territories African insurgents came to use mines and booby-traps as part of a strategy of maximizing enemy casualties while minimizing physical contact and their own losses. Still officially considered at a "tolerable" level, Portuguese losses from 1967 to 1974 totaled some 11,000 dead and perhaps four times as many wounded (including many amputees). Its home population shrunk by emigration to as few as 8.4 million, Portugal's casualty rates compared proportionately to those suffered by the United States in Vietnam.

However, nationalist efforts from 1961 failed totally to prevail upon Western powers to refrain from selling arms, granting loans, or exporting capital to Portugal until African rights to self-determination were acknowledged. In return for a tracking station (Azores) and air base facilities (Beja), respectively, France and West Germany provided standard NATO weaponry on favorable terms. African nationalists were left to pursue attritional guerrilla war against Portuguese forces well equipped for counterinsurgency (e.g., Alouette II/III and Puma SA-330 helicopters) through the expenditure of funds dependent to some extent on economic relations with the United States and Western Europe.

After ten years of guerrilla warfare in Angola, the Portuguese government appeared resigned to continuing "military police action" for an indefinite period of time. It remained confident that it could confine guerrilla action to peripheral border regions, forest redoubts, and relatively empty areas of the arid south and east, well outside the territories' major population centers. While using some 65,000 troops (including a growing component of African conscripts) and local militia units to isolate and limit nationalist action, the colonial administration counted on long-term economic, social, and educational change to secure Portuguese sovereignty.

From 1961 through 1963 the Angolan insurgency was led principally by the National Front for the Liberation of Angola (FNLA) based in the Bakongo area of the north and led by a Bakongo politician, Holden Roberto. The apex of its ascendancy came in mid-1963 when its Government in Exile (GRAE) at Kinshasa was recognized by the newly founded Organization of African Unity and offered exclusive support from a Liberation Fund set up by the OAU. Concentrating on military action and giving only minimal attention to political education, organization, or strategic planning, the FNLA failed to maintain its revolutionary momentum in the face of stepped-up counterinsurgency, including effective Portuguese use of air power, land mines, and fortified villages. The fall of the Congolese government of Cyrille Adoula and the assumption of power by Katanga's pro-Portuguese Moise Tshombe (1964) severely handicapped FNLA operations, especially its ability to supply its forces inside Angola. Concurrently, internal quarrels brought forth primordial ethnic-regional rivalry, and in 1964 Ovimbundu soldiers mutinied and most central-southern leadership left the FNLA movement. During 1964–65 desertions and an abortive internal coup to overthrow Roberto reduced the FNLA to a defensive strategy based on the several hundred thousand Bakongo refugees and émigrés living in the Lower Congo. At the same time, it lost much of its *élan* and promising leadership as Roberto eliminated all potential rivals and asserted his own conservative direction.

The FNLA's constituency had largely transplanted itself from Angola to the Congo (now Zaïre). Angola's total Bakongo population had numbered around 600,000, and by 1966 up to 400,000 of them had reportedly moved across the border to join their ethnic kin in Bakongo regions of the Congolese Republic. This external political base along with renewed support from the Congolese central government after General (Joseph) Mobutu Sésé Séko came to power in late 1965 accounted for the staying power of Roberto's movement. It continued to carry out minor military action, ambushes, and raids from mountainous bases in the north and sorties across the Kwango River and Katanga (now Shaba) border areas of Zaïre. But no coherent plan or cumulative political buildup seemed involved.

In return for exclusive use of Zaïrean territory and sole access to Zaïre's extensive borders with Angola, the FNLA cooperated closely with the Mobutu government. Perforce, it did not seek aid from foes of the Kinshasa government, in particular the Soviet Union. In the view of some observers, the FNLA constituted a rather safe, ineffectual organization that could be supported without provoking serious Portuguese reprisals. As Zaïre's economic relations with Angola and diplomatic contacts with Portugal improved in the early 1970s, the Kinshasa government seemingly increased constraints on FNLA actions. In March 1972 frustrated FNLA guerrillas mutinied and Zaïre forces occupied the FNLA's principal training base of Kinkuzu. In an apparent bid for Pan-African leadership at little risk,

Mobutu then reversed field and undertook to retrain and equip the FNLA army. To this end, he also sought the collaboration of the OAU and China. By early 1974 the FNLA under Zaïre's tutelage had recruited a new army, brought in new administrative leadership, and planned to make a bid to become once again the preeminent insurgent movement.

Led by an urban intellectual elite from Luanda and its Mbundu hinterland, the rival MPLA found itself initially disadvantaged by geography and, to some extent, its class and racial origins. Its exiled *assimilado* and *mestiço* leadership moved from European exile to the Congo only after the outbreak of fighting. Once in the Congo, it managed to establish links with and gain the allegiance of some Mbundu guerrilla units in the forested Nambuangongo-Dembos areas northeast of Luanda. A Marxist orientation and sympathetic left-wing press won it considerable support within Western Europe and Scandinavia, and also among more "radical" African states and from Communist countries. But this did not compensate for the lack of Congolese support essential for access to Angola's borders. Nor did it make up for the MPLA's slowness to build up military cadres. The result was a near debacle in 1963, when the OAU gave exclusive recognition to Roberto's militarily more active movement. The MPLA split into two, a loyalist wing led by Dr. Agostinho Neto and a smaller, Maoist-oriented faction led by the MPLA's original secretary general, Viriato da Cruz.

Regrouped in Congo-Brazzaville under Dr. Neto's leadership, MPLA loyalists mounted a significant guerrilla campaign in the Cabinda enclave by mid-1964. And then in 1966, following Zambian independence, Neto's movement opened up a new Eastern front. Emulating the program of political indoctrination carried out by the PAIGC in Guinea-Bissau, the MPLA trained political cadres from eastern communities (Luena, Luchasi, etc.), including émigrés in Zambia. It sent some of these cadres to Eastern Europe for military training, then equipped them with Soviet and Czech weapons and launched them (1966) upon a wide-ranging campaign in eastern Angola. This campaign carried MPLA patrols to the outskirts of Angola's population centers, notably the margins of the central Bie district. MPLA action extended from the Malange district in the north to Ovambo regions of the south. In addition, the movement continued minor guerrilla activity in Cabinda and the Nambuangongo-Dembos forests near Luanda.

In sum, the MPLA thus developed into the strongest Angolan movement. It was capable of hijacking an airplane and of disrupting the Benguela railroad (if Zambia had permitted), and it forced the Portuguese to resettle thousands of outlying peasants and pastoral peoples in fortified villages (*aldeamentos*). Moreover, the fact that it was the only Angolan movement that received OAU, Soviet, and Scandinavian aid significantly reinforced its advantage over its rivals. Beginning in 1968, the MPLA held regional party conferences inside the country. Its top leadership, however, like that of the FNLA, continued to spend most of its time in exile. And this absence, combined with military reverses in the face of Portuguese helicopter-borne search-and-destroy offensives in 1968–69 and 1972, produced internal schisms. In 1973 the MPLA eastern zone leader, Daniel Chipenda, openly broke with Agostinho Neto. The MPLA was thus in a state of political turmoil and military paralysis at the time of the Lisbon coup of April 1974.

Jonas Savimbi and most of the leaders of the Union for the Total Independence of Angola (UNITA), making a virtue of necessity, operated more or less permanently inside the country. UNITA's leadership enjoyed a strong ethnic base in the southern half of Angola. It was founded in 1966 by Savimbi, the former minister for foreign affairs in Roberto's exile government (GRAE), and by other Ovimbundu exiles and representatives from other southern and eastern communities (Chokwe, Luena, Ovambo). It lost its one contiguous exile base when the Zambian government closed its offices in 1967 after its forces had blown up the Benguela railroad and Savimbi had quarreled with Zambian officials. With a highly self-reliant, militant program, some press support, and a modicum of financial support from the Chinese, UNITA forces reportedly operated in areas west and south of Luso. Lacking any major external source of arms, and thus militarily the weakest of the three movements, UNITA concentrated on a relatively quiet strategy of building up a political underground. According to UNITA's own communiques, its guerrillas achieved an unprecedented series of "resounding victories" in early 1970. By 1972 it, like the MPLA, claimed to be operating militarily in both Bie and the Huila district (as far south as the Cunene-Namibia border regions) of the southwest. But its military action in reality was quite modest.

As of early 1974 then, guerrilla action still plagued large areas of northern and eastern Angola. Nationalists ambushed Portuguese convoys, blew up bridges, and raided military outposts. They were not, on the other hand, able to carry physical or psychological warfare to the more than 335,000 European town- and farm-dwellers, although in late 1969, and again in 1971, security police were obliged to move against persistent MPLA efforts to create and recreate a political underground in Luanda. Moreover, the nationalist movements were not able to thrust themselves deeply into the populous (over 2 million) Ovimbundu plateau areas west of the upper Cuanza River, a move that would have signaled real danger to the future of Portuguese rule.

PORTUGAL'S AFRICA POLICY AND THE NORTH ATLANTIC ALLIANCE

Despite Portugal's heightened economic stakes and continued military superiority in Africa, its Eurafrican "mission" was steadily challenged and eroded. Although the post-Salazar government of Marcello Caetano disappointed those who anticipated a political liberalization of substance as well as style, domestic opposition to the colonial wars became a major problem. Lisbon was of course aware that war weariness and political disaffection, not military defeat, prompted the withdrawal of France from Algeria and the United States from Vietnam. And if antiwar elements in Portugal were denied the intstruments of an open society—free press, mass demonstration, electioneering—with which to mobilize popular support, opposition became manifest in draft-dodging (*émigrés*), increasing army defections, and, most important, military sabotage carried out by the country's first really effective and disciplined political underground, Armed Revolutionary Action (ARA). The core of the ARA, which destroyed seventeen military aircraft at Tancos Field in one operation and bombed ships, attacked trains, blew up ammunition dumps, damaged NATO facilities, and disrupted communications, all with skill and drama, managed, unlike more amateurish precursors, to elude the police. Other revolutionary groups emerged. The government felt obliged to declare a "state of subversion," and the minister of interior warned that the discovery and arrest of subversive elements within the armed forces, universities, and labor organizations would cause the political police (DGS) to use its power to detain without charges anyone suspected of activities against the security of the state. Premier Caetano and other officials spoke of the *real* enemy as "anti-Portuguese [read antiwar] collaborators" *at home*.

While Portuguese army deserters joined American counterparts in Sweden, the military leaders and hardcore Africa-first elements led by former Foreign Minister Alberto Franco Nogueira and Minister of Interior Goncalves Rápazote continued to demand a military solution in Africa. But if Nogueira saw Portugal's claim to global status as residing in the hydroelectric power of Cabora Bassa and the oil of Cabinda, a growing number of young economists, businessmen, and politicians were concluding that Portugal's well-being would be best served by working for association with an economically integrated Western Europe. As *The Economist* noted in 1972, Western Europe provided some 58 percent of Portugal's imports and bought about 54 percent of its exports: "The comparable figures for Portugal's African provinces were 14 percent and 25 percent." Consequently, an Africa-versus-Europe debate over national priorities emerged. It was reminiscent of that which had taken place two decades earlier in France during the waning days of the French Union. And it was sharpened by the economic and political fact that Portugal had enough difficulty preparing for its own gradual association with the European Economic Community (EEC) without trying to fit its overseas "provinces" in too. Recognizing the benefits already accrued from membership in the loose European Free Trade Association (EFTA), Portugal's "European" advocates did not wish to be left sitting alone in the dust as Great Britain and other EFTA countries joined the EEC.

The dilemma underlying the Africa-versus-Europe debate, which increasingly polarized the ruling stratum of Portuguese society, was put thus by *Le Monde's* Marcel Niedergang: "The Portuguese state cannot at one and the same time maintain its war effort and assure an indispensable economic development." Seeking a way out of this dilemma, however, Lisbon turned to the United States and (1) found in "Vietnamization" a suggestive model for a new, less costly colonial policy and (2) obtained economic assistance that temporarily reduced the urgency for making tough guns-versus-butter choices.

As with its use of "strategic hamlets" (*aldeamentos*) and its threats of massive aerial retaliation against external support, Portugal borrowed from the United States' concept of Vietnamization and launched a program of "regionalization," or Africanization, that had three principal goals. First, in financial terms it meant that the "provincial" government of Angola, and Mozambique also, would bear an increasingly large share of the costs of counterinsurgency. Between 1967 and 1971 the percentage of defense costs borne by the overseas territories rose from 25.2 percent to 32.3 percent, and the secretary of state for the treasury, Costa André, predicted that it would be possible "to organize the defense of the overseas provinces more and more within the internal orbit of each province." Because of "the rapidly increasing military budgets of the overseas territories," Lisbon was able to channel more metropolitan funds into socioeconomic development, and in 1972, for the first time since the early 1960s, estimated development expenditure was almost 80 percent of the amount spent on defense and security.

In military manpower terms Africanization, already well advanced, called for gradual replacement of metropolitan troops by local recruits. By offering literacy and technical training along with entry into special status commando and paratroop units, the government was developing the armed forces as *the* avenue of upward social mobility for thousands of young Africans. In constitutional terms Africanization meant a modest devolution of administrative (as distinct from substantive) political autonomy to provincial authorities. Basically it represented a response to demands for a larger governmental role by local European settler interests—notably demands contained in a petition (1969) by predominantly white Angolan economic associations.

While its short-term expediency was patent, in the long term Africanization seemed likely to produce more problems than it solved. Could one recruit train thousands of African soldiers for counterinsurgency and yet continue to exclude Africans from meaningful participation in the political, economic, and educational processes and institutions of their country? Could one promise more autonomy to settler interests and yet maintain a mercantilist economic relationship under which Angola's diamonds, petroleum, and iron were processed in metropolitan Portugal while Angola was compelled to sell its exports cheaply to Portugal in return for Portuguese goods at inflated prices? The overt, latent, and contradictory forces of African nationalism and white separatism suggested ample reason for doubt. And Africanization notwithstanding, did a Portugal that was able to settle only 277 families in Mozambique in 1971 at a cost of nearly $3 million, and was forced to import Cape Verdean and African workers (some 15,000 by July 1971) to meet domestic needs for unskilled labor at the risk of opening a door to racial conflict and political subversion, have the manpower and financial base to pursue a successful Eurafrican mission?

Attempts to answer that question had to reckon with external variables. In December 1971, as a quid pro quo for a two-year extension of United States base rights in the Azores, the United States extended some aid to Lisbon, up to $400 million in Export-Import Bank loan-drawing rights, $30 million in PL-480 agricultural commodities, and $5 million or more in excess "nonmilitary equipment" such as road-building machinery. Little of the available loan was in fact drawn. The aid was more important psychologically than materially, reinforcing Portuguese resistance to mounting pressures against the pursuit of endless colonial war. To be fully appreciated, of course, this aid had also to be placed in the context of unregulated American private sector relations, which pumped an annual $300 million into the Portuguese economy through expenditures for tourism ($80 million), Azores base operations ($13 million), Cabinda oil (over $60 million), Angolan coffee (nearly $100 million), Mozambican cashews ($9 million), and so on. Moreover, it fell within the framework of a policy which, despite an embargo on arms for use by Portugal in Africa, provided specialized training for some one hundred Portuguese military officers annually (for a total of some three thousand by 1973–74), and access to U.S. jet transports, heavy-duty trucks, jeeps, and herbicides (defoliants) for use in Africa.

American assistance could be partially explained by a special desire to maintain antisubmarine, air-rescue, and refueling bases in the Azores, through which the United States routed supplies to Israel during the "Yom Kippur war" of 1973. But in a more general way, American policy simply reflected the thrust of strategic thinking and particular military and economic interests operating in the absence of any countervailing public pressures (notably the as-yet-unrealized potential for Afro-American political action). For fourteen years American policymakers paid scant attention to the small-scale wars for independence being waged by African guerrilla forces in Portugal's African colonies. With the advent of the Nixon administration in 1969, a major review of American policy toward Southern Africa (NSSM 39) concluded that African insurgent movements were ineffectual and not "realistic or supportable" alternatives to continued colonial rule. American policy became even more Eurocentric. The authors of the inter-departmental policy review, commissioned by then White House adviser Henry Kissinger, questioned "the depth and permanence of black resolve" and "rule[d] out a black victory at any stage." They did not question the depth and permanence of Portuguese resolve. They miscalculated because of faulty intelligence, in both senses of that word.

By the early 1970s there were ample signs—economic disarray, political restiveness, military demoralization—that Portugal's days as a Eurafrican power were numbered. These indicators were visible to those with eyes to see. But when in April 1974 Portugal's armed forces overthrew the government of Salazar's successor, Marcello Caetano, the American government stood surprised and embarrassed by its close ties to the *ancien régime*. The debacle of America's subsequent involvement in Angola flowed from the same propensity to view what was happening there through the distorting lens of a larger strategic concern—this time a global shoving match with the Soviet Union.

ANGOLAN INDEPENDENCE AND FOREIGN INTERVENTION

From the April coup until the end of 1974, the Portuguese moved steadily toward independence for Angola and attempted to lead Angola's national-ists into the unfamiliar arena of legal, electoral competition. In so doing they sought to achieve a degree of intermovement cooperation that a long series of conciliation initiatives by the OAU and its members had not. In early 1975 Lisbon's new military regime brought together the leadership of Angola's three liberation movements, first at Mombasa, Kenya, and then at Alvor, Portugal. The resultant tripartite accord created a transitional government to prepare the way for independence on November 11, 1975.

By July 1975, however, the transitional government collapsed, the victim of intermovement rivalry and external intervention. Enjoying an initial military advantage due to Chinese, Rumanian, and Zaïrean support,

Holden Roberto's forces occupied the coffee country of the Bakongo north, seeking FNLA ascendancy through military action. Finally able to organize freely in Luanda and its Mbundu hinterland, Agostinho Neto's MPLA (shorn of Daniel Chipenda's splinter group) implanted itself firmly within its own regional bailiwick and, as of late 1974, began receiving renewed arms and financial help from the Soviet Union.

In January 1975 the National Security Council's "40 Committee" had authorized a covert American grant of $300,000 to the FNLA, whose preference for a "military solution" and ostentatious spending spurred the Soviets, in turn, to increase their support for the MPLA. Partisan of a "political solution," UNITA, which had counted on an electoral victory based on its roots within the more than two-million-strong Ovimbundu population and a calculated appeal for support within the European community, found itself being squeezed out of contention by its better-armed, bitterly embattled rivals. With some belated assistance from Zambia and Zaïre, UNITA began building its own army. And in July 1975 the United States, eager to block the Soviet-backed MPLA from power, began funneling arms and money to both the FNLA and UNITA. In August South African troops occupied hydroelectric facilities near the Namibian border, and Cuban instructors began appearing among MPLA troops. At this point China stepped aside.

Finally, in late October a South African-led military column marched north from Namibia, turning the tide of battle temporarily in favor of loosely allied UNITA/FNLA forces. Before it was able to reach Luanda, however, thousands of Cuban soldiers equipped with heavy Soviet weaponry streamed in to reinforce the MPLA. By late 1975, MPLA/Cuban forces had smashed badly organized and badly led FNLA/Zaïre troops in the north. They then turned southward. Having underestimated Cuban/Soviet resolve and overestimated American nerve, South Africa found itself engaged in a lonely adventure that, given Pretoria's white supremacist racial policies, no African state was prepared publicly to support. South Africa pulled out. And UNITA's hastily assembled and outgunned army fled into the Angolan bush.

Following its military triumph, the MPLA controlled all major towns by February 1976. The OAU, previously split down the middle on the issue, recognized the MPLA government in Luanda. The United States alone among Western powers still refused to recognize the People's Republic of Angola, to the extent of first vetoing, then abstaining on its application for United Nations membership. In the view of the American Secretary of State, Dr. Henry Kissinger, who had vainly pleaded with Congress to counter Cuban intervention with increased American assistance to FNLA/UNITA forces, the MPLA's victory represented a Soviet victory. He had inexplicably failed to contact the Soviets to seek an agreement to support the transitional coalition government—the obvious political solution—until the tide of battle had already assured an MPLA victory. Having been defeated in what he viewed as a global chess game with the Soviets, Kissinger then refused to "reward" the victors with American recognition. He appeared to cling to the hope that ongoing resistance by UNITA and FNLA guerrillas would bleed Cuban forces in a protracted Vietnam-like rural insurgency.

ANGOLA FACES THE FUTURE

That independence came amid violence and chaos is directly traceable to colonial policies that were based upon divide-and-rule exploitation. Whoever ended up governing Angola was bound to face enormous problems, starting with the need to weld the country into a cohesive political entity. Convinced of the importance of political education, the MPLA, like its multiracial, Marxist allies in Guinea-Bissau (PAIGC) and Mozambique (Frelimo), plunged into the task of politicizing and molding a new, socialist society.

The constitution of the People's Republic of Angola (PRA) placed the MPLA, a "broad front" of "anti-imperialist" forces, "in charge of the political, economic and social leadership of the nation." After less than a year of independence, however, the powerful, long-time secretary of the movement, Lúcio Lára, announced plans to replace MPLA rule with that of a new "vanguard" socialist party. In November 1976 the MPLA Central Committee scheduled a congress for the second half of 1977 for the purpose of "transforming" the movement into a "Marxist-Leninist party." And in a new "action program" MPLA leaders stated that, given the "intentions" of external forces to impose "neo-colonial domination" on it, Angola was obliged to embark upon the road to "scientific socialism." This meant adopting "the socialism of Marx, Engels and Lenin, scientific socialism that explicitly entails the ending of exploitation of man by man." Inspired by an "internationalist" world view, MPLA leaders rejected regionalist notions of "African socialism" or Pan-Africanism as diluted and constricted approaches to the goal of collective human liberation. And to achieve their "liberation" goal, they planned a massive effort in political education among Angola's six million people, some 90 percent of whom remain illiterate despite an expansion of public education during the last years of the colonial regime.

Did all this signify that Angola, as Henry Kissinger had feared, was becoming a Soviet-style, communist state? The October 1976 visit of the PRA's poet-physician president, Agostinho Neto, to Moscow, where he signed a Treaty of Friendship and Cooperation with the Soviet Union, encouraged some to so conclude. The treaty included a military clause promising mutual support: "In the interest of strengthening the defense of the capability of the High Contracting Parties they will continue to develop cooperation in the military sphere on the lines of appropriate agreements concluded between them" (*Izvestia*, October 10, 1976).

But there was considerable evidence on which to base a contrary assessment. This view perceives Angola as setting out on a pragmatic, independent, and open-ended process of sociopolitical change. The MPLA Central Committee itself gave immediate priority to the task of "binding the wounds of war and getting the economy functioning again." Recognizing that Angola had only a very small urban working class, even the MPLA's principal ideologue, Lúcio Lára, warned against precipitous moves that would alienate such groups as the peasants, petits bourgeois, and intellectuals, whose participation was vital to national reconstruction. And it seemed reasonable to assume that the country's own particular historical, cultural, and experiential circumstances would play an important role in determining the final form that its socialist society would take.

Meanwhile, a visible measure of economic pragmatism was consistent with the PRA constitution, which "recognizes, protects and guarantees private property, including that of foreigners, provided these favor the economy of the country and the interests of the Angolan people." The fighting during 1975, or what the MPLA refers to as the "second war for national liberation," had left the economy in shambles. The departure of over 250,000 whites crippled production and transport, but also facilitated the nationalization of industrial and agricultural property. Repairing bridges, replacing transport vehicles, obtaining technicians were the sorts of problems that commanded immediate attention.

Just as Cuba's intervention was crucial to the MPLA's military victory, so its help was invaluable in coping with the postwar break in technical services. Cuban doctors, dentists, and medical technicians; education experts; and coffee, sugar, and forestry specialists arrived in force to join the battle of national reconstruction. They were joined by an influx of technical personnel from the Soviet Union and Eastern Europe.

Western business interests were also reported flocking to Luanda, lured by prospects of trade with one of Africa's potentially most wealthy countries. Scandinavian and Dutch firms had an advantage, given their countries' support for the Angolan cause prior to independence. But Luandan officials expressed a desire also to establish ties with the United States, which formerly imported much of the country's coffee, about one hundred million dollars worth annually. Indeed, the markets for many Angolan exports, including oil, diamonds, and iron ore, were perforce Western. And American fears that the Soviet Union would acquire a South Atlantic naval base at Lobito seemed overdrawn. Diplomatic sources have indicated that Soviet feelers pointing to that end were rebuffed. The PRA consititution, moreover, specifically prohibits "the installation of foreign military bases on its national territory." And Agostinho Neto has often stated that the PRA will "never be enslaved to any foreign country, be it the U.S.S.R. or any another power."

What should be expected, however, is a further expansion of the state sector of the economy, the creation of more state cooperatives in farming, manufacturing, and distributive enterprise. And through the medium of the National Union of Angolan Workers (UNTA), efforts are being made to infuse both technical training and greater discipline into the ranks of Angolan workers.

The long-term objective of the government is economic as well as political independence. Accordingly, firms such as the Gulf Oil Corporation face the prospect that their operations will ultimately be nationalized. But at present MPLA authorities are anxious not to disrupt the production of Cabindan oil, which translated into some $500 million in annual state revenue by early 1977. Indeed, in 1976 Cabindan oil accounted for some 80 percent of the country's export earnings (given the interruption of coffee and diamond production), or roughly 60 percent of the government's revenue. It seems likely, therefore that Luanda will follow the gradualist approach recommended by Algerian oil experts and negotiate for 55-percent stake in Gulf's Cabinda subsidiary for the duration of a new contract period. And a similar approach may be anticipated with respect to Angola's Cassinga iron and Launda diamond resources as well as the Benguela railroad.

Over the long haul Western as well as other capital and technology will likely be welcomed, but on strict, toughly negotiated terms of mutual benefit. The PRA gives every indication that it will seek diverse sources of participation in the development of its unexploited but promising wealth in copper, manganese, titanium, and uranium, and in agriculture (less than 2 percent of its arable land is now under cultivation). Though they view the world through the prism of Marxist ideology, Angola's new rulers are manifesting a flexible rather than a doctrinaire approach to foreign economic relations.

The building of a new, socialist order through the political mobilization of "people's power" (*poder popular*) constitutes an ambitious undertaking. It also faces some formidable obstacles. To begin with, the MPLA has been beset with dissidence within its own ranks and within its key Luandan political constituency. Since 1974 Joaquim Pinto de Andrade, named "honorary president" of the MPLA during his years as a political prisoner in Portugal, has led a group of largely *mestiço* intellectuals in quest of political power inside the MPLA. Known as the *Revolta Activa*, this faction has been joined in Luanda by the extreme left, quasi-Maoist Angolan Communist Organization (OCA) in opposing Agostinho Neto's leadership. And within the government itself, a former black (Mbundu) guerrilla leader and critic of perceived white-*mestiço* dominance in the Neto administration, Nito Alves, emerged as a serious contender for political power. His ambition, however, provoked his dismissal as interior minister in November 1976, a dismissal that came despite Alves' reputed pro-Soviet sympathies.

That the top levels of MPLA–PRA leadership are held by talented, well-educated, and dedicated men seems incontrovertible. That this leadership represents principally one elite, Portuguese-educated segment of Angolan society seems no less evident, if inevitable. The exclusion of Nito Alves may bring temporary respite from the challenge of "black power" advocates. But it also serves to highlight a dominant characteristic of the MPLA government: the prominence of *mestiço,* white, and *assimilado* ministers and the corresponding paucity of African names among those in senior positions. This fact of course reflects an historical continuity within the MPLA. And the elimination of the FNLA and UNITA as political contenders in a contest of force has sharpened and weighted an underlying social dichotomy that cleaved Angolan nationalism throughout the struggle for independence. The exclusion of leadership cadres of the vanquished FNLA and UNITA from government reinforces the preeminence of the MPLA's Portuguese-educated urbanites, who stress the centrality of class conflict as over against racial and ethno-cultural considerations. It reinforces the political ascendancy of the *urban/acculturated-intellectual/multiracialists* over the *rural/ethno-populist/uniracialists.* But it has not blinded MPLA leadership to what Lúcio Lára, himself a *mestiço,* has described as an urgent need to improve economic conditions throughout the country and to overcome "tribal prejudices" within its largely rural population.

Under the Portuguese the cultural values of Angola's diverse peoples were systematically denigrated. This practice has left a legacy of mutual ignorance and suspicion among ethnic groups. Consequently, any hope of building an integrated Angolan nation through a consensual as distinct from coercive process must rely on conscious, knowledgeable efforts to promote interethnic understanding and respect. To bind the wounds of war and construct a unified socialist society, the MPLA government will have to reach out, bring in new leadership, and transcend the limits of its Luanda/Mbundu/*mestiço* dimensions. But even if there is an awareness of the need and a commitment to do so, the task will not be an easy one.

A year after independence the PRA still confronted a residual military challenge to its authority. Small guerrilla forces—UNITA in the arid southeast, the FNLA in the forested northwest, and FLEC (the Cabinda Liberation Front) in the oil-rich Cabindan enclave—continued to harass the

MPLA army. Persistent reports that Zaïre was supporting, or at least condoning, the use of its territory by FNLA and FLEC guerrillas were matched by similar reports of continuing South African help for UNITA. Zaïre's hostility was evident as well in a refusal to allow its and Zambia's copper exports access to the Benguela railroad—meaning a loss of some thirty million dollars in annual revenue for Angola. Whether externally supported guerrilla forces represented a serious short-term threat or a harbinger of long-term instability was unclear. Much would depend on the ability of the MPLA government to promote an inclusive, integrative participation by all sectors of Angolan society within the political process.

One obvious consequence of externally-backed insurgency against the government, however, was to prolong, even increase, its dependency on the continued presence of over ten thousand Cuban troops. The Cubans, engaged in training an Angolan army of some twenty thousand were paving the way for their own eventual military withdrawal. But until the Neto government firmly established its authority throughout the country, the Cuban army would remain a vital guarantor of "law and order." Improbable as it might seem, a small island country of nine million people located six thousand miles away had become the arbiter of Angola's future, the decisive block to Ovimbundu, Bakongo, or Cabindan secession, the sole force preventing a return to foreign-fed civil war.

The punitive policy of nonrecognition pursued by Kissinger after the defeat of anti-MPLA forces in February 1976 has done nothing but nourish anti-American sentiment and discredit American diplomacy in Africa as a whole. One of the first foreign-policy decisions to be faced by the Carter administration, therefore, must be whether to continue that negative policy or to seek to establish relations based on the principle of "mutuality of interest." Among the arguments for entering into a more constructive relationship is the very role of Cuba that aroused so much hostility in Washington. If the United States will accept as a *modus operandi* the notion that it cannot and need not everywhere "shape events," to use one of Kissinger's favorite expressions, it may reduce or eliminate the phenomenon in which America's new "enemies" seek the support of its old "enemies" in violent reaction to its interventionist policies. Indeed, Angola suggests a good argument for "normalizing" relations with Cuba, for Cuba itself is only rendered perpetually dependent on the Soviet Union by a punitive but futile American economic and diplomatic boycott. Why is it necessary or useful to perpetuate hostile relationships with either country?

It must be anticipated that the MPLA's sense of "revolutionary solidarity" will lead it, without regard for what its relations with the United States may be, to play an active role in the regional struggle against South African apartheid. The MPLA has pledged itself to support the South West Africa People's Organization (SWAPO) in its efforts to liberate Namibia from white minority rule. In the words of one observer, journalist Robert Manning, as the MPLA "forges a socialist Angola" it will continue to perceive "its victory [as] part and parcel of the liberation struggle throughout southern Africa." Luanda's new rulers are committed to the creation of a radical new order—egalitarian, mobilized, disciplined—within Angola *and* all of Southern Africa.

But this objective represents no threat to legitimate American interests. In a lecture at the University of Dar es Salaam in 1974, Agostinho Neto set forth his political ideas. "What we want," he said, "is an independent life as a nation, a life in which economic relations are just both between countries and within the country, a revival of [African] cultural values which are still valid for our era." A revival of or rededication to "valid" American cultural values would suggest that the United States eschew the compulsion to "shape events" *for* others and, instead, identify and relate constructively with the efforts *of* others who seek in their own way to "abolish exploitation" and place "relations with all peoples on a basis of equality and fraternity."

It may be a long time before the United States and other Western allies of Portugal's old colonial order can be accepted as well-intentioned friends of an independent, socialist Angola. But the advent of a new administration in Washington offers the United States an opportunity to adopt new, nonimpositional policies that can foster cooperative relationships and can reinforce Angola's own efforts to construct a strong and independent state and economy. That opportunity should be seized.

[5]

Namibia

Impending Independence?

ELIZABETH S. LANDIS

IN MID-AUGUST 1976 newspapers carried the story that Namibia would become independent at the end of 1978 under a multiracial government. The story was based on a one-page announcement made by the constitutional committee of a mysteriously convened multiethnic conference that had met in Windhoek, the Territory's capital, for a year in order to produce that statement.

Within a few weeks representatives of one nation after another addressed the United Nations Security Council condemning the projected "independence" as fraudulent. They pointed to Security Council resolutions 366 and 385, adopted in the preceding year and a half, which had called on South Africa to take specified steps to end its illegal occupation of Namibia. The speakers indicated that the August statement did not in any respect meet the requirements of those resolutions.

At the same time Secretary of State Kissinger was engaged in various negotiations to bring about independence for Namibia in the near future. When ten members of the Security Council voted to impose an arms embargo against South Africa because of its failure to comply with resolutions 366 and 385, the United States, along with France and Britain, vetoed the draft resolution. They said delicate negotiations regarding Namibia were under way and should not be jeopardized by Security Council interference.

Meanwhile, Sam Nujoma, president of the South West Africa Peoples' Organization (SWAPO), which is recognized by the United Nations as a representative of the people of Namibia and is carrying out political and military activities designed to drive out the South Africans, declared that his organization was not beguiled by either the "independence" predicted for Namibia or Dr. Kissinger's "shuttle diplomacy." After a meeting with Secretary Kissinger, which he termed fruitless, he left the United Nations for Cuba to seek more weapons for SWAPO's guerrilla army.

This confused situation at the moment of Namibia's apparent transition to independence reflected, in fact, very deep and fundamental differences among those immediately concerned about Namibia: the Namibians themselves; South Africa, which through its military might and police-state tactics occupies the Territory in defiance of international law; the OAU, and particularly the African states south of Zaïre; the United Nations, which is the legal administrator of the Territory but is unable to eject South Africa; and the Great Powers, whose economic, strategic, and political interests extend to Southern Africa.

In order to understand these differences and what they may portend for the future of the Territory, it is important to visualize the area and to know a little of its relatively short recorded history. The name "Namibia" is said to derive from *Namib,* the Nama word for "shelter." Indeed, for hundreds of years, while Europeans were exploring other parts of Africa, the waterless, uninhabitable Namib Desert, which runs along the entire coast of the Territory, discouraged explorers and settlers from penetrating to its interior.

THE GERMAN ERA

Such isolation could not last forever. At the beginning of the nineteenth century, German missionaries entered the Territory, which was called South West Africa for obvious geographical reasons. Beyond the Namib they found an arid, sparsely populated interior plateau, which was bounded on the east by another desert, the Kalahari.

The Germans must have been struck by the stark and austere beauty of the country, which still moves inhabitants and visitors alike. In the drier south central part of the plateau sheep and goats grazed. (Today the valuable karakul sheep is raised there.) Farther north there were vast herds of carefully tended cattle. All around were the wild animals of the savannah. After a rain, the dry, dusty plains came alive in a carpet of grass and flowers.

The pressure of population, small as it was, was already causing episodic intertribal warfare to control the vast acreage needed for each ruminant. But at a time of relatively plentiful rainfall and little or no disease—disease periodically thinned the herds—the country looked inviting even if it was too dry for grain crops.

The missionaries came with the benevolent intention of bringing the Christian message to the area. Were they to be judged simply by how well they achieved that objective—a test that their present-day successors admit is inadequate—they would be considered uniquely successful. The Lutheran missions, along with Roman Catholic, Anglican, and a few others, were so thorough in their self-appointed task that Namibia is today perhaps the most Christian country in Africa.

Like missionaries elsewhere, however, they brought in their wake first traders, then settlers, and finally soldiers, administrators, and politicians, most of them Germans belatedly seeking a share of Africa. After the Berlin Conference of 1884–85 set the ground rules for colonial expansion in unclaimed or challenged territories, the German officials in South West Africa promptly induced or forced most of the tribes in the Territory to sign protection treaties. On that basis the Imperial German Reich proclaimed a protectorate over the entire area except "the Port and Settlement of Walfish [whale] Bay." (That enclave of 434 square miles had been claimed by Britain some ten years before.)

There followed a systematic looting of the local Africans. By the end of the century German traders and settlers had seized by legal trickery, guile, or force much of the best land and the cattle. In desperation, first the Hereros and then the Namas rose in rebellion against the government. But, fighting separately, they were defeated by superior weapons and organization and by Teutonic ruthlessness. The Hereros were literally decimated under an extermination order issued by the German command. The Namas were ruined because they had to forfeit all their cattle; landless and broken, they were reduced to acting as herdsmen for the very whites who had seized their traditional lands and their animals.

The Germans established their control over the entire Territory except the sector north of the "Red Line," which marked the limit of the area believed fit for white settlement. Within the "Police Zone" to the south of the Red Line they were unquestioned masters and treated the Africans as subhuman. They made only a partial exception for the Rehoboth Basters, a community of persons of part-white ancestry who had migrated from the Cape in mid-century; the German representatives signed a treaty with their leaders which gave that community substantial autonomy in their own area under the laws they had brought with them.

THE MANDATE ERA

When the South Africans invaded the Territory in 1915 as their contribution to the Allied war effort, they were hailed as saviors by the Africans. Their reputation was enhanced by the official Blue Book published in 1918, which documented German atrocities during the protectorate period.

The Union expected to take over Namibia at the war's end. But in the name of a peace without annexations, and under the mandatory concept devised by General Jan Christiaan Smuts of South Africa, President Wilson prevented South Africa from absorbing the Territory as a fifth province. Instead, the newly created League of Nations entrusted Namibia to South Africa as a mandate for the latter to "promote to the utmost the material and moral welfare and the social progress" of the Territory's inhabitants. The closest analogy is a court's entrusting the care of an orphan to a guardian. South Africa was allowed to administer and legislate for the former protectorate as if it were an integral part of its own territory.

It was clear almost from the start that South Africa had no intention of treating its mandated territory as "a sacred trust of civilization" (President Wilson's term), except as and when compelled to by the international community. The Africans despoiled by German rapacity did not regain their lost lands or cattle. Instead, they were treated as vagrants and impressed into labor in the mines and on the farms of new South African settlers or of the many Germans who had remained. All other Africans were relegated to inadequate, poor-quality native reserves, and whenever the land-hungry whites desired land in a reserve, the borders were shifted, always to the detriment of the black inhabitants. The Blue Book on German atrocities was soon suppressed—long before the South African air force put down a rebellion by a few hundred Bondelswarts Namas armed with knives and clubs by bombing their women and children. The Africans learned that they had exchanged an overseas tyrant for one from next door.

After the Second World War, South Africa was the only mandatory power that refused either to grant independence to its mandated territory or to place it under the somewhat more rigorous trusteeship system of the United Nations. At the first session of the U.N. General Assemby the South African representative sought permission for his country to annex South West Africa, but the General Assembly refused. The Union government thereupon refused to recognize the right of the Assembly, in substitution for the defunct League of Nations, to supervise its administration of Namibia.

The South African government also refused to accept the 1950 Advisory Opinion of the International Court of Justice concerning the legal status of South West Africa. That Opinion had held that the mandate continued to exist even after the dissolution of the League; that the General Assembly had the right to supervise South Africa's administration of its mandate; and that South Africa could not unilaterally change the mandate's status by annexing it without Assembly approval.

The Union government was, however, unmoved and soon began applying its own system of apartheid to the territory. It extended to Namibia its own laws mandating discrimination, either directly or through similar legislation enacted by the all-white territorial Legislative Assembly. (Discrimination had, of course, been rife in South West Africa ever since the German era, but the South African laws were more extensive, ideological, and vengeful and left little or nothing to more flexible local practice.)

As one facet of extending apartheid to the Territory, South Africa introduced the pass system, long functioning within the Union itself. The pass laws require Africans, but not whites, to carry on their persons and to produce on official demand numerous passes, i.e., permits, certificates, receipts, etc. Failure to produce them is punished by a fine or imprisonment. Pass laws function to prevent or restrict the movement of Africans, who may not leave their reserves or areas of employment without an appropriate pass. They serve at least three major purposes: compel Africans to take particular jobs in particular areas only; serve as "influx control" measures, to prevent unwanted Africans (wives, children, the elderly, and the incompetent) from entering or remaining in the white urban centers; and facilitate political control by limiting African movement and contact.

Along with the pass laws, the government expanded the contract labor system. Under this system Africans from the north were recruited by white employers' organizations, which were later consolidated into the South West Africa Native Labourers Association (SWANLA), for work on the farms and in the mines of the Police Zone. Africans had no choice as to the kind of work or even as to their employers. They were involuntarily separated from their families, who were prevented by the pass laws from accompanying them for the duration of the contract (a year or more). They were subject to imprisonment if they left their jobs, regardless of the justification. Nevertheless, poverty drove them to the recruiters; and if it did not, their chiefs or headmen might deliver them anyway to fulfill their quotas.

South Africa also undermined, if it did not alter, the international status of the Territory by having white representatives of the Territory in the South African Parliament and by making *all* Namibians involuntary South African citizens.

For over a decade the United Nations tried to reach some accommodation with the Union, alternately employing criticism, cajolery, and mediation, but in vain. Finally, in 1960 Ethiopia and Liberia brought a proceeding against South Africa in the World Court under an untried provision of the mandate agreement that provided for a binding judgment. After six years of arguments and one interim decision, the court eventually concluded that the two complainants had no status to bring the proceeding. It therefore refused to rule on the issue, leaving unanswered the basic legal question: whether South Africa was maladministering the Territory in violation of its obligations under the mandate agreement.

POST-MANDATE ERA

After years of being warned against taking any action that would preju-
dice judicial consideration of the *South-West Africa Cases,* the General
Assembly was outraged by the court's ultimate nondecision. By 114 votes
to 2 (South Africa and Portugal) and with the United States voting affirma-
tively, the Assembly on October 27, 1966, adopted resolution 2145 (XXI)
(1966), which revoked South Africa's mandate on the political ground that
by its maladministration of the Territory, the Republic had repudiated the
mandate agreement. The Assembly also resolved to take over the administration of South West Africa until it should attain independence. A few
months later it established an eleven-member Council for South West
Africa to act on its behalf, and in 1968 it changed the name of the Territory
from South West Africa to Namibia.

Resolution 2145 established the unique international legal status of
Namibia. By removing the Territory from South African jurisdiction, the
resolution automatically converted South Africa's presence in the Territory
from a legal *administration* into an illegal *occupation.* It made the Territory
the direct responsibility of the international community, which was legally
obligated to bring the Territory to independence and self-determination.
South Africa thus became a foreign state vis-à-vis Namibia.

South Africa is occasionally referred to as the "de facto administration
(or government)" of Namibia. This designation is technically incorrect and
misleading if used to indicate that South Africa exercises control there by
reason of its superior force. A de facto government, in proper usage, is one
that is recognized in international law as having *some* justified claim or
right to govern. South Africa lacks *any* such claim or right vis-à-vis
Namibia.

On June 21, 1971, the International Court of Justice confirmed this
analysis in an Advisory Opinion presented to the Security Council on the
"Legal Consequences for States of the Continued Presence of South Africa
in Namibia." The court held that South Africa was obligated to withdraw
its administration from the Territory immediately; that United Nations
members should recognize the illegality of the South African presence in

Namibia and the invalidity of its acts on behalf of or concerning Namibia; and that they should refrain from any acts implying recognition of the legality of the South African presence or giving support or assistance to that presence.

Not surprisingly, South Africa, which had defied the United Nations for the two decades before revocation of the mandate, refused to yield to the international community thereafter. On the contrary, it began to put into effect a plan, published in 1964 during the long Ethiopian-Liberian proceedings in the World Court, for a complete reorganization of the administration of the Territory.

IMPLEMENTING THE ODENDAAL PLAN

The Odendaal Plan—named for F. H. Odendaal, the chairman of the commission that drafted it—consisted of two parts: the first part completely revised the legislative, administrative, and financial relations between the Territory and the Republic, greatly reducing local, white autonomy and binding Namibia far more closely than before to South Africa. The second part established a Bantustan system within the Territory very much like that evolving in the Republic (see Chapter 3). The first part of the Odendaal Plan was implemented primarily under the South West Africa Affairs Act of 1969, which rewrote certain key provisions of the South West Africa constitution.

The original constitution, granted by the South African Parliament in 1925, had created an all-white territorial Legislative Assembly elected by universal adult all-white suffrage. The Assembly had broad legislative authority, effectively limited, however, to whites and the "white area" of the Territory. In 1954 Africans in the reserves were placed under the jurisdiction of the South African Ministry of Native Affairs (now Bantu Administration and Development). Subject to veto by the governor-general (now the state president), the Assembly could legislate on all matters of territorial concern, with the exception of those in which the Republic insisted on identical laws, such as "native affairs," courts, police, defense, immigration, and currency.

The 1969 Act amended the constitution by returning to the South African government both legislative and administrative authority over virtually all subjects previously under territorial control. It left only those of purely limited, local concern. The Legislative Assembly and Territorial Administration were effectively reduced to the status of the four South African provincial governments. As a consequence of this change, there was a great increase in the next few years in the amount of South African legislation extended to Namibia or applied in the Territory by executive proclamations issued under a special provision of the 1969 Act.

In addition many sources of territorial revenue—in particular the corporate income tax on firms doing business in Namibia—were taken from the Territory and allocated to Pretoria. This was done ostensibly to compensate the South African government for performing the many functions the territorial government had performed before 1969; but the effect was to integrate Namibia with the Republic economically, as well as legislatively and administratively.

The second part of the Odendaal Plan was implemented by the Native Nations Act of 19. This Act provided for the allocation of parts of the territory as ethnic "homelands" to nine separate African groups and to the Rehoboth Basters. These homelands were alleged to represent, with certain modifications, the ancestral lands of those groups. Only the territorial Coloureds, who are of mixed racial descent, can claim no ancestral lands, in the South African view; and for that reason they were allocated no homeland, but continue to be scattered in urban and rural ghettos.

All the land not assigned to the Africans or Basters was considered to constitute the "white area." The 100,000 whites, who constitute some 10 percent of the total population, hold about 60 percent of the territory's land surface, while the remaining 40 percent of the land is divided among the black 90 percent of the population. The white area contains most of the best farming land, all of the urban centers, most of the known significant mineral deposits, the entire seacoast (with all its alluvial diamonds), and most of the Territory's economic infrastructure, such as roads, railroads, airports, electric lines, and boreholes. Black homelands are overcrowded, overgrazed, underdeveloped, lacking in basic amenities, and, in some cases, waterless or with soils lacking in the chemicals needed to raise healthy animals.

The ostensible purpose of the Act was to allow each ethnic group ("peo-

ple" or "nation") to develop separately, according to its own culture and
genius. The decision as to which persons constituted a separate nation was
made by South Africa, which also decided where each homeland was to be
located. Thus, all whites, regardless of linguistic, cultural, and political
differences, are considered to constitute one people; but, as designated in the
Odendaal Plan, there are nine African peoples, including one referred to as
"Tswana and other."

In theory, each homeland was to be uni-ethnic. In fact, the extensive
population transfers that would be involved in some areas to limit the
inhabitants to one group have prevented full application of the theory in
some of the black homelands in the Police Zone. However, the government's stated intention was clear: that each people should advance, according to its own desires and capabilities, from simple tribal structure through
regional "authorities" to lesser, then greater "self-government," and possibly eventually to "independence." To facilitate this development only members of the ethnic group for which a particular homeland had been
established could be citizens of the homeland and enjoy citizenship rights
there.

The unstated intention of the government was to apply a more sophisticated version of the basic colonial strategy of "divide and rule." By isolating African groups from one another and by restricting common endeavors,
the Republic was seeking to divert their common hostility from itself and
refracting it among the blacks. In particular, the South Africans combined
this strategy with a constant barrage of propaganda about the "Ovambo
menace." The Ovambos, who represent some 40 to 50 percent of the total
black population, have for years been accused by the whites of seeking to
take over the Territory and dominate all the other blacks, a fate which has
been made to sound far worse than the present oppression by the white
minority. Government propaganda has been aimed at linking the Ovambo
menace with SWAPO, which had its start as an Ovambo association before
it became a national organization opposed to any ethnic orientation.

The effect of the law has been, for all practical purposes, to strip the
Africans of their common Namibian citizenship. It has transformed them
into rightless aliens in the white area, where, given the economic realities
of the Territory, they are compelled to secure work. While whites are

theoretically aliens in all the homelands, the fact is that whites are never without rights anywhere in Namibia. In any case, virtually the only whites who have reason to go to the homelands are government officials or wealthy businessmen or tourists, whom no African can afford to antagonize.

"TERRORISM"

By the late sixties the full scope of Odendaal-style apartheid, by then called "separate development," had became apparent. At that point the fledgling black political movements faced a major political, practical, and philosophical decision: whether to resort to armed struggle or to limit themselves to exclusively nonviolent means. SWAPO opted for armed struggle; the others were against it.

The possibilities for successful armed struggle seemed very limited when SWAPO took that fateful decision; Portugal still controlled Angola, and the struggle for independence there seemed unpromising. Nevertheless, it was possible for SWAPO to infiltrate across the Angola border into Ovambo-land, since by reason of ethnic origin SWAPO had strong sympathy among the Ovambos, who straddled the border. Infiltration of the Eastern Caprivi Strip from Zambia was also possible despite the fact that Eastern Caprivi, which had been administered as part of the Transvaal since 1939, was protected by a major air base near Katima Mulilo. The western portion of the Strip, a boggy, nearly impassable area with much close vegetation, was ideal for guerrilla movement but contained no significant targets.

The first guerrilla activities ended with the capture of a number of the inexperienced freedom fighters and the roundup of hundreds of Africans believed to support them. Although there was no law authorizing the action, many were detained incommunicado for periods of up to several years and tortured during their detention. Eventually several were brought to trial in South Africa, not Namibia, under the Terrorism Act. This law, enacted in 1967, was made retroactive to 1962 in order to convict many of the detainees against whom no existing statutory or common-law crime could be proved.

The Terrorism Act created a crime of "terrorism" so broad that virtually any political or social act falls within the definition. Such normally innocent behavior as cooperating with UNICEF to reduce infant mortality, undertaking an advertising campaign to secure an increased share of the detergent market, or revealing misconduct by a state official can be so construed. Under its provisions accused persons are presumed guilty and required to prove their innocence beyond a reasonable doubt. Section 6 of the Act permitted indefinite detention incommunicado of persons for interrogation, and it denied them the right to habeas corpus. Under the authority of that section government ministers have refused, on the grounds of state security, to give any information whatsoever about detainees—even their names—to inquiring families or even to members of the South African Parliament. One much-criticized provision permitted the retrial of persons already acquitted of an offense under the Act, while another permitted joint trials of persons accused of different crimes under the same Act. The same section authorized the trial in any place in the Republic or Territory of persons accused of terrorism, regardless of where the alleged crime was committed.

Although the Act defined the crime of terrorism broadly enough to cover virtually the entire range of social conduct, by and large only selected political dissidents have been *tried* under it, although thousands have been *detained* under section 6 and threatened with trial. The first prosecution, against Eliasar Tuhadeleni and thirty-six other Namibians was a "show" trial; it was designed to intimidate Namibian nationalists and to persuade whites that guerrilla activity on the border required further and more repressive action and legislation. While the failure of the first SWAPO guerrilla incursions did not—as South Africa confidently expected—put an end to such action, it did compel a period of consolidation and reevaluation of strategy.

THE ADVISORY OPINION

At the same time the momentum that had been generated at the United Nations by the revocation of the mandate was also halted. Although most countries wanted some quick and effective follow-up on resolution 2145, the Western Powers insisted that, given the new situation, negotiations with South Africa should precede any other action. Ultimately numbers prevailed in the Assembly, and the Council for Namibia was created in a special session in the spring of 1967. But no Western country accepted membership, thereby denying the Council the political effectiveness and prestige that their participation could have assured.

The position of the United States, which had actively supported resolution 2145, was particularly resented by the Africans as hypocritical. Its delegate argued that the Council was a futile organization because it could not operate inside Namibia, and the United States did not believe in engaging in futile activities, he said, which would only lower the prestige and credibility of the United Nations as a whole. This argument ignored the Third World position that the American failure to join the Council was a primary source of its impotence. In a related argument the United States justified repeated refusal to cooperate with the Council on the grounds that resolution 2248 directed that body to proceed to Namibia and to administer the Territory there, and that therefore actions taken by the Council from New York were technically not within its power.

As post-revocation doldrums set in, the General Assembly appealed to the Security Council for assistance. But Britain and France, two of the permanent members, still questioned the validity of resolution 2145, and the other members were unwilling to support any steps involving compulsion. So the Council, as a means of temporizing, decided to seek the advice of the International Court of Justice on the obligations of U.N. members in relation to Namibia.

It was at this point, in 1971, that the court specifically upheld the validity of the resolution, advised that South Africa should end its occupation of Namibia forthwith, and informed the Council that other states should refuse to assist the Republic to remain in Namibia or to recognize any action taken by the Republic on behalf of Namibia.

THE ROLE OF THE MISSION CHURCHES

The court's opinion was quickly made known throughout the Territory and was greeted enthusiastically by the Africans. Shortly thereafter bishops Leonard Auala and Lukas de Vries of the Lutheran Mission Church addressed an open letter to Prime Minister Vorster. Taking a purely pastoral position, they asked for an end to discrimination, pass laws, and the contract-labor system as the sources of poverty, marital instability, and general social disorganization among the Territory's inhabitants.

The bishops' letter reflected the growing involvement of the mission churches—primarily Anglican and Lutheran—in the Africans' political and social problems. White pastors, teachers, and doctors in Namibia were excluded from the territorial "establishment." Unlike the local whites, the missionaries lived among the Africans. Lacking preconceptions as to color-based abilities or proprieties, they quickly and sympathetically responded to the moral and material problems of their parishioners, most of which seemed to originate in the political system imposed upon them.

The Africans, in turn, rallied to the church, which provided sympathy, education, doctoring, and a vision of a new and better way of life. In the church they were introduced to the concept of wider communities—African, Namibian, and Christian—and, more concretely, they met their contemporaries and coreligionists from other parts of the Territory and developed friendships and common interests across ethnic lines. It is not surprising, therefore, that the liberation movement has for years numbered among its most influential members black pastors and lay persons, as well as African mission teachers, nurses, and students. Nor is it surprising, given these facts, that three Anglican bishops and innumerable missionaries of both churches have been expelled from the Territory, and that dozens of other missionaries have been denied visas to enter Namibia. Afrikaner officials in the Territory have been particularly hostile to mission education in English, which they commonly believe to be the language of subversion.

THE GENERAL STRIKE

At the end of the same year, 1971, the Africans began a general strike against low wages, the pass laws, the labor system, and the separation of workers from their families. Offered their choice between returning to work or being sent home, they chose the latter. From all over the country—the mines, the farms, and the towns—Africans streamed back to their homes. Because the rains had been adequate, and newly harvested crops were relatively plentiful, there was no immediate pressure to return to work. Consequently, the stoppage lasted far into the spring of 1972.

In Ovamboland the restless strikers who returned tore down the border fences, streamed across the frontier, and vented their wrath against some unpopular homeland officials. Without consulting Parliament, which was then in session, the South African government issued a proclamation (No. R 17 of 1972) which established quasi-martial law in Ovamboland. It prohibited entering or leaving the area except by special permit; banned all meetings except church ceremonies, sporting events, and local assemblies; permitted indefinite detention incommunicado; and made it a serious crime to make "subversive statements" or to treat a chief with "disrespect, contempt, or ridicule."

As soon as the proclamation was issued, journalists and other observers were banned from Ovamboland and have seldom been allowed in since except on a limited or official-tour basis. South African police then freely rounded up hundreds of strikers, SWAPO members, and others believed to sympathize with them. They were detained in special camps, most of them tortured, and many executed. It was a method of control to which South Africa would revert more frequently and more ruthlessly in succeeding years.

Meanwhile, every effort was being made to end the strike and, even more important, to convince the world that it had ended and that Namibia still remained a good place for foreign investment. When it was determined that the strike could not be broken by imported labor, a conference of employer representatives, South African representatives, and Ovambo and Kavango officials was held at Grootfontein. It excluded representatives of the workers and of SWAPO, which had obviously played a role in the strike. A settlement was announced at the end of the meeting; but it was another month or more before industry was operating normally again, and far longer before sporadic walkout and wildcat strikes ceased.

The "settlement" claimed to end the contract-labor system. In fact, however, it modified the system cosmetically but maintained its essentials: SWANLA, the employers' association, was abolished, but labor recruitment in the homelands was not; it was carried out (for the first time among the Namas as well as in the north) through labor officers in the homelands —a change that substituted corruptible local individuals for the impersonal cruelty of a large organization. A worker could no longer be assigned to a particular employer against his will, but the operation of the pass laws and of the newly established labor bureaus achieved substantially the same results. The law that made it a prison offense for an African to breach his labor contract was repealed; but the requirements for official permission to leave before the end of the contract period were almost impossible to fulfill, and the administrative penalties for quitting without permission were only marginally less severe than the former criminal penalties. Although promises were made to allow at least some families to accompany their breadwinners to the mining centers, they were never carried out, ostensibly due to objections by homeland authorities.

OVAMBOLAND ELECTIONS

With the restoration of an uneasy calm in 1973, Pretoria decided to allow the Ovambo (renamed "Owambo") and Kavango homelands slightly more "self-government" by electing some members of the homeland legislative councils. These councils were empowered by the Native Nations Act to enact ordinances on some matters of local concern and application. In a challenge to both South African and homeland authorities, SWAPO called for a boycott of the elections in Ovamboland. It also held rallies to support the boycott, in violation of the continuing ban on meetings.

Against these SWAPO actions the South African police also employed a new tactic. They arrested anyone believed connected with the movement and turned over such persons to the local Ovambo chiefs to be punished for that "offense." The chiefs, resurrecting a tribal "tradition" unknown to other Ovambos, sentenced the alleged "offenders," usually without even the pretense of a trial, to public floggings. Old and young, male and female, church deacons and student nurses were stripped and whipped in public, many until they lost consciousness.

The Lutheran and Anglican bishops, on behalf of their coreligionists and a victim of the floggings, joined in seeking an injunction against this practice. Their plea was refused by the local courts, thereby giving new life to the tradition, but it was finally granted on appeal by South Africa's highest court.

Despite this cruel use of local chiefs as South African surrogates, the

Ovambos were not intimidated, and the boycott was fully effective. Less than three percent of the eligible voters went to the polls—a number that hardly exceeded the roll of office-holders and their families and retainers. By way of contrast, in the neighboring Kavango homeland, where SWAPO did not mount a boycott campaign, a majority of the Africans voted.

In the period that followed, South Africa worked to undo the political damage done by the boycott. It set out to break SWAPO within the Territory, first by the floggings, then by mass arrests and political trials for offenses ranging from pass-law violations to sabotage. At one point the entire internal SWAPO leadership was either banned or detained in prison under the Terrorism Act. At the same time soldiers were sent to Ovamboland and began a new course of intimidation and violence that sent thousands of Namibians fleeing across the border.

When this program was well under way, the Ovambo authorities requested South Africa to promote their homeland to the highest level of "self-government." Pretoria promptly acceded to their wishes and, in connection with this change, scheduled new elections at the beginning of 1975 for members of the enlarged legislative council.

SWAPO was unable to mount another effective boycott campaign. According to South African figures, somewhat more than half the eligible population went to the polls. After the election new and released SWAPO leaders complained that the Ovambos had been dragooned into voting, some by sheer force and others by threats and intimidation, such as the denial of passes, refusal of hospital admissions, etc., to nonvoters. The International Commission of Jurists, which investigated the elections, graphically reported a classic pattern of force, fraud, and intimidation, nonetheless real because the purpose was to compel the unwilling to vote rather than, as in so many cases, to prevent potential voters from exercising the franchise.

PRO-LIBERATION FORCES 1974–75

As of 1974–75 an altered balance of forces was becoming evident in Namibia, one that presaged either confrontation or some form of accommodation in the not too distant future. Starting soon after the 1971 Advisory

Opinion of the World Court, the Africans had shown new militancy and organization within the Territory, as witnessed in the general strike and the boycott of the first Ovamboland election. Even the temporary disruption of SWAPO preceding the 1975 elections had not prevented an obvious increase in SWAPO's support throughout the Territory. A British observer who toured the Territory, including Ovamboland, while the flogging was in progress reported that everywhere the children chanted SWAPO's slogan, "One nation, one Namibia."

At about that time a fragile coalition of virtually all the black political parties and groups in the Territory formed as the National Convention (of Namibia). It ultimately broke up, leaving the abbreviated name NCN to the groups that gathered around Chief Clemens Kapuuo, and creating a new Namibian National Convention (NNC), in which SWAPO and SWANU (South West African National Union) were leading members. (Subsequently a smaller group, originally brought together under the title of the "Okahandja summit," renamed itself the Namibian National Council [also NNC], to add to the alphabetical confusion.)

Outside Namibia SWAPO's quasi-diplomatic representatives at the U.N. and elsewhere were beginning to win increased humanitarian assistance in the West and more military assistance elsewhere. SWAPO was accepted by the OAU and the U.N. as the sole authentic representative of the Namibian people pending independence and elections (although not without objections from other Namibian political groups). It was allowed to participate in U.N. debate (but not to vote) on Namibian issues, and it was brought more closely into the work of the Council for Namibia. The U.N. General Assembly upheld the right of the Namibian people to seek, by whatever means necessary—including force—the liberation of their country.

SWAPO's military arm, PLAN (People's Liberation Army of Namibia), was also becoming more effective. Raids across the border were more frequent and more successful, and the mining of roads used by South African troops also increased. Both civil and military members of the SWAPO command were able to hold an undisturbed week-long conference in the Caprivi Strip while a large part of the South African army and air force searched for them in vain.

At the United Nations also, the naming of a full-time commissioner, Sean

MacBride, who had had practical experience in the liberation of his native Ireland, brought a burst of new activity to Namibian issues. Within twelve months the Council for Namibia had created a Namibia Institute in Lusaka. The Institute was designed to engage in fundamental research about the Territory and to prepare untrained Namibians in exile to participate in the administration of a future independent Namibia. The council also adopted a Decree for the Protection of the Natural Resources of Namibia. That decree provided that no one might exploit or export Namibian natural resources without the consent of the council; that mining or exporting concessions or licenses issued to Namibia by South African authorities were invalid; that resources removed from Namibia without council consent could be seized and forfeited on behalf of the council for the benefit of the Namibian people; and that anyone contravening the decree might be held liable in damages by a future government of an independent Namibia. No proceeding has yet been brought under the decree; but it already appears to have had some influence on speculative investment in the Territory and on insurance and shipping of Namibian products.

ANTI-LIBERATION FORCES

On the other hand, as long as the Portuguese held on in Angola and Mozambique, South Africa appeared to have a sound, if not wholly comfortable, position politically, economically, and militarily both in Namibia and at home.

Changes proposed in the Odendaal Plan were being carried out relatively smoothly, despite considerable temporary embarrassment caused by the general strike and again by the boycott of the 1973 Ovambo election. The northern homelands (except the Kaokoveld, a poor and sparsely populated area) were marching steadily along the "self-government" path. The chiefs and homeland officials, along with their dependents and retainers, were developing into a sizable group whose fortunes and futures were tied into the success of the South African separate development policy. South Africa appeared to envisage a cluster of weak "independent" client states in Namibia as the possible outcome. In the case of the Ovambos, who are also settled over a considerable area in southern Angola, a rash of irredentist

statements led some observers to believe that a "greater Ovambo" encom-
passing the groups on both sides of the border was a feasible political
possibility.

At home South Africa had begun to break out of the political isolation
to which its apartheid policies and its unlawful occupation of Namibia had
consigned it. Its policy of black-white détente in Africa was beginning to
bring the more conservative African states into a sympathetic, potentially
semi-client relationship. The generous economic assistance that bought
quasi-clandestine support by some African states was, by South African
standards, money well spent.

So was the increasing amount spent on propaganda and public relations
in the United States and Europe. Perhaps as a consequence, the United
States' position, announced in 1970—that American investment in Namibia
should be discouraged—never advanced beyond the formal-letter-to-poten-
tial-investors stage. Certainly, it remained a secret from other government
departments in Washington. And State Department representatives, although having no positive alternative suggestions to offer, continued to
oppose United States participation in the U.N. Council for Namibia.

South Africa was also successfully implementing the Odendaal Plan in
the economic sphere. It liberalized territorial policy in order to attract
additional investment capital; hastened the development of the Cunene
River project, which would supply electric power to the major mining and
industrial centers of Namibia; and undertook to involve the power-hungry
West and Japan in the development of uranium deposits found at Rossing,
a short distance north of Walvis Bay. In addition, the price of gold was
skyrocketing, and every increase strengthened South Africa's overall position.

Militarily, South Africa had begun in the late fifties or early sixties to
fortify the Territory in defiance of the express prohibition in its mandate
agreement. A major naval base was established at Walvis Bay, backed by
an air force base a few miles away in the desert, and now tied by advanced
electronic communications into South Africa's main naval base at Simons-
town, in the Cape. An air-army base was built at Katima Mulilo in the
Eastern Caprivi Strip, with another major airfield nearby. A major army
base was also constructed at Grootfontein, close to the valuable copper
mines at Tsumeb and not far from the border separating the Kavango and

Ovambo homelands. All these facilities were greatly expanded over the years. In addition other lesser bases, connecting roads, military airfields, and airstrips were added until in 1976 it was calculated that there were at least ten major and fifteen secondary military bases in Namibia.

THE IMPACT OF THE PORTUGUESE COUP

The Portuguese coup affected the psychological and political balance of forces in Southern Africa long before the decolonization of Luso-Africa was in fact accomplished. It utterly undermined the basic American premise shaped by the option selected in the 1969 National Security Study Memorandum on Southern Africa that had argued that Africans could not change their condition in Southern Africa by their own efforts. Thus it assumed that, except as the outside world could convince the ruling white minorities in Southern Africa to change their ways, blacks would always have to be satisfied with handouts. Therefore, American policy should aim at increasing the handouts rather than pressing for basic change.

The basic South African premise that the Republic would be protected by the Portuguese from large-scale contact with black liberation forces was also shattered. Not only was the Portuguese buffer crumbling; white-ruled Rhodesia, which had constituted an additional barrier to black advances (thanks in part to South African undermining of sanctions and limited military assistance) was also, and immediately, endangered.

On the other hand, Africans were finally able to confirm, by their brothers' experience, that the whites of Southern Africa were not invincible. The planned African celebrations in honor of Frelimo and Mozambican independence and subsequent violent confrontations between white police and black demonstrators in South Africa reflected a new attitude on the part of Africans toward themselves, their white bosses, and their ability to determine their own future.

Even before the final form of the Portuguese African settlement was entirely clear, Pretoria had recognized the need for at least outward accommodation with the forces of change. Thus, in the fall of 1974 Prime Minister Vorster began to suggest that change was in the offing for Namibia; and he referred, somewhat vaguely, to a six-month interval for achieving it.

In December the U.N. Security Council took him at his word. In resolution 366 the Council gave South Africa until May 31 to make a solemn declaration that it would terminate its unlawful occupation. The resolution also required the Republic to take certain specific steps—releasing political prisoners, repealing apartheid legislation, etc.—toward that end. In particular it required the holding of territory-wide elections, under U.N. supervision and control, for delegates to a constituent assembly that would draft a constitution for a free Namibia.

During the spring of 1975 South Africa leaked word that the government had taken a first step toward change by repealing the pass laws and ending segregation of certain public facilities.

The vaunted changes turned out to be meaningless. Obsolete pass laws no longer used were repealed, but modern laws were retained. Optional desegregation of cafes, restaurants, and hotels was finally adopted with continued misgivings months after announcement. But general segregation was hardly affected: late in 1976 a theater where a Christmas concert was being given was still closed to nonwhites, and swimming pools were shut down rather than opened to all races.

As the end of May approached without the required declaration by South Africa, the African states decided to back an uncompromisingly tough line in the Security Council. They presented a draft resolution calling for an arms embargo against South Africa. When the draft gained the necessary nine votes for adoption, France, Britain, and the United States cast a triple veto. Since there was no backup draft resolution, the Council session closed without acting on South Africa's failure to comply with resolution 366. However, the speeches of the representatives of the three Western countries were read, signaling the Republic that they would not continue to protect it indefinitely from similar attacks if it did not move on Namibia.

THE TURNHALLE CONFERENCE

At the same time that Prime Minister Vorster asked for six months, he also made an obscure reference to some future time when South Africa would step aside to let Namibians govern themselves. Shortly thereafter the territorial leader of the National Party, apparently under pressure from

Pretoria, announced a vague proposal to hold a constitutional conference to determine the future of "South West Africa."

The proposal, which progressed very slowly through party congresses and the otherwise defunct multiracial territorial Advisory Council, surfaced again in concrete form after the triple veto. By September 1, 1975, the conference was called into session in a converted gymnasium (*Turnhalle* in German, hence the popular name of the conference) in Windhoek.

According to the convenor, the conference was designed to represent all the "people*s*" of Namibia. *Peoples* spelled with an "s" is a code word in Southern Africa indicating that the persons involved are considered only as members of ethnic ("tribal") groups and not as individuals. This restriction automatically excluded SWAPO and SWANU from representation unless they were willing—as of course they were not—to seek selection as delegates of a particular ethnic group.

Not only were the Namibians to be represented tribally whether or not they believed in the ethnic approach, but they were also to be represented at the conference whether or not they wanted to be represented at all. Thus, when the Damara Advisory Council and the Damara Tribal Executive at the behest of their people refused to participate, twenty-six hitherto unheard-of "Damara leaders" were recruited by the Damara United Front (itself a new organization allegedly created by the South African secret police) to represent the homeland at Turnhalle.

Most of the black delegates were chiefs or notables on the public payroll; some were teachers or civil servants also dependent on the government. Many were unable to adequately understand or speak Afrikaans, the working language of the conference, and required interpreters. None had had any sophisticated parliamentary experience, and few had dealt with whites in other than a subordinate-superior relationship.

The size of the delegations varied greatly but had no necessary relationship to tribal population; and the manner of the delegates' selection, when known, varied from one homeland to another. The largest delegation, numbering forty-four, represented the Hereros and the closely related Kaokovelders, who together constituted less than 8 percent of the Territory's total population; these delegates were chosen by the homeland authorities entirely from one of two groups competing for the chieftaincy of the Hereros.

The Namas, who quarreled bitterly over alleged South African interference in the selection process, sent a delegation of twenty-six. Ovamboland, with some 40 percent of the Territory's population, sent a delegation composed of fifteen members of its legislative council; and the Rehoboth Basters and Coloureds sent slightly smaller delegations reflecting the results of recent communal elections. The Kavango and East Caprivi homelands were represented by a handful of members of their legislative councils, and the Tswana and Bushmen had the smallest delegations of all, chosen in an unknown manner. The whites, who started with only two delegates, both members of the territorial Legislative Assembly, ultimately included the whole assembly membership in their delegation.

Of the more than one hundred and fifty members, only a few became household names. Among the whites were Dirk Mudge, chairman of the conference constitutional committee; Eben van Zijl, a hardline *verkrampte;* and A. H. du Plessis, official head of the enlarged delegation. Among the blacks were the "autocratic" Dr. B. J. Africa of the Rehoboth Basters; A. J. F. Kloppers, a skilled politician from the Coloured community; Chief Clemens Kapuuo of the Hereros, head of NCN and of NUDO (the National Unity Democratic Organization, a once revolutionary party that had become largely a mouthpiece of the Herero Chief's council); and Pastor Cornelius Ndjoba, prime minister of Ovamboland.

Chief Kapuuo created a stir when he brought a white American lawyer, Stewart Schwartz, described as a constitutional expert, to the conference. But after some wrangling the lawyer was allowed to attend the sessions. After observing Chief Kapuuo, a number of the other black groups indicated that they too would like legal advice. Rather than face the risk that unknown and aggressive counsel might be chosen by any of them, conference officials arranged to supply counsel to any group that requested it. The lawyers, who were paid by the South African government indirectly through the homeland authorities, were all South Africans; most of them had previously represented their government against Namibia's interests before the World Court. Only the Chief's lawyers—the full complement of the team included a senior partner of the American lawyer, a Namibian junior counsel, and a London barrister—were not subsidized directly or indirectly by South Africa, according to their testimony before Congressman Fraser's Congressional subcommittee; they declared that the Chief or his party, NUDO, had available small "private contributions."

The first session of the conference adjourned less than two weeks after it opened. It produced a Declaration of Intent which urged that a constitution be drawn up within three years. But it was important primarily for its clear and unequivocal rejection of force to obtain independence or change.

It was not clear what the South Africans expected to emerge from the Turnhalle conference, probably some kind of loose, confederal system of semi-autonomous client states. Presumably such an arrangement would have protected the whites against any major change. In any case Pretoria must have been prepared to let the conference atrophy if external pressure eased.

South Africa itself, however, ensured that the external pressure would increase, rather than decrease, by intervening in the Angolan civil war. Crossing the border in August 1975, ostensibly to protect the Ruacana dam on the Cunene, it quickly converted that limited action into a major invasion with what it subsequently intimated was the implied, if not the express, blessing of the United States. In attempting to wipe out the MPLA and radical nationalism, it made common cause with UNITA, which had joined FNLA against MPLA in a two-front war for the control of Angola. The strike at MPLA in collaboration with UNITA enabled the South Africans at the same time to destroy many of the SWAPO guerrilla bases in southern Angola; SWAPO soldiers had previously shared certain UNITA bases, and UNITA was now willing to point out those bases in exchange for South African assistance against MPLA.

There were two major flaws in this military stroke: The MPLA was able, with outside help, to defeat both Angolan opponents. And the American Congress prohibited United States intervention in Angola. South Africa suffered a major military defeat when the troops it was using became bogged down in central Angola; in danger of being wiped out, they had to retire to Namibia, suffering considerable losses.

In January 1976, when information about South Africa's role in Angola was becoming clearer, the Security Council again took up the subject of Namibia. International outrage led to a new resolution, numbered 385, which was similar in content to resolution 366. The new resolution gave the

Republic until the end of August 1976 to start its withdrawal from the Territory.

The South African military humiliation, combined with the unanimous adoption of resolution 385, put pressure on the Turnhalle conference to end its procrastination and produce positive results before the new deadline. A constitutional committee of thirty-six members representing all the population groups was established under the chairmanship of Dirk Mudge. It began to work on plans for a limited-power interim government, as well as on longer-range plans that alternatively or together might satisfy the Security Council.

With tight time-constraints, punctuated by sharp public criticisms and temporary walkouts, the committee finally produced a short statement of principles on August 18, 1976. It was described in the media as a "promise" of independence for the Territory by December 31, 1978, and a unitary state. The latter "promise" ostensibly complied with repeated General Assembly and Security Council demands that South Africa preserve the national unity and territorial integrity of Namibia. In fact, of course, the statement did not constitute a promise or agreement of any sort whatsoever. It was at best a statement of the wishes and hopes of one committee, which had not even been approved by the conference plenary. The South African government, which *officially* had no role in any of the discussions—whatever its role behind the scenes—was not bound by statements of the committee or even by decisions of a plenary session of the conference. It was noticeable that when the statement of August 18 was presented by the South African ambassador to the secretary-general of the United Nations, it did not carry any South African approval or endorsement of its conclusions.

A close reading of the committee statement, in fact, made it clear that independence must wait on an agreement on constitutional principles (not yet achieved); the drafting of a constitution based on those principles; successful negotiations with South Africa on that constitution and a vast number of difficult issues (such as financial matters, the future of Walvis Bay, the division of property, the protection of South African property, etc.); and selection of the government of the future Namibian state.

Further analysis made it clear also that the statement did not promise a unitary state, but merely announced the "desire" of the committee that

Namibia be "maintained" as a unitary state. Since Namibia was divided into Bantustans at the time the statement was issued, it was difficult to understand how it could be "maintained" as something which it then was not. Indeed, a new Rehoboth Bantustan was created by Parliament over serious conference objections, and the Namas were advanced toward full Bantustan status, both actions taking place while the Turnhalle conference was in session. Thus it was difficult to understand how Namibia could be "maintained" as a "unitary" state.

Contrary to media headlines, the statement, when read with the evidence —including news stories, conference documents, and the testimony of Chief Kapuuo's lawyers in Washington—suggested quite a different future for Namibia: the continuation of essential, if concealed, South African control of the Territory even after formal "independence"; the continuation of white domination of blacks; the continuation of Bantustans; and the continuation of foreign exploitation of Namibia's vast mineral resources without benefit to the general black population. The major differences would be the existence of formal independence and the creation of a government in which a number of blacks would play visible roles.

Continuing South African domination has been and will continue to be assured by acceptance of the advice given the black delegates at the conference by the lawyers supplied and paid by the Republic as well as by the overwhelming South African military presence in Namibia. Black and white Namibian leaders at Turnhalle have agreed that "protection" of the new state by South African troops will be necessary for many years to come, even after "independence." Moreover, a decision has been reached—in direct contravention of resolutions 366 and 385—that U.N. supervision and control of the first Namibian elections under the interim government will not be allowed. It seems inevitable that South African police and military will provide necessary safeguards for the election of politicians who, when they form a new government, will be expected to "invite" their protectors to continue in that role.

Continuing white domination of blacks was assured in the first instance by persuading conference members to act by consensus. Since it was the blacks who wished to change the political, economic, and social situation in the Territory, the white delegates held an effective veto over conference proposals. They exercised that power in at least two matters of major importance: by barring integrated education, thus assuring the educational inferiority of succeeding generations of blacks, and by blocking a move to end the contract-labor system, which, over the protests of the blacks, government authorities decided was too efficient to give up. Even when the delegates decided on a territorial minimum wage, the white farmers' organization announced that its members had no intention of raising their black workers' pay to the set minimum.

Continuing white domination has also been assured by the draft constitution proposed by Chief Kapuuo, which is believed to form the basis for the government of a future Namibia. While Chief Kapuuo is being heralded by his American public relations firm as the first president, the presidency is a mere figurehead position mentioned only once in the document. Under the proposed plan Dirk Mudge, the white chairman of the constitutional committee, will be prime minister and will control the government and the administration. In view of the inadequate education of most blacks, few will be able to qualify for positions of any importance. Those who receive portfolios will undoubtedly operate in the way homeland ministers do now, with a white adviser at their sides controlling every move.

Continuation of the Bantustans was implicit in the August 18 statement; in Chief Kapuuo's draft constitution, which includes an elaborate bicameral parliamentary structure representing Ovambos, Kavangos, and East Caprivians in one house and the rest of the Territory in the other; and in a subsequent three-paragraph-long committee proposal of September 16. That proposal envisaged a three-tiered government structure, the second level of which would consist of homeland governments.

Moreover, the continuation of foreign exploitation of Namibia's vast, still largely unexplored mineral resources was stated as a primary goal by Chief Kapuuo's lawyers. It seems possible that present or potential investors, rather than South African subsidy, are the source of the "private contributions," which, his lawyers claimed, enabled him to engage expensive legal counsel and public relations firms and to commute frequently to Europe and the United States with his retainers. It seems equally possible that after "independence" these contributors will have claims to make on the Chief and on territorial mineral policy based on those contributions. The refusal to end the "efficient" contract-labor system, which offset the Territory's sometimes high nonlabor costs, has also been interpreted as a sign of the intention to exploit the Territory's wasting assets without benefiting the black laborers involved.

The unanimous reaction to the Turnhalle statement of August 18 was that it was inadequate, if not actually insulting to the international community. At best, the Republic's supporters feebly argued that it constituted a step forward.

SWAPO: WAITING IN THE WINGS

The conference was harshly criticized because it failed to include SWAPO, which after all had been specifically recognized by the OAU and the U.N. as the authentic representative of the Namibian people. By the spring of 1976 some Turnhalle members were seeking SWAPO participation, although the basis on which it could have participated with ethnic delegations was far from clear. At one point it appeared that the South African government would withdraw its understood objections to such a development; but the failure to issue a formal invitation suggests that it finally held to its original position that it would never deal with SWAPO and particularly its president, Sam Nujoma. In any case it was clear that SWAPO would not have accepted an invitation to participate in the conference.

SWAPO objections to Turnhalle were well worked out. The ethnic basis of the conference was merely the first objection. Equally important was the fact that the conference was powerless to bring about independence or to effect fundamental change, particularly in view of its early decision to eschew the use of force. SWAPO felt, therefore, that the only relevant discussions would be those held with the South Africans, who had the power to grant independence, and not with other Namibians.

Furthermore, any detailed discussions held before independence concerning a post-independence government were bound to be subject to South Africa's constraining influence; conference members would constantly have to consider proposals not on their intrinsic merits but on the basis of whether they would improve or hinder the possibility of obtaining independence. An interim or final government set up under those circumstances was bound to serve South African rather than Namibian interests, and the persons who participated in setting up such a government were at best, in SWAPO's view, oblivious to Namibia's best interests.

Evidence to support SWAPO's objections was not hard to find. Thus, conference delegates meekly accepted data and analyses made by South African or territorial officials on economic and social questions affecting the future of Namibia instead of insisting on studies by their own experts. They also accepted without question the South African position that Walvis Bay, the Territory's only deep-water port and the key to its economic independence, if not survival, was part of South Africa, since it had been included in the Union in 1910 and never formally ceded to South West Africa. In fact, a strong argument can be made that under international law Walvis Bay has become part of Namibia, based on its administration, with South African consent, as part of the Territory since 1922, as well as on modern doctrines of self-determination, the international illegality of apartheid, and economic necessity; consequently, the conference should have insisted that Walvis Bay is part of Namibia and claimed concessions from South Africa if the Republic wanted to use the port.

U.N. members also criticized the conference for its advance refusal to hold elections under U.N. supervision and control. The element of "control" in this phrase implied more than mere observation of the conduct of elections. "Control" implied a process lasting a year or more that would ensure free territory-wide elections based on universal suffrage and full participation by all Namibians. It would involve establishing election districts and voters' rolls; educating illiterate and inexperienced Namibians about the purpose and procedures of elections; supervising campaigning and actual voting and ballot-counting; and dealing effectively on the spot with such irregularities as intimidation or fraud.

Confident of its claim to majority support throughout the territory, SWAPO was prepared to stand against all other parties in U.N.-supervised and -controlled elections, as called for by General Assembly resolution 2248 (S-V) (1967), to select members of a constituent assembly that would draft a constitution for Namibia. But it is quite possible that it may not continue to hold to this position indefinitely. If an interim Turnhalle government should be established under the aegis of South Africa and ultimately displaced by force, SWAPO might thereupon claim the legitimacy that arises out of politico-military success, as Frelimo did in Mozambique.

Since winning South African backing for his claim to the Herero chief-taincy, a claim which the government long opposed, Chief Kapuuo has echoed Pretoria's line that SWAPO is a communist (or Marxist) organiza-tion, as well as the agent of Ovambo hegemony. In fact, SWAPO appears from various kinds of evidence, including the draft constitution it has circulated as a "discussion document," to be moderate in its political and economic attitudes. The draft has strong human rights provisions, which would have precedence over other provisions in case of conflict; and it allows for an optional second house of the proposed legislature to represent chiefs and traditional elements. Its position on foreign investments has not been extreme, considering that Namibia's minerals, which are exploited entirely by foreigners, are its most important source of wealth.

SWAPO has cooperated with the U.N. through years of delay and disap-pointment. It has vainly sought aid from the West for its liberation struggle. It is likely, therefore, to become increasingly dependent on the communist bloc and radical nationalist states for military equipment if the U.N. cannot bring about the peaceful withdrawal of South Africa.

South African propagandists have consistently played down SWAPO support in the Territory despite evidence of its growing strength, particu-larly among the young. During the second half of 1976 alone, thousands of Rehoboth Basters and Namas merged their own political parties into SWAPO, and a white territorial official admitted that he found more sup-port for SWAPO than for Turnhalle in the Eastern Caprivi. During the same period SWAPO and SWANU inched toward a closer rapprochement than had previously existed.

It has long been recognized that with SWAPO divided among those inside Namibia and those outside (and the latter further divided among members of the guerrilla army), those in SWAPO headquarters in Lusaka, those in refugee camps, and others scattered around the world, some differ-ences in perception were bound to occur. It was inevitable, therefore, that the South African secret police and their allies would try to exploit these differences to destabilize the movement. It is astounding that they have had so little success.

The civil war in Angola offered extraordinary opportunities to exploit any serious differences in the organization. SWAPO leaders in Lusaka were affected by Zambia's strong pro-UNITA stance as well as by the traditional ties of northern Namibians with their Angolan kinsmen in UNITA, whereas SWAPO soldiers at the fluid Namibian front were concerned with the more immediate problems caused by the then generally unrecognized UNITA-South African collaboration. It may be speculated that destabilization tactics operating to take advantage of the conflicting pressures generated in this situation led ultimately to the arrest, detention, and subsequent transfer to Tanzanian detention of about a dozen SWAPO leaders, including Andreas Shipanga (then minister of information), Solomon Mifima (secretary for labor), and Shangula Sheeli (secretary-general of the Youth Wing). Up to another thousand SWAPO members from the front were alleged to be interned in camps guarded by Zambian soldiers near the country's northern border as a result of their connections with the imprisoned leaders.

Nevertheless, unlike the liberation movement in Zimbabwe, SWAPO did not split as a result of this drastic action affecting so many of its leaders and followers. The need for unity proved stronger than any pressures for fission. Even some members who were adversely, if peripherally, affected continued to support the movement although they criticized its handling of Shipanga and others. More significant, perhaps, is the continuing support of internal SWAPO, which has not yielded to the temptations held out to it to participate in the Turnhalle conference. In its convention held recently at Walvis Bay the party that operates legally within Namibia expressed its confidence in the part of the movement operating militarily and diplomatically outside the Territory by reelecting the present leadership.

WAR IN THE NORTH

While the Turnhalle conference was meeting sporadically in Windhoek, war was being waged in northern Namibia. It had begun years earlier with the infiltration of the first freedom fighters across the border and had continued in low-key, spasmodic fashion ever since. It accelerated greatly with the South African invasion of Angola. Although the alliance with

UNITA enabled South African troops to wipe out SWAPO's Angolan bases, the push into central Angola made it impossible for the troops to exercise continuing control of the border area. Therefore, SWAPO fighters soon filtered back. When South Africa finally retreated out of Angola, SWAPO at last found itself with a friendly government to its rear.

When South Africa crossed back into Namibia in retreat, it promptly invested the entire northern part of the Territory. "Operation Cobra" placed some fifty thousand troops in the area; they have been there ever since except when some were hurriedly but temporarily recalled to Soweto in the early summer.

Proclamation R 17, issued during the general strike, was extended to Kavango and the Caprivi and made more rigorous in its application. A half-mile-wide free-fire zone was declared along the Angolan border. Africans living there (generally the best farming area) were forced to leave; within the area anything that moved was shot, and every male that was caught alive was hauled off to detention and torture.

By the summer of 1976 it was widely known that South African troops were sporadically raiding western Zambia and parts of Angola. Eventually Zambia brought a complaint before the Security Council, which condemned South Africa for its hostile act and for mounting it from Namibia, which it continued to occupy illegally. SWAPO has also charged that South Africa was training UNITA troops in Namibia to fight in southern Angola against both SWAPO and the new Angolan government. South Africa replied that the MPLA was persecuting UNITA partisans, causing them to flee to Namibia for refuge, where Pretoria was merely giving them humanitarian aid.

On the Namibian side of the border, meanwhile, land-mine explosions, ambushes, and exchanges of fire between small groups had become everyday occurrences, with both SWAPO and the South African government issuing sporadic accounts of military action. By the beginning of December, South African military officials were anticipating increased military action on the border during the coming summer rainy season (northern-hemisphere winter), and they were threatening to exercise "the right of hot pursuit" across the border in such event.

AMERICAN POLICY TOWARD NAMIBIA

For a number of years United States policy toward Namibia has been characterized by a visible stand against discrimination and illegal occupation of the Territory combined with behind-the-scenes dilution of almost every action taken which would work toward fundamental change. In 1966 the United States supported Assembly resolution 2145, which revoked the South West Africa mandate. But, as indicated above, it opposed the establishment of the Council for Namibia, refused to join the Council, and repeatedly impeded or refused to cooperate in its activities. Consequently, the political and psychological momentum developed by the revocation of the mandate was dissipated.

In 1970 the United States ambassador to the U.N. announced that the American government would henceforth discourage investment in Namibia; in particular, it would not protect those American investors in Namibia whose post-mandate titles derived from the illegal South African authorities against claims by a future Namibian government. Unfortunately, this policy was never conveyed to or enforced by the Commerce Department, which advises potential investors, nor to the Small Business Administration, which has assisted American investors in the Territory. And even the State Department's followup on its own policy has been no more than a letter informing potential investors of it and then asking them to treat their workers well if they invest anyway.

In 1971 the United States supported the Advisory Opinion of the World Court, which called on U.N. members to treat the South African occupation regime as illegal. However, the following winter the United States backed a proposal that the secretary-general go to South Africa to negotiate concerning Namibia, thereby once again dissipating the pressures on South Africa that had arisen out of the Opinion and the Namibian general strike that followed soon after. The ultimately fruitless negotiations of the secretary-general and his personal envoy dragged on for two years while U.N. action was largely suspended.

In 1974 the United States supported Security Council resolution 366, which called on South Africa to start dismantling its occupation regime within six months. But in June 1975 it joined in the triple veto of a proposed mandatory arms embargo to compel South Africa to act. The United States announced that it had voluntarily embargoed arms shipments to South Africa for a decade but ignored mounting evidence that it was constantly enlarging the definition of equipment excluded from the definition of arms.

In January of 1976 the United States joined in adopting Security Council resolution 385, again directing South Africa to end its occupation within six months. But in September 1976 it again vetoed a proposed mandatory arms embargo, claiming that it would jeopardize the delicate negotiations regarding Namibia in which Secretary Kissinger was then engaged as part of his "shuttle diplomacy." This veto ignored the fact that by barring the mandatory arms embargo the United States was removing a vital pressure needed to move South Africa to conduct meaningful negotiations. At the same time, according to U.N. gossip, the United States was maneuvering behind the scenes at the United Nations to drive out the commissioner for Namibia, Sean MacBride, and either abolish the post or fill it with a "safe" candidate. In December 1976 a new commissioner was selected, Ambassador Martti Ahtisaari.

Ironically, when in the spring of 1976 Secretary Kissinger announced his conversion to majority rule for Southern Africa, he did not necessarily imply—whatever the media may have inferred—that he favored national liberation. It appears from the evidence that he felt the survival of white South Africa could only be achieved by a major change in tactics. No longer could South Africa impose upon Namibia its blatantly discriminatory regime administered by an unsympathetic white administration; it must operate behind a moderate black government, which would respond to white exigencies. In other words, he seemed to give his implicit support to the Turnhalle formula, provided at least that it could obtain a modicum of international legitimacy. In order to make the Turnhalle formula viable, it was clearly desirable that SWAPO should be associated in some way with the conference or with the new government to be created. But neither the movement nor the South African government could be budged from their mutual rejection of SWAPO participation.

Meanwhile, during the summer a proposal was put forth at the U.N. that the secretary-general should call a conference in Geneva of the South African government and SWAPO to determine the modalities of future negotiations between them relating to Namibian independence. Secretary Kissinger seized on the idea, transformed it into a Geneva meeting between SWAPO and the Turnhalle participants, and presented it to the General Assembly as part of his shuttle diplomacy although, when he spoke, this version of the original proposal had already been turned down by SWAPO. It seemed possible too that the United States might be prepared to accept and support an interim Turnhalle government even without SWAPO participation. The United States is alleged to have assisted in various indirect ways the public relations campaign of Chief Kapuuo to make him known and accepted on Capitol Hill and by the media as the president-to-be of the interim government.

In addition, the United States was known to be contemplating large-scale financial support for the interim government. As of the fall of 1976 it had allocated over a million dollars of AID funds for studies of programs of political, technical, and economic aid to Namibia and Zimbabwe during their transitional periods before independence. The studies and the aid they envisaged were bitterly opposed by most Africans as intervention designed to ensure the advent to power of moderate leaders in those territories. Despite official denials, the draft studies which have been made available indicate that certain assumptions had been made by their authors: that there would be an interim Turnhalle government, and that the contemplated aid would (and should) be related primarily to growth of the modern mining and white farming economy, exactly the sectors Chief Kapuuo's lawyers indicated would be protected and stimulated under his proposed constitution and governance.

Finally, it has been rumored that the United States was also contemplating military aid to the Turnhalle interim government. There were repeated reports that in order to minimize the South African military presence, which would give the lie to purported independence, the United States would be willing to send black American army experts and instructors to train a Namibian army. Although Ambassador William Scranton flatly denied at the United Nations that the United States is training Namibian soldiers, he did not refer to plans for future action.

THE FUTURE: TURNHALLE AND CONFRONTATION

Recent South African announcements have indicated that a Turnhalle interim government will be established during the spring 1977 session of Parliament (when necessary enabling legislation can be enacted). Most observers believe that such a government will not be accepted by the vast majority of the Namibian people. Certainly SWAPO will continue to oppose it and will step up its military activity, particularly as it continues to gain popular support.

There is some speculation that South Africa may decide to try to crush SWAPO militarily and at the same time create a buffer zone against incursions from southern Angola beyond the boundaries of Namibia. South Africa's military authorities have called for increased numbers of volunteers and have threatened to call up army reservists if there are not enough volunteers; they have also warned of "hot pursuit" across the border. Together, these announcements could presage a major preemptive strike. It is possible that the idea of a revived UNITA–greater Ovambo "state" could once again be resurrected in such a case. If conflict breaks out there is also the possibility that South Africa might "Namibianize" the war, as it appears the United States would prefer. "Loyal" homeland troops, who could be used for such a purpose, are being trained by the South Africans in the old Augustineum College buildings at Okahandja. And many homelands are forming their own militia, some trained by foreign counterinsurgency experts. To Namibianize the war would, of course, be to convert it from a war of national liberation into a civil war.

Either possibility raises the specter of foreign intervention, whether Angola seeks assistance to fend off South African aggression or SWAPO, as the authentic representative of Namibia, seeks assistance to oust the usurper in a civil war.

A peaceful solution for Namibia, which will remain an international responsibility until true independence is achieved, depends on international action aimed at establishing a government legitimized by genuine public participation and consent.

Botswana

Democratic Politics and Development

E. PHILIP MORGAN

BOTSWANA, LESOTHO, SWAZILAND: THE COMMON BACKGROUND

BORDERING ON, or embedded in South Africa are three independent African-controlled states—Botswana, Lesotho, and Swaziland—that, despite their economic dependence on their giant neighbor, sharply oppose apartheid and uphold nonracial policies. Although long expected to form part of South Africa, their people rejected this alternative in favor of separate independence, which was granted to Botswana and Lesotho in 1966, and Swaziland in 1968. Up to that time, however, the British administered them as a unit known as the High Commission Territories because the top-ranking British official in the area was the high commissioner (after 1961, ambassador) to South Africa. In consequence, the section of the British home administration responsible for these territories was the Commonwealth Relations Office, not the Colonial Office as would otherwise have been appropriate for protectorates and colonies.

Comparable if not identical circumstances brought these territories into the orbit of British protection in the late nineteenth century, circumstances in which the present Republic of South Africa played a pivotal role. The common administration of the three territories resulted in certain institutional linkages with South Africa, some of which persist today.

The first of the three to come under British control was Lesotho (then Basutoland) when King Moshoeshoe, a man of great ability and diplomatic skill, requested British protection in 1868. His kingdom was faced with encroachment from the Afrikaner Republic of the Orange Free State.

Botswana (or Bechuanaland, as it was called between 1885 and 1966) came next. It was the missionaries' "road" to central Africa. It was also an avenue of Afrikaner expansion for settlers from the Transvaal area seeking more land. Rhodes's dream of a central Africa as rich as the Rand led to the ill-fated Jameson Raid of 1896, which attempted to overthrow President Kruger's government in the Transvaal and bring it under *uitlander* control (see p. 95). This abortive attempt by the British South Africa Company to thwart collusion between Kruger and the Germans in South West Africa (today's Namibia) to deny Rhodes access to the north is an index of the strategic location of Bechuanaland.

Both Afrikaner encroachments and the intentions of Rhodes's company led the Batswana chiefs to appeal to the British for assistance in the protection of their lands and traditional autonomy. In response, the British declared the land of the Batswana, or Bechuanaland, a protectorate of the Crown in 1885. Bechuanaland was not thought to be valuable for either industry or agriculture, but the fact that it represented a corridor between the Cape and the northern territories led the British to act.

Swaziland was the smallest of the three territories. For years there was an active dispute as to who should control it: the Afrikaner Republic of the Transvaal or Great Britain. In 1894 Great Britain recognized the right of the Transvaal to protect Swaziland, but at the conclusion of the Anglo-Boer War, the country came under the administration of the British governor of the Transvaal. In 1906 Swaziland became a British protectorate.

These territories shared common features that distinguished them from the neighboring "native" reserves in South Africa. They had a common British civil administration, and there were no passes or other racial restrictions common within South Africa. Nonetheless, they had close ties with

South Africa and to a great extent were dependent. Their posts and tele-graphs, currency and banking, customs and tariffs were operated by the South African government.

Moreover their peoples' opportunities for industrial wage labor and higher education were available only in South Africa. South African news-papers and radio programs were their principal sources of communications. White farmers in these territories belonged to the South African Farmers' Union and received the subsidies South Africa gave to its farmers. Such transterritorial interdependency made it logical and convenient for white South Africans to perceive the three British territories as the equivalent of their own African reserves.

Contributing to this view was the very tentativeness of the British com-mitment to the territories. The South Africa Act of Union of 1909 carried an addendum explicitly noting that the three High Commission Territories were expected to become part of the Union in due course. The British seemed to share the white South African view that the logic of geography, economics, and ethnic ties between the peoples of the High Commission Territories and those in the Union pointed to incorporation as the sensible path for their development.

It was precisely their fear of incorporation, however, that led the people of the High Commission Territories to resist any such move. The chiefs of the three territories continued to remind the British that the latter had an obligation to protect the autonomy, independence, and basic human rights that would be denied their people if they were to be formally incorporated into South Africa.

After 1948, when the Afrikaner Nationalists came to power in South Africa, the incorporation issue took on a different and more menacing meaning as apartheid restrictions were steadily increased. From the South African side, incorporation became more attractive as the white National-ists planned the Bantustan, or homeland, program. This was made explicit in the Tomlinson Commission report of 1956, in which maps of the three territories were included in the overall separate development strategy.

By then, however, a number of external events had contributed to strengthening their leaders' resistance to incorporation of the three territo-ries. African nationalism in British colonies to the north was pressing for political independence. The modern spirit of nationalism in the High Commission Territories made it more difficult for the British to yield to South African plans. Also, apartheid had now become an international issue, and pressure on Great Britain not to turn over these territories to white supremacist hegemony came from many capitals as well as the United Nations.

By 1962 Prime Minister Verwoerd finally declared that he was reconciled to the High Commission Territories becoming separate self-governing states. However, in a famous speech in 1963 he asked Britain to allow South Africa to appeal directly to the African people of the territories and explain how they would benefit from the Tomlinson formula for incorporation in his country. The formula involved both economic incentives and threats in a gambit that was intended to yield precedents for apartheid in a single stroke. But the tactic was transparent and came at a time when Britain was already moving toward constitutional changes in each of the three territories which would result in their political independence.

As the three countries moved toward statehood in the mid-1960s, a number of the institutional linkages between them and South Africa were altered, while new ties among the states were forged.

The most important regional institution is the South African Customs Union Agreement. At the time of South African Union in 1910 a customs union was established that provided for the free interchange of goods between South Africa and the territories and a percentage sharing of the area's total import and excise duties accruing from the common external tariff. (The territories collected their own duties only on alcoholic beverages.) Although the percentage share of the three smaller territories varied slightly, in each case the respective share of revenues was less than 1 percent, leaving about 98 percent for South Africa.

In 1969 the Customs Union Agreement was renegotiated at the collective insistence of Botswana, Lesotho, and Swaziland. The objective was to improve the revenue position of the three smaller states relative to South Africa or, more accurately, to reduce the inequalities so apparent in the 1910 formula. The new agreement is complex. In brief, instead of the former straight-percentage basis, customs duties are now divided among the four members according to a formula based on the actual imports and taxes in each of the countries in relation to those of the common customs area as a whole.

Although this new customs union formula still allows South Africa to benefit disproportionately due to its large industrial economy, income from the duties represents a significant portion of the recurrent public revenues of the three countries and has enabled the two stronger members—Botswana and Swaziland—to terminate their dependence on British subsidies. The agreement also provides that the three smaller members can impose protectionist measures against South Africa for selected infant industries.

Botswana, Lesotho, and Swaziland ultimately buy most of their consumer goods from South Africa even though South African products might be higher in price than those produced elsewhere because of the high external tariff. Any economic arrangement which includes one large industrial country and several nonindustrial ones tends to perpetuate inequalities wherein the poor to some extent subsidize the rich. The problem for the three smaller states is the high cost of going it alone. This is a condition all three countries are attempting to alter, some more successfully than others, as can be seen in Chapter 7.

A functional linkage among the three countries which was compatible with political independence was that of the University of Botswana, Lesotho, and Swaziland. The core campus at Roma, Lesotho, evolved from long-established Pius XII College in the mid-1960s. Satellite campuses were established in Botswana and Swaziland in the early 1970s. This arrangement greatly expanded the opportunities for higher education in the three countries. It also represented a more economical alternative to establishing separate national universities in countries with small populations.

However, by 1975 the centrifugal forces of nationalism had begun to affect the cohesion of the institution. Disagreements over proposals for devolution in the interest of more equitable sharing of facilities and programs led to the precipitous withdrawal of Lesotho in October 1975, and establishment of the National University of Lesotho. The University of Botswana and Swaziland presently reflects a plan to develop two separate university colleges but not duplicate professional schools such as the College of Agriculture and the Faculty of Law. A surviving regional legacy of the university is the Institute of Development Management, a tri-country institution specializing in higher-level administrative and management training for both the public and the private sectors.

The three countries are also moving inexorably, if at different paces, toward their own currency and central banking systems. Swaziland issued its own currency in 1975, Botswana in 1976. Although the former still accepts the South African Rand as legal tender, Botswana does not and may or may not maintain the value of its currency equivalent to the Rand.

Thus, apart from some additional plans to establish scheduled air links among the three national airlines, the common characteristics and functional linkages of Botswana, Lesotho, and Swaziland are fading. Emerging national identities, differential resource endowments and development, different politico-geographic locations, and, perhaps most important, different political systems more aptly characterize the three distinct national entities. The rest of this chapter is devoted to an analysis of Botswana's vulnerabilities and opportunities.

BOTSWANA'S POLITICAL VULNERABILITIES

As in the early days of the protectorate, landlocked Botswana occupies a strategic position. It is almost surrounded by the three white-dominated territories in which there is dramatic pressure for change: Rhodesia to the north and east, South Africa to the east and south, and Namibia to the north and west. Botswana thus has hundreds of miles of exposed borders. Given the proximity of South African military might, the Botswana Government has decided it would be futile to build up an army except for a paramilitary police mobile unit.

Nonetheless, within Southern Africa, Botswana occupies an increasingly prominent position although its population is less than three quarters of a million. Its president, Sir Seretse Khama, is one of the "front-line presidents" involved in the delicate negotiations over the transfer of power to majority rule in Rhodesia. This distinction is a tribute both to President Khama's personal stature and to the respect accorded the country's efforts to overcome great economic and political obstacles while maintaining a nonracial, open society.

Botswana is a large country, roughly the size of France. As the vast Kalahari Desert occupies the southwestern quarter of the country, the bulk of the population is distributed along the "green strip" to the east and across the well-watered north. Communication is thus difficult, though radio helps to bridge these physical divisions since most Batswana speak a version of the same indigenous language: Setswana.

The location of the country, the specter of incorporation with South Africa, the salience of color, and the effects of British "protection" have combined to shape Botswana's position and prospects. These antecedents provide the framework for those contemporary structures of vulnerability and opportunity which together generate a combination of anxiety and optimism about the country's future.

Much depends on what happens to the railway. Until recently, the railway running north-south through Botswana was a lifeline for the illegal regime in Rhodesia. In 1974, however, a rail link was opened across the South African and Rhodesian frontier at Beitbridge that added direct rail to the road transport between the two countries. So Botswana no longer has the potential lever on the white Rhodesian regime that it once had.

Ironically, however, the railway connection to Rhodesia is more of a lifeline for Botswana than for Rhodesia. It is the principal carrier of goods between Botswana and the seaports of South Africa. Within the country "Rhodesia Railways," as it is still called, consists of the tracks running the length of the country, a few stations, and some housing for Batswana maintenance workers. The Rhodesians own the rolling stock and all the repair facilities are located in Rhodesia.

Because of this real and symbolic affront to the independence of Botswana and the tension between white Rhodesian railway staff and the Batswana passengers and workers, the Botswana government has been under pressure for some time to take over the railway. The government is on record as planning an eventual takeover; it was a campaign commitment in the election of October 1974. The reasons why it has not occurred to date relate to money and manpower. Official statements after an extended study by Canadian National Railways consultants put the costs at P60 ($69) million* and three hundred and fifty trained technicians.

The transfer of Rhodesia Railways to "Botswana Railways" will thus require assistance from some outside power. President Khama raised this

*Currency equivalents between the Botswana pula and the U.S. dollar have been computed at the rate of 1P = $1.40 prior to 1975 and at the rate of 1P = $1.15 after 1975.

issue during his visit to the United States, Canada, Britain, and the People's Republic of China between June and August of 1976. For Botswana, in the short run, there is also the special problem of what would happen to its supply situation if the present violence in Rhodesia should escalate to the point of terminating the operation of the railway from the Rhodesian side. The northern part of Botswana depends on certain food imports from Rhodesia, especially dairy products.

As part of an official strategy of outreach to its African-governed neighbors to the north, Botswana has given high priority to a road project connecting Francistown with Kazungula on the Zambian border. The project is being financed by the United States Agency for International Development and several other Western countries and should be completed within the next year, giving Botswana an all-weather road running the north-south length of the country. The importance of this road is more strategic than economic. Although it is a costly route, Botswana would then have access to the sea via Zambia and the Tan-Zam railway to Dar es Salaam, Tanzania, in the event that political forces should interfere with its usual routes through South Africa. While the "freedom ferry" across the Zambezi River to Kazungula would represent a bottleneck to any large-scale movement of goods, this route would provide an important alternative.

Another aspect of Botswana's geographic vulnerability is the prospect that it might become a staging area for assaults by the contending sides in the liberation of Rhodesia, Namibia, or South Africa. The government provides political asylum for what it calls "genuine" political refugees. But it has not condoned the use of Botswana territory as sanctuaries or training bases for active guerrilla fighters. President Khama has many times expressed the "moral" support of the people of Botswana for the freedom fighters, but candidly says his government cannot participate more actively for fear of giving the whites (whether from Rhodesia or South Africa) a pretext for violating Botswana territory.

Many such violations have occurred since 1975. Rhodesian forces embarked upon a general policy of "hot pursuit." In so doing they attacked a United Nations High Commission refugee camp inside Mozambique in the belief that it was a guerrilla base (see p. 86). This policy has resulted both in shooting attacks from across the Rhodesian border and in actual incursions into Botswana territory by Rhodesian security forces. The Botswana Government is taking measures to shore up its border-police posts, but there is little it can do to stop such intimidation. Perhaps because of this, Sir Seretse Khama publicly identified his government with the front-line presidents' endorsement of armed struggle to achieve majority rule in Rhodesia.

Apart from location, the legacy of South African efforts to incorporate Botswana into the Republic also affects present relations between the two countries. Botswana has only arms-length relations with the Republic of South Africa. There has been no exchange of diplomatic representatives. Botswana is unalterably opposed to apartheid and has not recognized the so-called independent Transkei. This belief applies by extension to the independence of any of the homelands, including that of the Batswana people in South Africa: Bophuthatswana.

Although the chief minister of Bophuthatswana, Lucas Mangope, once indicated a willingness to become federated with Botswana, the latter did not respond because such a move would legitimize the balkanization of South Africa and more than double Botswana's population all at once.

ECONOMIC AND SOCIAL VULNERABILITIES

Although Botswana is politically aloof, its economic interdependence with South Africa forces continuous contact. In addition to being Botswana's principal general market, South Africa accounts for a greater percentage of foreign investment in Botswana than any other country. This investment is preponderantly in the emerging industrial sector of mineral exploitation, where profits are highest, and secondarily in light manufacturing and service industries. The majority of the engineering and building contractors who bid on development projects that are not tied to donor agency contractors are also South African.

Over fifty thousand Batswana, who represent nearly 25 percent of the adult male work force of Botswana, work annually in the mines of South Africa (gold, coal, diamonds). The Rand mine organizations need foreign mine labor, and the Botswana Government does not feel it can restrict the movement of its citizens to the South African mines so long as it cannot provide jobs for them at home. Despite the hazardous living and working conditions for the Motswana worker in South Africa, he can make more money there than at home. Taken in conjunction with the common customs union described above and the dependence on South Africa both for goods and as a market, there remains an almost client relationship in commerce, industry, and employment. This inhibits Botswana's efforts to establish genuine independence.

PROBLEMS OF MANPOWER AND SKILLS

Among the economic constraints independent Botswana faces is that of skilled manpower. Although this is a general phenomenon in new states, it is particularly acute in Botswana for peculiar historical reasons. Relative to the financial commitment Britain made to most of its other colonies in Africa, Bechuanaland was sorely neglected.

Whereas in West Africa, British-inspired and -sponsored secondary education goes back to the early years of this century, there was no government secondary school in Botswana until after independence in 1966. There were a few poverty-stricken ethnic and missionary secondary schools, but the protectorate government spent very little on the development of human resources.

Nor were there development expenditures of any significance related to the creation of local wage employment. In fact, the colonial government cooperated with the South African mine labor-recruiting organizations in the mobilization of Batswana for mine work so that they would have a source of cash income with which to pay their head tax.

The lack of British commitment to the development of Bechuanaland goes back to the incorporation issue. Moreover, the land and climate of Bechuanaland were inhospitable to large-scale white settlement; thus, the territory never attracted a large European community that would have made developmental demands of its own on the British. Such migratory settlement as occurred was composed of South Africans who established large cattle ranches and looked south for protection of their interests rather than to Great Britain.

Thus at the very time an independent Botswana is attempting to pursue a rapid development policy—certain aspects of which are highly capital intensive and technologically complex—it must invest heavily in the basic social overhead capital to develop human resources that many other African countries enjoyed by the time of their independence: schools, clinics, roads, communications facilities. This state of affairs has resulted in a heavy reliance on expatriate manpower in the short run, and has serious implications for the country's future labor and race relations.

Soon after independence the new government talked about self-sufficiency in manpower and articulated a policy of recruiting qualified Batswana first and only resorting to expatriates secondarily. But the Public Service Commission itself was staffed by many expatriates and was not very effective. The Public Service Commission could only appoint; it had no recruitment plan, nor could it criticize standards or training programs. By the late sixties morale among the Batswana in the civil service was very low and the Civil Servants Association was sending increasingly militant signals to the government that something had to be done.

Perhaps chastened by having lost four seats in the election of October 1969, the president issued a directive calling for a consultant to "review Government's policies on recruitment, training and staff development and to make a recommendation for any changes necessary to secure the fastest possible localization compatible with Botswana's development objective. . . ." The consultant's recommendations resulted in a major overhaul of the machinery of government, which affected policy in the development of local manpower resources. The Public Service Act of 1970 established a directorate of personnel responsible for recruitment, appointments, promotions, and training, all centralized in the office of the president. Recruitment and promotions were rationalized through systematic job descriptions and promotion criteria that would be the principal tools of the director of personnel. In addition, a Bursaries Committee was established to secure school output in a rational way through earmarking students for certain types of posts, funding their training, and bonding them to government service on completion of their training. Government departments would continue to do some of their own training, but the personnel directorate now controlled access to all training opportunities for which public funds would be used, both local and external.

Finally, this major adjustment in the interests of rationalized manpower recruitment, localization, and training was complemented by some new consultative machinery for civil servants. In 1971 a Presidential Commission on Localization and Training was established to review localization programs, examine the relevance of training programs, review the operating arrangements of the bursaries system, and determine the entry qualifications to technical and professional cadres in the service. The commission is a permanent body, is to make annual reviews of progress in localization, and is to insure that approved training programs and recruitment policies are fully complied with. These official measures are noted because the report of the commission in 1973 had an extraordinary feature for a public document: it included detailed references, by name, to individuals in the service who, with stipulated augmented training, would succeed to particular posts.

Despite these efforts the relevance of race politics in the region still emerges from time to time in Botswana. There is an open and still healthy debate about the wisdom of importing increasing numbers of foreign technical assistance people, most of whom are white. The foreigners who appear most credibly to be impeding the upward mobility of local people are those on contracts who do semiskilled or technical work that can rather readily be learned, e.g., posts and telecommunications, works, mining, construction, and similar jobs. Too often such technicians do not train counterparts. Perhaps they perceive it is not in their interest to do so because they have nowhere else to go if they localize themselves out of a job.

Racial problems are created when this particular skill group of expatriates is also made up of a particular nationality and concentrated in one place, such as South Africans at the copper-nickel mining site. However, the Botswana government does not hesitate to remind the foreign community as to who is in charge and that foreigners are in the country only at the indulgence of the Batswana.

To the extent that there have been vocal protests about white *citizens* in positions of public power, the government has held to a firm line. The president defends the few white citizens who are in pivotal positions on the basis of their loyalty to the country in the early days of independence and their competence. Since he married a white woman in 1949 and was persecuted for it by denial of his chieftainship and banishment from his own country by the British (1950–56), Sir Seretse Khama is particularly sensitive to the development of "anti-whiteism" in Botswana. He defends the policy of nonracialism out of conviction and holds out Botswana to the region and the world as an example of moral commitment.

The Botswana government tends to tolerate the idiosyncracies of foreigners only so long as they do not include racialism. People in Botswana are prosecuted for the use of racially pejorative terms. Black employees can use the law in defense of their own dignity in the event of racial slurs made by employers or supervisors.

Given the national and international environment, racial attitudes in Botswana are still encouraging. Whether this continues, however, will depend on three things: whether the technical requirements of an industrial economy outstrip the ability of a country with such a small population and human resource development infrastructure to keep up a rapid pace of localization; whether the resolution of the struggle for democracy in the neighboring states is relatively more benign or bitter; and the endurance of Sir Seretse Khama, who is not in the best of health, thereby leaving the succession problematic.

POLITICAL OPPORTUNITIES

Botswana is symbolic in the region as a liberal democracy, an African state that has enjoyed successive popularly-elected governments. The openness of the Botswana political process stands in sharp contrast to that of both Swaziland and Lesotho, as well as that of the countries on its periphery. It provides a refutation of the paternalistic assumptions underlying the ideology of white supremacy.

TABLE 1:   National Assembly Election

	BDP		BPP		BNF		BIP		IND	
	1969	1974	1969	1974	1969	1974	1969	1974	1969	1974
Total Vote	52,518	49,047	9,329	4,199	10,410	7,358	4,601	3,086	–	321
Percent of										
Total Vote	68.3	77.7	12.1	6.6	13.5	11.5	6.0	4.8	–	.5
No. Contested	31*	32	15	8	21	14	9	6	–	3
Returned										
Unopposed	3	4								
No. Won	24	27	3	2	3	2	1	1	–	0

*BDP contested all constituencies both times. One new constituency was added in 1974.

The Botswana Democratic Party (BDP), headed by Sir Seretse Khama, formed the government after the preindependence election of 1965 and has been in office ever since. There was little doubt in either 1969 or 1974 that the BDP would emerge with a majority. However, the three opposition parties—the Botswana People's Party (BPP), the Botswana National Front (BNF), and the Botswana Independence Party (BIP)—and independent candidates collectively contested thirty-one of the thirty-two elective seats for the National Assembly in 1974. That fact, arithmetically at least, offered the possibility of an alternative government (see Table 1). In a political system where the governing party is constantly returned, opposition votes are nonetheless interesting as indicators of issues and of the extent to which the governing party is meeting the perceived interests of the public.

TABLE 2:   Turnout

	National Elections		Local Elections	
	1969	1974	1969	1974
Total Registered Voters 　Contested Constituencies	140,428	205,050	103,084	143,197
Total Vote	76,858	64,011	53,594	43,412
Percentage of Turnout	54.9	31.2	52	30.3

The data presented in these tables are compiled from two reports on the general elections of 1969 and 1974 respectively, prepared by the supervisor of elections. They were published in March 1970 and December 1974, respectively, by the Government Printer, Gaborone.

Despite an increase of 64,622 registered voters between 1969 and 1974, there was an absolute reduction in total voter turnout from 76,858 in 1969 to 64,011 in 1974 (from 54.9 percent of the registered voters in 1969 to 31.2 percent in 1974) (see Table 2). All parties experienced a lower absolute vote in 1974 compared with 1969. However, as a percentage of the total vote, the BDP did better in 1974 than in 1969 (77.7 percent *vs.* 68.3 percent), whereas the opposition parties, both individually and collectively, did worse. In 1969 the opposition parties collectively commanded 31.6 percent of the total vote in the national election; in 1974, only 22.9 percent. Because the BDP had received a setback in 1969, having lost four seats from 1965, the 1974 election was considered by many to be especially important. The outcome reversed any potential trend to an electoral defeat.

Botswana has a pragmatic and pluralistic party system. The preoccupation with ideology is very limited indeed. The BDP speaks of its "national philosophy" in terms of four concepts—democracy, development, self-reliance, and unity—but there is little attention to developing or propagating these themes apart from the party manifesto at election time and preambles to public documents. The media are clearly government instruments, but they are not used as channels for ideological cant. BNF and BPP documents, and especially the utterances of the leadership of the BPP, are more ideological than the BDP. Opposition statements are often fragmented, their issues diffuse, and the tone of debate more contentious than ideological. Ten years of independence seem to have attenuated the previous affinities between the BPP, BIP, and African nationalist sentiments in South Africa, although they might be rekindled by events.

In terms of popular participation, the degree of mobilization is low and popular response to public policy is partial if not passive. There are more interest and activity at election time, but the turnout figures for the 1974 election raise many questions about the governing party's success in mobilizing public opinion. Individual participation is increasing among the elite, e.g., civil servants' associations, teachers' organizations, and so forth, but such pluralist activity is inchoate. The mass public is still unmobilized except for localized interests such as self-help projects here and there.

All four Botswana parties can be characterized as hierarchical and centralized in principle, but loose and undisciplined in practice. Local Botswana Democratic Party branches are not well-organized between elections; the party is simply not an identifiable instrument of governmental/developmental policy at the village level. After the last election the government announced its intent to change this situation, and the BDP congress of May 1975 included exhortations to maintain effective local-level organization. The lack of vital local party organizations between elections does not seem to affect the ability of the BDP to pull itself together when it counts most. Tsholetsa House, one of the two new high-rise buildings in Gaborone, is owned by the Botswana Democratic Party, testimony to an ability to mobilize resources that sets it apart from the other three party organizations.

The electoral successes of the BDP indicate that Botswana has a one-party-dominant system. Is it, in fact, changing into a one-party system?

The two systems have marked differences. One-party-dominant systems include only one party truly capable of governing, but that party cannot afford to ignore other parties; and interests are articulated *both* within the major party and through the smaller parties. One-party systems, on the other hand, do not exclude the existence of other parties, but the major party can ignore them. Interests are articulated exclusively from within the major party.

In the case of Botswana it is difficult to make a clear-cut decision based strictly on these criteria. The BDP is clearly the major party and the only one capable of forming a government. The experience of three elections confirms this. But whether the Botswana Democratic Party can ignore the smaller parties is less clear.

The turnout in the 1974 election is a sign of the declining importance to the political system of two of the opposition parties, the BPP and the BNF. The BIP as an organization can be ignored. Although Motsamai Mpho plays a vocal role in parliamentary debate, he is the only Member of Parliament representing the Botswana Independence Party, having barely won reelection in 1974.

Although the turnout in general was down from 1969, the fact that the opposition parties did worse in 1974 than in 1969 might reveal something about the extent to which they are perceived by the public as articulators of their interests. It is possible that Chief Bathoen II, leader of the BNF, is too traditional and confusing in his posture for many voters. The BPP is perhaps too sectional for others. So the BDP benefits from those who feel unrepresented but are still willing to vote. In addition, the two principal opposition parties do not appear to be identifying and grooming new political leadership to strengthen their cause.

There is also a constitutional provision which over time could add to the attitudes of cynicism about the value of voting opposition. Four seats in the National Assembly are filled by presidential appointment, not by election. This allows the president to bring into Parliament and the cabinet people who are not otherwise politically inclined. It also gives him the opportunity of "saving" a member who has been defeated at the polls. The most frequently cited example of the use of this provision was the appointment of

Quett Masire as Member of Parliament, minister of finance and development planning, and vice-president of the Republic after he had been defeated in the 1969 election. Fortunately for the BDP and the president, Dr. Masire regained an elective seat in the 1974 election.

The power of appointment has also been used in local government elections. Here the power of nomination lies in the hands of the minister of local government and lands, but the result is the same. The use by the BDP of the power of nomination to convert electoral defeats into majorities in district and/or town councils has caused some bitterness.

A tendency toward criticism within the government party suggests new possibilities of opposition. In the first session of the National Assembly after the 1974 election (March 1975), there appears to have been a marked increase in vocal opposition from majority party back-benchers. For the first time since independence, a Member of Parliament, a BDP back-bencher and former mayor of Gaborone, was expelled from the House by the Speaker for unruly behavior in debate. An unusually large number of queries from the majority back bench was also directed at the minister of finance and development planning during the budget debate. This trend toward more vocal opposition within the governing party is matched by continuing admonitions from the opposition despite their reduced numbers.

There are at least two cleavage patterns that must be identified as holding possible clues to the direction of party system change in Botswana: ethnicity and socioeconomic class. The casual observer might think that, because most Batswana speak the same language, there is little or no ethnic dimension to social and political life. The Batswana themselves, however, distinguish nine separate "tribes." There is a considerable degree of ethnic consciousness and an awareness that the Bamangwato, Sir Seretse Khama's group, is the single largest ethnic group in the country. At the same time the governing party has not used an ethnic spoils system in political appointments; rather the Botswana Democratic Party has attempted to capture loyalties all over the country, as is reflected by BDP performance in non-Ngwato constituencies. Although ethnic arithmetic is important and is a potential basis for bifurcation, obvious polarities are confined to the northeast. Even so, while the BNF has been an essentially Bangwanketse party, the majority party has two cabinet ministers from that ethnic group.

The second potential cleavage is socioeconomic. The salaried group, principally civil servants and politicians, are enjoying an urban life style and investing in cattle. Despite a wages-and-incomes policy designed to avoid a lopsided distribution of wealth, the cost of living in urban areas is high enough so that the government has yielded to demands by civil servants for increased salaries on two occasions since 1973. After the first increase the ratio between remuneration for super-scale posts and messenger-grade posts in the civil service was about ten to one, whereas in most European countries the ratio is about five to one. As young career civil servants put their savings into cattle over the next decade, a modernized landed gentry might emerge in Botswana. If rural incomes do not increase more than they have in the past decade—from about $39 per capita per annum ten years ago to about $56 per capita now—there will indeed be cumulative cleavage. So the potential bifurcation that could become self-reinforcing is less likely to be ethnic than socioeconomic; the haves pitted against the have-nots.

In the sort of bifurcation outlined above, the interests of the salaried become identical to those of the ruling party. The civil servant who chafes under an awareness of the maldistribution of income is only rarely likely to quit his job on principle in a situation where the alternatives to government employment are so meager. The choice is presently one of co-optation or returning to the land. As long as the major party provides the monetary inducements, the bureaucracy allies itself tacitly with the governing party. The governing party can rely on the bureaucracy to do the work of the government, essentially ignoring the party between elections. It remains true, however, that maintaining a one-party-dominant status in a multiparty setting, rather than ignoring the opposition, is seen by the regime to be necessary to legitimize the political system.

ECONOMIC PROSPERITY?

Until recently Botswana was among the countries on the United Nations list of the world's twenty-five poorest countries. Per capita income was about P60 ($84) in 1966-67, the first year of political independence. (One Pula=one Rand.) Botswana suffered large balance of trade deficits because it had to look abroad for supplies of capital. In 1966-67 the national budget included P17.8 ($24.9) million in expenditures, and only P11.6 ($16.2) million in revenues. There were no development funds at that time.

However, in ten years what was an extremely bleak picture has become much more encouraging. National budget estimates for 1975-76 show P73.2 ($84.2) million for recurrent expenditures plus P51.8 ($59.6) million for development expenditures. Revenues were expected to match expenditures in both accounts. Also, the GDP doubled between 1971 and 1975, from P103.6 ($145) million to over P200 ($280) million. Economic growth in the early seventies has been at 15 to 18 percent per year in real terms.

The remarkable improvement in Botswana's economic position results principally from a number of mineral discoveries. Diamonds, copper-nickel, and coal are now being commercially exploited under complex agreements with a number of multinational corporations. The diamond mine at Orapa is the second largest in the world, generating about three million carats per year. Revenues of about P30 ($42) million in 1972 will increase as a second pipe is developed. The copper-nickel complex was producing about 2400 tons per month by the end of 1975, although that represents only about 70 percent of capacity because of technical problems. Revenues were expected to reach P40 ($46) million by the end of 1976.

This large-scale investment has improved Botswana's ability to raise financing for its complementary support infrastructure. In 1968-69 development revenue obtained from external loans was only P140.6 ($197) million. In 1973-74 development loans peaked at P30.7 ($43) million. In addition, the imports of capital goods related to the mineral industry substantially increased Botswana's revenues from the customs duties. Almost half of the country's recurrent public revenue came from these duties in 1974-75: P30.2 ($42.3) million out of a total recurrent revenue of P62.9 ($88) million.

Botswana's traditional exports of beef and beef products have increased annually since the drought of 1965–67. The national herd recovered from under one million head of cattle in 1966 to an estimated two and a half million in 1975. Botswana Meat Commission sales in 1974 were P37 ($51.8) million.

In fact, Botswana's beef industry has become so attractive to a traditional cattle-holding people that expanded grazing has created problems of potentially irreparable damage to the country's limited range. The need for systematic range management and water resource development has caused the government to embark on a far-reaching Tribal Grazing Land Policy. Under this new land-tenure arrangement what was always regarded as communal grazing land for respective ethnic groups will now be subject to surveying, fencing, and allocation by commercial lease. There are a number of mechanisms to protect the small herder, such as syndicates where several persons take out a lease collectively and graze their cattle in a more systematically managed arena. Some communal land will be set aside also for those who have only a few cattle and do not join any group. Finally, there is "reserved" land as well, which will be held for future use. This fundamental change has been compared to the eighteenth-century enclosure movement in Britain.

Marketing Botswana's beef has been a problem over the last two years. In the past, beef products have been exported to essentially two markets: South Africa and Britain, with 64 percent going to the latter. When the British entered the European Economic Community, Britain's imports of agricultural products became subject to the common agricultural policy of the EEC. That policy subjects those foreign imports of beef which are admitted to the market to a 46- to 51-percent levy on sales receipts. During much of 1975 and 1976 the minister of commerce and industry and the permanent secretary of the Ministry of Agriculture negotiated in Europe for a reduction of this levy. The basis for the argument is the hard-fought-for article of the Lome Agreement of 1975 between the EEC and the African, Caribbean, and Pacific countries dealing with trade preferences. The outcome of their exhausting effort was a 90-percent reduction of the levy for Botswana's beef, but only for six months at a time.

The uncertainty of the European beef market not only requires that several of Botswana's thinly spread senior officials spend many months of the year in Europe; it also makes it very difficult to plan for the future. The Botswana Meat Commission has had to postpone the construction of a second abbatoir at Dukwe because it cannot be sure of markets for Botswana's increasing beef production. Until now, the only abbatoir has been in the southeastern corner of the country at Lobatse. The decision to build a second abbatoir in the north represented the culmination of fifteen years of political and economic debate. The United States Agency for International Development had already committed the funds for the venture. But with a market for the country's principal agricultural export guaranteed for only six months at a time, the situation became untenable and the project had to be postponed.

Botswana continues to seek a long-term agreement from the EEC. Without it the country's principal agricultural industry is threatened with massive curtailment in production at the very time when the population has developed a true commercial sense for cattle holding. Botswana is attempting to develop markets in other African countries, but the amounts involved compared with the transport costs have not yet made it a viable option.

The concerted efforts in both mineral development and livestock production must be seen in the context of Botswana's need for export earnings. Without these earnings Botswana cannot diversify its economy in order to increase its total economic capacity. Until earnings from the two principal classes of export products begin to help expand the country's limited economic capacity, Botswana will be faced with limitations on its overall economic development, social objectives, administrative efficiency, and foreign-policy options.

FUTURE CONSTRAINTS AND OPTIONS

Since the reason for much of the foreign investment in Botswana is to exploit nonrenewable resources, it is important that the terms are such that the nation gets an adequate share of the earnings from those resources. In the original agreement between Anglo-American (DeBeers) and the Botswana government for the exploitation of the diamonds at Orapa, the government secured only a 15-percent equity interest for itself. Fifty percent (of the 15 percent) of the dividends to be paid the government by the company were to be withheld in payback installments for the P2.25 ($3.15) million loan the company gave to Botswana for the construction of the road from Francistown to Orapa.

Given such meager terms, when the opportunity to exploit a second and richer pipe came up in 1975, the government took the opportunity to oblige DeBeers to renegotiate the terms to the greater advantage of Botswana. The new agreement involves an almost 50-percent equity share for the government, as well as a flexible schedule of taxes and royalties depending on profitability. The result is a share of between 65 and 75 percent of all profits for Botswana.

The Botswana Government has only a 15-percent equity interest in the copper-nickel complex. When the venture becomes more profitable, no doubt some renegotiation of that arrangement will be undertaken, since the alteration of the diamond concession resulted in a new adjustable sales royalty policy that could have general application to extractive industries.

Another dimension of this learning process in the exploitation of non-renewable resources is a new policy on prospecting. When the initial copper prospecting agreement was signed, the exploring firm automatically secured a mining lease in the event of success. Future prospecting licenses will no longer carry such a guarantee. This will allow the government more flexibility in setting terms for the actual exploitation.

A number of technical constraints are delaying realization of the full benefits from the mining sector. A decision to begin open mining of a surface seam at the copper-nickel site resulted in new costs. In addition, chemical changes in the ore and subsequent uncontrolled combustion required redesign of the smelter. These technical problems combined with the current poor price of copper have resulted in disappointing short-term losses. Likewise, the quality of the local coal is requiring adjustments to boiler machinery necessitating continued imports of coal from South Africa until remedial measures are completed.

Botswana still has one of the most lenient tax structures for new investment. At the close of the 1976 annual Gaborone Trade Fair the minister of commerce and industry made a speech inviting foreign investors to come to Botswana. She indicated that Botswana's company tax was among the "lowest in the world and that land in Botswana is at present plentiful and cheap." The question arises as to whether the tax policies of the government are progressive enough to turn that private foreign investment into national gain. The tax department has been the focus of American aid and advice for a number of years.

Another future set of constraints relates to the effects of technology transfer. Much of the technology required for modern mineral exploitation is capital intensive. What are the effects of this on employment? Is the employment of, say, two thousand local people in the service of a several-hundred-million-dollar investment a fair capital-to-labor ratio in a country with severe employment problems? Is the technology being transferred increasing employment and per capita real income as well as decreasing the unemployment rate in the country? Is the nature of the technology conducive to a wide sharing of the benefits, or will they accrue largely to a small class of people who understand and arrange to benefit from its use? Finally, what are the side effects of the technology on the environment, on rural-urban migration, on food production, as more lucrative industrial employment is sought?

Another potential constraint is that of debt service. Many developing countries have found themselves faced with severe difficulties in honoring interest payments coming due on loans secured to finance capital development. Botswana will have an increasing debt bill for the rest of the decade because of the large influx of loan capital in the early 1970s. Allowances have to be made for meeting repayment schedules even in the face of unanticipated drains on public funds, for example, oil price increases, shortfalls in revenues, or reduced national income deriving from a drought.

This list of potential problems suggests a number of options, most of which are being explored or implemented to some extent by the Botswana government. The government could encourage foreign investors to employ more local people in the construction industries and mining ventures. Many of the experienced Batswana mine workers still going to South Africa can be utilized in similar industries of their home country.

Because of the incomes policy in Botswana, local mining companies do not pay Batswana miners as much as they are getting in South Africa, so they prefer to work outside the country. If the mining companies really wanted to pay locals a competitive wage, the government would no doubt accede. This paradox derives from the country's location; the effort to maintain equity in incomes is having negative effects on the development and use of local labor because of the proximity of South Africa and alternative employment.

Another option which needs exploration is that of encouraging foreign investors to use more "appropriate technology" in their investments. This suggests the use of more labor-intensive methods of mineral exploitation, house construction, road building, and dam construction. It also points to the need to identify local resources as substitutes for imported ones in the design of technology.

On the financial side the Botswana Government has made a number of moves in the direction of taking greater control of its financial affairs. In July 1975 it established the Bank of Botswana—a new institution that will gradually take on all the functions of a central bank—governance of exchange controls, size of money supply, management of foreign exchange reserves, regulation of financial institutions operating in Botswana, and repository of government funds. As a first step, the bank issued its own currency on August 23, 1976: the Pula (meaning "rain"). The value of the Pula was originally on a par with the South African Rand. However, now that Botswana has taken control, it can decide whether to continue this equivalency. There are also controls on the repatriation of profits and wages.

Finally, there is a very large and forbidding option that needs thoughtful and rigorous analysis: whether to remain a member of the Southern African Customs Union Agreement. Does Botswana really benefit over the long run from the renegotiated agreement of 1969? The answer to this question not only rests with an assessment of the revenue generated by the new formula as compensation to Botswana for its loss of fiscal discretion and for having to import some commodities from South Africa at prices greater than those on the world market. It also depends on an analysis of the extent to which the customs union has inhibited, or will inhibit, the growth of industry in Botswana.

The analysis implicit in whether Botswana should remain in the customs union is extremely difficult. It must examine the effects of withdrawal in terms of the potentially enlarged domestic market, reduced exports to South Africa, changes in revenue resulting from setting up its own import-duty structure and administration, and changes in the cost of living in the country. An exploratory analysis suggests that the results are most encouraging in the area of "shiftable" industries; those for which, though presently located in South Africa, the magnitude of Botswana imports would justify shifting production to Botswana. Examples include dairy products, milling industry products, beverages, pharmaceuticals, soap and candles, rubber articles including tires, and so on. The preliminary analysis is not so encouraging in the areas of export markets, revenue, and cost-of-living projections.

The best economic analysis does not yield a forecast of the possibility of outright retaliation by South Africa in the event of a Botswana withdrawal. Such a move could cripple the landlocked country. Nonetheless, more economic analysis of the kind suggested might allow the Botswana Government to move from a strategy of risk-avoidance based on extreme uncertainty to a strategy of calculated risk in its economic planning.

While Botswana remains a part of the customs union the potential costs of withdrawal will be higher in the long run than in the short. Membership in customs unions always involves a certain amount of interdependence that derives from specialization. But the extreme differences in the economies of the members could, even with the new aspects of the 1969 agreement, stunt the development of the three small members and render their relationship to South Africa one of acute and increasing dependence.

The resolution of who is to govern in Rhodesia and Namibia will give Botswana a clearer picture of its immediate and potential economic environment. Whether the risks of withdrawal from the customs union are worthwhile depends on these imponderables. What economic relationships will emerge between Botswana, Rhodesia (Zimbabwe), and Namibia when the latter achieve majority rule? As the changing political situation is consolidated over the next few years, prospects for new economic alliances will be greatly enhanced, affecting markets and access to the sea.

Such questions lead to a consideration of the political options open to Botswana for enhancing its circumscribed position. Since independence, Botswana's leaders have attempted to compensate for the country's vulnerability by using the tools of statecraft on the international stage to alert the world to their own plight and that of the African majorities in the region. The president, his ministers, and the tiny but very able external affairs staff have constantly attempted to put a global construction on the crisis in Southern Africa. Sir Seretse Khama's speeches have in the past few years become less oblique and more categorical regarding the universal issues at stake of race, human rights, and democracy.

Botswana has attempted to remain true to the general Pan-African principles of noninterference and nonalignment, as well as self-reliance. Its representatives have attended most of the international conferences of the nonaligned nations and Botswana has been an active member of the Organization of African Unity and the United Nations. Although it wasn't a preferred option, Botswana broke off relations with Israel in 1973 along with most of its African colleagues.

At the same time, Botswana's foreign policy is not rigidly ideological and can be quite independent of other African countries. Botswana did not attend the OAU meeting in Kampala in 1975 because it might have contributed to legitimizing Idi Amin of Uganda as a spokesman for Africa.

Botswana has not been intimidated by South African reactions to its outreach policy. When it established relations with the Soviet Union in 1970, the outcry from Pretoria would have suggested that the Soviet army was in Gaborone. (The only development assistance arrangement with the Soviets to date is in fact scholarships for a small number of Batswana to study in the U.S.S.R.)

In 1974 Botswana recognized the People's Republic of China after having supported its claim to the China seat at the U.N. Unlike the Russians, the Chinese have a residential mission in Gaborone. There are as yet no visible China-supported technical assistance projects under way although President Khama did visit Peking in July 1976.

It can be said in conclusion that Botswana has been moving consistently in this decade from a posture of risk-avoidance to one of more calculated risk-taking. This is no doubt the result of both external circumstance and improved domestic prospects. Whatever the cause, the credibility of President Khama among African leaders and others is a vindication of his tireless diplomatic efforts and vision. Botswana has exerted its symbolic and moral force effectively and with dignity.

Yet ironically Botswana is in the center of great political uncertainty. The government's ability to maintain vigilance against threats to its own security and still support a democracy is constantly being tested.

[7]

Swaziland and Lesotho

From Traditionalism to Modernity

ABSOLOM L. VILAKAZI

LIKE BOTSWANA, Swaziland and to a lesser extent Lesotho occupy strategic and sensitive positions within Southern Africa. While the white redoubt was still firmly under white and colonial control, the scope for independent action by the two countries was circumscribed by their economic dependence on South Africa, although Swaziland's outlet to the sea through Lourenço Marques (now Maputo) gave it a major advantage. Since Mozambique became independent, Swaziland has found itself in the unenviable position of forming a corridor between its giant apartheid neighbor and a Marxist-oriented state that is sympathetic to South African liberation movements.

Lesotho, like Swaziland and Botswana, has provided protection for South African refugees, whose numbers have been vastly increased by the battles between embittered African youth and riot police in South African townships. Whether Lesotho's encirclement by foreign territory will ultimately be somewhat relieved through Transkeian independence, which it originally refused to recognize, remains to be seen.

Swaziland and Lesotho have two distinctive features in common: each has a monarchy and each consists of a single ethnic group. There are also Swazis and Basutos in the Republic; however, the former are in their own Swazi Bantustan, or homeland, while the latter are divided between Qua-Qua and the Transkei. The Swazis in the Republic, who number about half a million, show little disposition to join the half million in Swaziland, since they do not acknowledge the Dlaminis, the ruling house in Swaziland. The Basutos in the Republic, however, have clan relationships across the Lesotho border that would facilitate such a regrouping.

Swaziland and Lesotho have distinctive physical terrains, which account for their widely differing economic prospects. Swaziland's verdant landscape, stretching from the hills on the west through the forested central slopes to subtropical sugar-growing plantations in the east, affords a variety of sought-after products that underwrite the country's prosperity. Lesotho, in contrast, is largely mountainous with precipitous slopes that impede travel and tend to separate its more than a million people into sections that are psychologically as well as economically diverse. Its major resource, water, has never been sufficiently exploited either for power or for irrigating its neighbor's lands. Lesotho exists precariously, therefore, on the earnings of its migrant workers in the Republic, the proceeds from livestock (in particular high-grade merino wool), and international development funds.

Socially also, Swaziland and Lesotho differ sharply. Although Lesotho has a monarchy, it plays a much more subordinate role than does the king in Swaziland. This distinction and its effect on the political life of the two countries make it necessary to analyze their characteristic features separately.

SWAZILAND

THE SWAZI SOCIAL ORDER

The social order of Swaziland has always been overwhelmingly traditional, and the social, political, and economic actions of its people are generally carried out as result of ingrained habit. Undergirding all their actions is the "value-orientation" of traditionalism, which ensures that the social actions of persons will be determined by what seems to them to be required by duty, honor, personal loyalty, and proper standards of right and wrong. Value-orientation acts as a binding social imperative. This social order derives from the sacredness of tradition, whose validity is reinforced socially and psychologically by fears of the anger of the ancestral spirits that brings with it magical evils if tradition is transgressed. The living symbol of all tradition and of unity of the nation is the King (*Ingwenyama*), who is draped in "the mystical credentials of authority," which give unquestioned legitimacy to whatever he does or says. When the Swazi speak of "our way of life" and of "our traditions," they refer to the social relationships and social actions that take as their point of departure age-old customs validated by the ideology of traditionalism and legitimized by the King. Tradition is the unshakable pillar of their social, political, religious, intellectual, and moral order.

The social hierarchies that derive from this structure are the King, the Queen Mother, and the royal household. Although the literature puts the King and the Queen Mother on an equal footing, the position and power of the Queen Mother are in fact derivative. As the wife of the King's father, who was also the King, she acquires the awesome dignity and ritual sacredness of the King's person. She is a very important political and religious figure without whom certain religious rituals cannot be performed.

Next in the social hierarchy are members of the aristocracy. They are the Dlaminis, or members of the King's extended family; that is, his brothers and cousins and other princes of the realm who have been elevated for meritorious service. Such, for example, are war heroes, army generals, powerful medicine men, and commoners who marry royal women.

The traditional political structure rests on the social structure described above. The King is supreme ruler and all the people owe fealty to him. He is the symbol of the unity of the nation and is its religious leader; so he is "hedged around with divinity," which gives him his mystical powers of authority.

PREINDEPENDENCE DEVELOPMENTS

The traditional order was interrupted by colonial rule and control from 1900 to 1968, when Great Britain was the administering authority. The

King was reduced to the status of paramount chief, who was subordinate to the British resident commissioner, who had ultimate responsibility for policy. The British administrators in Swaziland did not practice the traditional British system of indirect rule but developed a type of dual administration. Because of the large number of European settlers who were allowed to buy land in Swaziland, and because it was expected that the protectorate would ultimately become part of South Africa, the British administration issued proclamations and enforced them directly, set up a national police force in 1907, and controlled the system of criminal justice. Although British administrators often consulted with the paramount chief, the responsibilities of the traditional Swazi authorities were limited in practice to the collection of taxes and to matters that were strictly within the traditional sector, always providing that tradition was not "repugnant to natural justice."

The colonial period introduced for the first time in Swaziland a new form of legitimacy, that is, legal authority that rested on the acceptance of the validity of certain concepts. According to these concepts, a given legal norm may be established outside of traditional authority, and claim obedience from the population. Moreover, the top authority, whether the King or British administrator, is himself subject to an impersonal order of law. In other words, the King's powers are limited by law. It is assumed further that persons who obey the authority do so as members of the state, and therefore their obedience is to the law not to the individual who represents it. Thus, there is no personal loyalty required of the people to the man in authority; rather, there is loyalty to an impersonal country, a code, a flag, or even a set of laws.

These concepts introduced a dualism between the traditional and the modern in the social, cultural, political, religious, intellectual, and economic sectors of the social order. The dualism continues to this day but with the difference that the King presently is at the top of both structures.

Initially, however, the new legal concepts were such a radical departure from Swazi norms that they almost (but not quite) dealt a death blow to the influence of traditional authorities. It is significant that the beginnings of political unrest and political agitation in Swaziland were during this period. It is also important to note that the Swazi political "agitators" criticized not just the colonial presence in Swaziland. They raised the much more serious question of the basis of legitimacy in Swazi society. The idea that legal norms can and should be established by agreement became popular, and people began to question the right of the King and the aristocracy to hold absolute power. The political agitators were admittedly a small minority, but they became the vanguard for a new kind of social and political order that was at variance with the traditionally held view about the basis of legitimacy, and they represented a growth of the educated and urbanized sections of the community.

By 1963 five political organizations had emerged: the Swaziland Progressive Party (SPP) led by K. T. Samketi; the Ngwane National Liberatory Congress (NNLC) under the leadership of Dr. Ambrose Zwane; another Swaziland Progressive Party (SPP) led by John Nquku; the Swaziland Democratic Party (DSP) led by Simon Nxumalo; and the Mbandzeni National Convention led by Dr. George Msibi. Their programs were variations on a common theme. Notwithstanding differences among them, they agreed at constitutional talks in London to form an alliance, with Simon Nxumalo as chairman. The alliance made three basic demands: that the King would become a constitutional monarch under the new constitution; that Britain would be asked to give independence immediately to Swaziland; and that all forms of discrimination on the basis of race and color would be abolished forthwith.

Nonetheless the dominant figure in the whole Swaziland struggle for power was the King. He accepted the challenge of the Pan-Africanists for an elected legislature, organized his own Mbokodvo Party, and decisively defeated the other parties. All of their candidates lost their deposits because they did not receive the necessary minimum number of votes, and the King's party became the sole ruling party.

After the elections of 1964, conducted under a constitution that gave 30 percent of the seats in the legislature to the white community, 30 percent to the Swazi hierarchy, and 30 percent to the national roll, the Mbokodvo Party, which had been dismissed everywhere as subservient to South Africa, pulled off what was almost tantamount to a coup. They disenfranchised all the white South Africans living in Swaziland and challenged the provisions of the 1964 constitution on the grounds that they were racist. They then declared for "independence now" and demanded that the King be designated head of state. The British later acceded to the demands, and they became the basis of the constitution, which the British accepted on February 22, 1967.

It is important to note that the Swazi rejected radicalism and Pan-Africanism as a basis of national policy. They voted for moderate policies that would ensure coexistence with their white-controlled neighbor. The defeat of the Pan-Africanist leaders did not mean that the Swazis endorsed racism and the apartheid policies of their white neighbors, but simply that the Swazi, like the Basuto and the Batswana, rejected both apartheid and radicalism. The fact that they rejected incorporation into South Africa is meaningless otherwise. The policy of coexistence was dictated to them by their political and economic circumstances.

What happened in Swaziland after the victory of the Mbokodvo Party was that many young and dynamic Swazi left their old parties and joined the King's party. The King, characteristically, welcomed his people "back home," saying, "It is their land, their party, their government. Even if they are communists, as some people tell us, they are our sons and therefore our communists."

The injection of this new blood had an important influence on the Mbokodvo. The members with Pan-Africanist leanings broadened the general political and ideological outlook of the party and moved it from its original rightist and traditionalist position toward the center. Thus, young radicals could find a home in the Mbokodvo. They became a very important influence in orienting the party toward the black states of Africa and toward positive positions on questions of Pan-Africanist ideology. They were also instrumental in developing disengagement strategies, especially in the economic sphere. Moreover, by the rejection of any racist reservation of seats in the constitution, the premise was enunciated that to be a Swazi was not simply a matter of color or race but an act of commitment to the aims and purposes of the Swazi state. The party therefore followed a nonracial policy.

The liberalization of the Mbokodvo made the South African government rethink and even modify its assumption that it is a protector of African peoples everywhere against communism or any form of radicalism. There was a time when South Africa assumed the right to decide who could or could not be admitted into Swaziland based on its own definition of communism. When the Swazi King and the Mbokodvo Party showed that they were not afraid of Swazi radicals and that they could, in fact, find a home within the ruling party for them, South Africa had to relax its arrogant assumption of guardianship of the peoples and policies of Swaziland. Finally, the new blood injected into the Mbokodvo Party made it possible for the government of Swaziland to accept South African refugees so long as they did not use Swaziland as a base to launch attacks on South Africa.

INDEPENDENCE, SEPTEMBER 6, 1968

When Swaziland achieved independence in 1968, it accepted a constitution drawn on the Westminster model. The constitution reinstated the monarchy and recognized the King as a constitutional head of state. This, it should be noted, was insisted on by the new elite, who even now proclaim their loyalty to the King and wish to retain the monarchy. It created two houses of Parliament, the members of which were to be elected by the general population on the principle of universal franchise. It institutionalized a two-party system, with the majority party being the ruling party. The effect was to legalize the opposition (a fundamental departure from Swazi tradition) and to establish the right of commoners to share in power and government. It introduced a civil service that was appointed by a civil-service commission according to well-established bureaucratic rules and standards.

This latter feature inevitably created a class of government workers who were outside traditional control, and so created a dualism with Swazi National Council (SNC) employees, who were directly under the control of traditional authorities. The creation of the civil service helped somewhat to eliminate nepotism in government and introduced moral norms alien to Swazi traditional culture and society.

The changes had far-reaching effects on the government of Swaziland and on the country's social structure. The immediate result of having a popularly elected government was that many people who previously were only commoners now assumed positions of power, influence, and wealth, which under the old precolonial order had been the prerogatives of the King and the aristocracy. Members of the royal house and most of the aristocracy did not have the necessary education for exercising power. The King, chiefs, and aristocracy in general had disdained education mainly because for a long time education was in the hands of the missionaries and the King and the aristocracy were not attracted to any new religion. The aristocracy also disdained hard work because they were accustomed to ascriptively acquired privileges. Furthermore, the discipline of schooling and being under teachers who were commoners caused problems for royal children, who often did poorly in school and failed their examinations.

For the King the legalization of the opposition was the most resented feature of the constitution because opposition was seen as *umbango,* an illegitimate contest for power that rightfully belonged to the King and the aristocracy. The legalization of the opposition was the extension of the principle of legal authority, which had first been introduced by the British as a new form of legitimacy in Swazi life. It soon led to trouble, for in order to contain the opposition the King's party deported dissident people, who nevertheless regarded themselves as Swazi citizens. This led to court cases where the King's party lost. Thus, the King and the aristocracy felt that their powers had been subverted by the constitution and by the judges who ruled against them in court.

At the last election held in Swaziland, the Vuvulane Irrigation Farms, owners of the Lebombo district, returned to Parliament a man who was ultimately declared a prohibited immigrant by the government. At the court case on his status it was pointed out that he had been certified a citizen before the election and allocated a plot in Vuvulane on the basis of this citizenship, for no foreigners are allowed to own irrigated plots in Vuvulane. Nonetheless the government reacted with traditional rhetoric of *umbango* (an illicit disputation for power), thereby rejecting the constitutional restraints on the King's power and the role of opposition within a democratic political system that assumes sociocultural pluralism.

It was this attitude that led to the overthrow of the independence constitution and the takeover of the government by the King on April 16, 1973. In the preamble to the proclamation of the takeover, it is stated, among other things that

> the Constitution has permitted the importation into our country of highly undesirable practices alien to and incompatible with the way of life of our society and designed to disrupt and destroy our own peaceful and constructive and essentially democratic methods of political activity; increasingly this element engenders hostility, bitterness and unrest in our peaceful society.

The overthrow of the constitution and the takeover by the King of decision-making in day-to-day government was an attempt by the traditionalists to contain change and especially to deal with the harsh intrusion of new forms of legitimacy that industrialization, urbanization, modernization, and Western-style education are forcing onto the Swazi sociopolitical landscape.

It had the effect of subordinating the modern arm of government to the traditional structure, which is dominated by the Swazi National Council. The SNC is the supreme sociopolitical body of the Swazi nation and meets once a year between July and August at Lobamba, the King's ritual and ceremonial capital. The council is analogous to a national parliament, but it is also the Swazi highest court of appeal. Because land is a particular concern and involves serious sensitivities, any development in Swaziland that has to do with land use is thwarted unless it has the explicit approval of the King and the concurrence of the Swazi National Council. It is the citadel of Swazi traditionalism and conservatism.

In theory, every adult male Swazi can attend and participate in the deliberations of the SNC; but in fact, due largely to geographic factors, attendance tends to be limited to those with special functions, the aristocracy, and those who live near Lobamba.

The effective body that conducts day-to-day SNC business is a small executive committee composed mostly of members of the aristocracy and headed by an executive secretary who keeps the minutes and records and manages the offices.

Whenever there are matters of regional or national importance to be discussed, the Swazi National Council gets its communication links with the rest of the country through the *tinkundla,* which are meeting places in the different rural areas throughout the country. Such meetings, which are attended by local adult males and their chiefs, are presided over by a special King's appointee, but none of the local chiefs is given that honor.

A new trend in the country is to make the *tinkundla* focal points not only of socioeconomic organization but also for the dispensing of rural social services. It is also planned that in the future they will be used increasingly as rural employment centers where rural youth can go to find out about job opportunities in the country.

By tradition the King rules the land through the chiefs, whom he invests with authority. The chiefs are district administrative officers and all are subject to the King. He has effectively "castrated" them politically and economically by refusing to pay them regular salaries, so most chiefs have been reduced to penury. The chief's most important function is allocating land to the people through what is known as the *khonta* system. A man who wishes to get land customarily gives the chief a *khonta* beast or an equivalent R10 ($11.50; Swazi currency Emalangeni equals Rand).

The *khonta* custom establishes a feudal relationship between the chief and his subject. He can *memeta*, or call on the men in his area to give free labor on his fields; and he expects occasional gifts of food, beer, and meat, especially when one of his subjects has a feast. At harvest time the people on the chief's lands are expected to *ethula*, or give a portion of their produce, normally one bag of whatever has been reaped from the field, to the chief. In Swaziland it is often a two-hundred-pound bag of maize or sorghum. Failure to perform these feudal services strains relationships between subject and chief and may, if persistent, result in the eviction of the man from the chief's land, although everybody has theoretically a right of appeal to the King. The right is rarely exercised; for, as a matter of practical politics, appeals follow certain procedures and a man can go to the King only through the very chief against whom he has a complaint. Cases are known of men who have gone directly to the King, but the simple peasant generally despairs of ever getting near the King through the complicated protocol.

A commoner has the political right to attend and participate in the *libandla* (chief's council) and to express his views. Again, theory differs from practice in that although most adult men attend the *libandla,* the real discussions are carried out by a few outstanding men, and the multitudes register their agreement by vociferous choruses of "*elethu*" (hear! hear!) or, if they disagree, by a discreet silence.

Economically the social order is based on subsistence farming and characterized, like all traditional orders, by low productivity. Rational agricultural techniques are unknown and much of agricultural activity is accompanied by magical ritual. Swazi agriculture still reflects conservatism, self-sufficiency, and traditionalism. But at the same time, important changes are taking place in Swaziland. Many traditional Swazi have sought changes because they have seen the resulting advantages. Many others, however, have had change imposed on them by industrialization, Christianity, and education. At the present time most Swazi remain outside the factory system and even outside the rapidly growing towns of Manzini, Mbabane, and others. But new socioeconomic groups have been created by the mining industry in neighboring South Africa, by the large sugar estates in Swaziland, and by growing industrial development in the country itself. These groups depend mainly on earned incomes for their livelihood although they still practice some agriculture, particularly cattle-keeping and subsistence farming.

There is a growing system of market agriculture that in some rural areas has replaced the traditional system of local subsistence production. In the south, for example, tobacco and cotton have become important cash crops. The growing trend toward market agriculture, especially with respect to tobacco and cotton, is due largely to new market opportunities. Similarly, a growing interest in the cash-crop production of green maize, potatoes, and beans for an increasing number of urban consumers has created new social and cultural developments in the country. Market agriculture raises new problems for the social structure and much more acutely for the traditional land-tenure system. For example, the concentration in the south on cash crops not for consumption enraged the traditional rulers and brought an angry outcry against nonfood crops from the highest political authorities in the land. Their indignation fortunately was short-lived, and the farmers were allowed to continue raising their cotton and tobacco. The point is that the traditional rulers were powerless to stop this development. The need for more production of high-value crops like cotton, tobacco, and sugar means that more land is needed and ultimately improved methods of production alien to Swazi agricultural technology.

Another direct challenge to the traditional social hierarchy results from the fact that enterprising farmers are almost exclusively commoners and they become conspicuously wealthier than either their immediate chiefs or the neighboring aristocrats. These new men clearly find it impossible to support the present feudal-aristocratic structure, a situation that creates in the community a new source of power: the rich farmer who becomes more prestigious than the traditional leaders and on whom the chiefs become dependent for handouts in the form of bribes camouflaged as traditional *ethula* gifts.

Successful people are resented in traditional societies, and they become the targets of social attacks ranging from accusations of witchcraft and sorcery (for that is the only logical explanation to a peasant for the sudden riches of a neighbor whose grandfather and father were known to be as poor as the rest of the community) to charges of disloyalty to the King.

But traditional attitudes and solidarities have been very much shaken by new developments in Swaziland. The migration of the young to the towns and to the South African mines and cities gives rise to social alienation, for the mobile ones tend to develop contemptuous attitudes toward traditional culture and traditional attitudes. They desert rural areas and prefer urban residence, which frees them from the impositions of rural authorities and from an empty and largely unmonetized existence in the rural areas. Material acquisition remains a less-important goal for rural peasants and they are reluctant to sell their cattle in spite of the high prices their cattle can fetch in the market. Most rural peasants seem content with a lower standard of living. Not so their children and the urbanized section of the population.

MODERN ECONOMY

A recent study by the World Bank shows that up to mid-1975 Swaziland was less affected by the downturn in worldwide economic activity than many other developing countries, largely because prices received for its major exports remained high, and also because South Africa, with which Swaziland's economy is closely linked, continued a moderate growth rate. While several indications are that external influences may not be so favorable in the immediate future as in the past, the economy is now in a stronger position to withstand an export-induced downturn than it was only a few years ago. During the recent period of high real growth the base of the economy has broadened, as demonstrated by sectoral GDP trends, and manufacturing activity has diversified.

The main sectoral development has been the expansion of the proportion of manufacturing in the GDP from 15 percent in 1971–72 to 22 percent in

1974–75. Although much of the increase stems directly from the higher prices for sugar and wood pulp, real output in manufacturing is estimated to have increased by around 10 percent a year. Agriculture and forestry, as well as community and social services, have grown at roughly the same rates as GDP, and they have continued to provide about 32 percent and 17 percent, respectively, of total production. The share of mining and quarrying fell from 10 to 5 percent, mainly reflecting a leveling off of production, stagnation in prices, and an increase in intermediate consumption.

The pattern of resource utilization shows that the ratio of investment to GDP has remained roughly at about 23 percent, with private fixed investment accounting for nearly three quarters of the total. The share of consumption declined slightly from 67.2 percent in 1971–72 to 65.2 percent in 1974–75, whereas the share of net exports of goods and services increased from 8.8 percent to 11.4 percent.

Agricultural and pastoral production still form the major economic activity in Swaziland, accounting directly for an estimated 29 percent of GDP, while the processing of agricultural products forms the basis for much of the manufacturing sector. Agricultural products, both raw and processed, comprised more than half of total exports in 1974. Approximately twenty-three thousand persons are employed by the modern agricultural subsector, while about half the total population depends directly on traditional agriculture.

Swaziland's land and water resources are only partially exploited. About 20 percent of the total land area of 1.7 million hectares is considered suitable for intensive agriculture, but only half of this area, or about 170,000 hectares, is currently under cultivation. About 25,000 hectares of this land is irrigated, and there is potential for irrigating an additional 15,000 hectares. A further 65 percent of the total area is utilized for cattle grazing.

The agricultural sector consists both of larger-scale, cash crop-oriented farms, which are mainly expatriate-owned, and of traditional farms (mainly subsistence) on Swazi nation land. There are about 790 individually-owned farms covering 45 percent of the total land area, with an average size of about 800 hectares. Approximately half of the farms are considered to be fully utilized, with an average of only about 140 hectares per farm being cultivated. Nevertheless, they account for some 60 percent of the total value in the agricultural sector. The remaining approximate 40 percent is produced by some 39,000 Swazi farmers working communal land. On the average these farmers cultivate less than three hectares each.

This dualism results in part from nineteenth-century land concessions made to Europeans. In 1907 less than 40 percent of the total land area was under Swazi control. This land is still held by the King in trust for the Swazi nation, and its use is determined according to traditional arrangements. Various programs have been formulated over the years to transfer additional land to the Swazi nation, including a E2.6 ($3.9) million grant from Great Britain in 1970 to finance the purchase of non-Swazi-owned land for incorporation into Swazi nation holdings. The programs have resulted in a rise in such holdings to about 55 percent of Swaziland's land area today. The government also enacted legislation in 1974 to tax underutilized land in an attempt to force expatriate landowners either to cultivate idle land or to sell it. The original legislation has not been implemented and is at present in the process of being redrafted.

The government is focusing its agricultural policy on developing the traditional sector from subsistence to semicommercial and commercial farming. Agricultural development expenditures have been about E4 ($6) million in recent years, with about three fourths financed from abroad, mainly by Britain and the United States. In addition substantial technical assistance has been provided through various UNDP-administered programs.

The government is concentrating its development efforts in a few large Rural Development Areas (RDAs) located on Swazi nation land. In these areas an integrated approach includes road improvements, water-resource development, construction of terraces, and provision of extension services for both animal husbandry and crops. After a slow start due to planning and implementation constraints, the program is now progressing more rapidly. In the northern RDA, where most of the effort has been concentrated thus far, output and yield of a number of crops have improved significantly, as have farmers' incomes. There is evidence that the results obtained with the RDAs have motivated farmers in other areas as well; for example, the increase in the number of farmers outside the RDAs seeking information and advice on growing cotton has been so great that it exceeds the capacity of the extension service staff of the Ministry of Agriculture to respond to all requests. The government is presently planning to divide the

RDAs into "High Input Rural Development Areas" and "Minimum Input Rural Development Areas," the difference being to reflect population density, resource bases, and physical development potential.

Animal husbandry is the largest source of cash income in the traditional sector. An estimated 80 percent of the nation's 600,000 head of cattle belong to Swazis. Cattle have traditionally been highly valued more for social than for economic reasons, which in some cases has led to overgrazing and soil erosion. It has also resulted in a low annual offtake (slaughtering and exports) of around 10 percent. Recently, however, the government programs for introducing new grazing systems, new breeds, cattle-fattening farms, and sales yards appear to have led to an increasingly commercial attitude among Swazi farmers. Estate ranches account for the remaining 20 percent of cattle. Management standards on the estates are high, and the annual offtake is almost 15 percent. Swaziland's disease-control programs are extensive; nevertheless, periodic epidemics and droughts result in stock losses, and the ratio of deaths to offtakes has not declined much in recent years.

National projects are to be launched in the fields of dairy farming, beef production, and marketing. The government is trying to spread the use of better-quality cattle breeds to Swazi nation farms and to improve the returns for animal husbandry by establishing fattening ranches where the cattle can be taken for finishing before sale to the abattoir. In addition educational efforts are being increased to promote a more commercial approach to livestock management, stressing quality and increased offtake rather than quantity.

One of the world's largest planted forests is located in Swaziland. Large coniferous forests, developed progressively since the late 1940s, constitute the basis of a major forest-products industry. At the end of 1973 the commercially exploitable area of the forest was estimated at 100,000 hectares, of which more than 90 percent consisted of coniferous trees. Forest development has taken place in two areas of the country: in the north at Piggs Peak, where the output is mostly in the form of logs; and in the south at Usutu, where a large pulp mill is located. This Usutu forest was initially developed by the Commonwealth Development Corporation, but at the time the pulp mill was established a major British fiber corporation (Courtaulds) acquired a 50-percent shareholding. The Usutu forest, together with the attendant processing facilities, represents one of the largest foreign investments in Swaziland. The direct contribution of forestry to GDP was estimated at E4.4 ($6.6) million in 1974–75, but if the pulp-processing industry is included, the total rises to E22 ($30.8) million, or 14 percent of GDP at factor cost. Employment in the forests is about 4,000, with a further 2,500 in the pulp mill and in the sawmills. Forestry exports are mostly wood pulp and amounted to E36.2 ($50.68) million in 1974, or 30 percent of total exports. This represents an increase of 77 percent compared to 1973, mainly due to a sharp increase in the price of wood pulp. In spite of a small increase in export volume, the value of exports of other wood products declined by 4 percent because of a reduction in the unit price received.

Despite the depressed wood-pulp market in 1975, the long-term prospects are good, and the existing pulp mill plans to increase its capacity for processing an ever-greater number of trees reaching maturity. In addition a Japanese company is tentatively considering plans for a second pulp mill, with an annual production of 250,000 tons (substantially above the output of the one in production now). The second mill would be situated at Piggs Peak, where enough log-producing trees are available.

Although mining was formerly a leading sector, in recent years both its relative and absolute roles have been declining. In 1971–72 mining and quarrying contributed nearly 10 percent to GDP, and minerals accounted for about one third of total exports; by 1974–75 mineral extraction's share in GDP had declined to 5 percent, and export of minerals had declined to about 15 percent of total exports. In terms of value the three main minerals extracted are iron ore, asbestos, and coal.

No new mining ventures of any significance have commenced in recent years, partly because of a freeze on new mineral concessions, which are granted by the Swazi nation, during most of the post-independence period. The government's policy is to secure a greater share of the benefits of mineral wealth for the country as a whole and to discourage the holding of inactive concessions. With these objectives in mind, in 1969 the Swazi National Council acquired a 20-percent share in the iron ore mine and in 1972 a 40-percent share in the asbestos mine. In 1973 a nondevelopment tax of E10 ($14) per hectare on all mineral-rights holdings was introduced.

In addition, a minerals committee has been set up by the government to advise the council on matters relating to the development of the mining sector. Recently a number of new concessions have been granted, and prospecting for additional mineral deposits is being accelerated.

Manufacturing has rapidly become the second most important activity in Swaziland. Although much of the increase in value added can be attributed to increases in prices, particularly for sugar and wood pulp, there has also been a substantial real increase estimated at between 8 percent and 10 percent a year. Employment in manufacturing has increased from 5,800 in 1971 to 7,500 in 1974, an increase of 29 percent. The two largest industries are sugar refining and wood-pulp processing; other important processing industries are meat packing, cotton ginning, and fruit canning. Together these industries account for more than 90 percent of the value added by the manufacturing sector. Although fluctuating from year to year, the production of processed sugar and cotton has shown a steady long-term increase. The processing of meat has also grown substantially, more than doubling between 1970 and 1973, whereas wood processing has remained about the same.

Although the manufacturing sector is now largely based on primary products, there has been a significant diversification over the last few years. A number of new industries have recently been established. A TV factory, financed by Finnish capital, has started production of color sets mainly for the South African market, where after hard bargaining Swaziland has been granted a share of twenty thousand sets a year. In the future the production may be increased to include black-and-white sets for export to other African countries. An E12 ($16.8) million fertilizer plant has just started production, mainly for export to South Africa. Investors from Hong Kong have established an E6 ($8.4) million cotton-spinning plant, which will eventually employ about two thousand persons. An interesting development is the start of production of the Tinkabi, a locally developed small tractor particularly suited to the needs of the developing countries. About two hundred Tinkabi tractors have been produced so far, and the prospects for large-scale production and marketing are presently being explored. Because of a small domestic market, new industries on any significant scale must be export-oriented. Swaziland, as a member of the customs union with South Africa,

Botswana, and Lesotho, enjoys access to the large Southern Africa market, and this fact has contributed to its success in attracting foreign investments. Swaziland has also signed the Lomé Convention with the EEC, which offers preferential treatment in that market and promises also to help the inflow of private investment. An additional attraction for some investors is the fact that goods manufactured in Swaziland are generally accepted by other African countries where imports from South Africa are banned.

Swaziland offers a number of generous tax incentives to investors. Over and above normal depreciation allowances, investors are allowed to deduct 30 percent of the cost of new industrial buildings and plant and machinery during the first year. The recent Income Tax Consolidation Order, 1975, introduced a number of modifications favorable to investors, including accelerated write-offs for capital investment (beyond the 30 percent during the first year), increased deductions for company housing for employees, and a new deduction for money spent on employee training. The company tax rate remains at 33⅓ percent of taxable income.

Tourism has been one of the most dynamic sectors of the economy in recent years. The number of hotel guests, coming mostly from South Africa, more than doubled between 1969 and 1974, from 43,000 to 96,000, a growth rate of about 18 percent per annum. At the same time the number of hotel beds increased from 900 to 1,630, a growth rate of about 13 percent per annum. The industry's income from room rental was about E3 ($4.2) million in 1974. Including ancillary services such as food, entertainment, and souvenirs, total earnings from tourism may be about E6 ($8.4) million. About 1,500 persons were directly employed in tourism in 1973.

Planned investment in the tourism sector suggests a continued rapid pace of expansion. A Tourism Development Authority has recently been established to promote the development of tourism and to strengthen the basis for sustained development. As heretofore most tourism has consisted of weekend visitors from South Africa, the Authority is seeking to solve the problem of low midweek occupancy of rooms by promoting longer-duration package holidays. The Authority is also promoting a diversification away from the well-developed Mbabane-Manzini area which will be aided by the planned expansion of the road system to the north and to the south, thus opening up new scenic areas, and by the development of another hotel-casino complex in the south near Big Bend. The government is also studying the possibility of opening a second game park, which would provide another focus for tourism.

Although there is no general minimum wage, minimum wages are speci-fied by the government for selected industries. Such minimum wages were largely unchanged between 1967 and 1973, at which time they were in-creased by between 9 and 40 percent. For the most part, wages in the private sector are determined by negotiation, and after three years of virtual stagna-tion actual wages received by semiskilled and unskilled workers increased by about 20 percent in 1974. Substantial additional increases of up to 60 percent occurred in 1975. The Swazi authorities attribute part of the recent increase in wages for unskilled labor to competition from South Africa for labor and to the demonstration effect of higher wages there on wage claims in Swaziland; however, even more fundamental has been the pressure on wages created by the increased demand for labor in Swaziland.

There has been a steady increase in paid employment in Swaziland, from a reported forty-seven thousand in 1971 to sixty-two thousand in 1974, when it equaled about one third of the active labor force. In addition to this domestic employment, some eight thousand Swazi workers find paid em-ployment in the mines in South Africa. About 80 percent of domestic employment is provided by the private sector. In 1974 the public sector employed thirteen thousand, equivalent to just over 20 percent of total paid employment. While most of the growth has been concentrated in the pri-mary sectors of the economy, where during certain peak employment peri-ods (such as the sugar-cane harvests) actual labor shortages appear, there has been significant growth of employment in industrialized sectors as well. In the immediate future commercial production of small-scale tractors, expansion of plant capacity for processing agricultural produce, and contin-ued growth of the SEDCO-sponsored small-scale industries will probably all contribute to a more rapid growth of employment opportunities in manufacturing than in most other sectors of the economy. This growth in employment opportunities has allowed and is expected to continue facilitat-ing a gradual shift in employment from the subsistence sector of agriculture, where labor is often underemployed, into paid employment, both in primary production and in manufacturing.

THE IMPACT OF CHANGE

At present the Swazi political scene is fraught with many ambiguities, if not uncertainties. The choice of the new prime minister after some delay was an indication that the King was looking for a trustworthy traditionalist who would help bolster the traditional government and traditional institutions. That he chose a Dlamini aristocrat and the chief of the army indicates that the King is uneasy about the assaults that have been made by modern political leaders on traditional institutions and on the legitimacy of his authority. Therefore, to ensure the stability and continuity of Swazi tradition, he selected as head of government a traditionalist and a military man. The clear aim here was to tie the army to the traditional instead of to the modern political sector. The problem of financing the army and thus ensuring its loyalty to the traditional sector of society has been met as well. The Swazi National Council has developed the Tibiyo Farms (bought out of the proceeds of the Tibiyo Fund) into commercial enterprises, and one of the purposes is to use the proceeds from such farms to maintain the army. In this way the King hopes to keep the army away from the modern sector and loyal only to him as head of the traditional sector. The difficulty with such plans and calculations is that the revenues from the Tibiyo Farms, even when they become fully developed and have reached maximum profitability, will not be sufficient to maintain an army of several thousands and equip it adequately. The traditionalists perceive a modern army as an unpaid volunteer force that needs only to be fed and supplied with guns. But the range of modern weaponry, army uniforms, army equipment, and transportation would very quickly deplete the resources built from the Tibiyo Farms. It would seem that for a viable army the modern government will have to use its greater resources.

The perceived dangers to Swazi security at the moment come from the Mozambique border, where President Samora Machel's policies seem threatening. There is also some uneasiness in Swaziland as a result of the arrest of South African refugees in Swaziland and the discovery in the last few months of a cache of arms at Sidwokodwo, a rail head between Swaziland and Mozambique. Some hand grenades were seized from South African refugees at St. Christopher's School, which is used by South African refugees. It is not yet clear where all these arms were destined to go, but the fact that they were found in Swaziland has become cause for concern.

The real problems in Swaziland arise from massive threats to traditionalism posed by the new kinds of men and women who are emerging from the schools and who are molded in the new urban areas that are growing rapidly in the country. The ruling elites are finding that the old assumptions and the old values around which traditional life was built do not meet the new demands of an industrializing society. But the problems that arise cannot be addressed in any meaningful way because political parties or political alternatives for the meeting of contemporary problems are proscribed.

The socioeconomic circumstances of the country are developing favorably for the emergence of political dissatisfaction with the traditional status quo. In Swaziland the teacher dissatisfaction in June, July, and August of 1976 and the unimaginative way in which it was handled by the government is merely one example of the problems ahead. Another factor likely to be a cause for popular dissatisfaction and possibly violent expression has to do with the control of the minerals in the country and the control of royalties paid by mining companies. The secrecy that surrounds these matters is seen by the average Swazi, particularly students and those outside the government, as creating suspicion about the government. The feeling persists that if the matters were controlled by the modern government instead of by the Swazi National Council, the people's interests would be better served.

Politically, the most important problem for Swaziland is political direction when the present King dies. He is the oldest reigning monarch in the world. There is nothing to show that the problems which are building up now will be handled with any assurance when the King goes. It means clearly that there will be a power struggle in which some radical Pan-Africanist leadership might emerge. The traditionalists who are now firmly in the saddle are kept there by the power and personal prestige of the King. There does not seem to be anyone on the horizon who could take over and exercise the same power and command the same respect from the people.

LESOTHO

PREINDEPENDENCE POLITICAL DEVELOPMENT

Lesotho's political development, like that of Swaziland and Botswana, took a different turn as soon as it became clear that there was to be no forced incorporation within South Africa. The British then moved forward cautiously and sent a commission to inquire "where ... they were going and how to get there." The commission's terms of reference made clear that it was expected only to tinker with the existing traditional system of government and to report "on the existing system of native authorities and consider, in particular, the problems of local government." The wider question of the need for a legislative council was ruled out from the start.

Political parties had emerged in the meantime. The first was the Basutoland Congress Party (BCP) founded by Ntsu Mokhetle. Its closest and much more conservative rival, the National Party, was formed six years after the BCP and was led by Chief Leabua Jonathan. The BCP was radical, Pan-Africanist, and supported mostly by schoolteachers and what may be called the "urban" population of Basutoland—mostly people who had worked in South Africa and had learned their politics in the African National Congress of South Africa. The alleged militancy and the authoritarian character of the BCP leader caused a split in the party and the emergence under a physician, Seth Makotoko, of the Marematlou Freedom Party (MFP), which was close to the King and was composed of the principal chiefs and some disaffected followers of the BCP.

The majority of the organized groups in Lesotho agreed on the maintenance of kingship as an institution because, as the BCP said in evidence before the commission, "it is inseparable from the land rights of the people since the land is also of the people, owned by the people, for the people. The oneness of hereditary chieftainship and the land rights of the people is elemental in any African society, and so it is with the Basotho." There was also general agreement among the Basotho that there should be fewer petty chiefs and that legislative institutions should be established.

As in other African countries, personalities have played a very important role in the politics of Lesotho. This was especially true in the BCP because

Ntsu Mokhetle has been the most influential force not only for the strength of his party but also for its weaknesses and failures. Having learned his politics in South Africa with the African National Congress and having traveled to the Pan-Africanist Ghana of Kwame Nkrumah, he was militantly Pan-Africanist. His program envisaged a severing of ties with the Commonwealth and a Pan-Africanist approach to the African liberation struggle. Mokhetle alienated many Basotho by attacking the Roman Catholic Church so that one of the strongest Sotho institutions turned against him and supported his rival, the BNP. Mokhetle's policies also threatened to provoke a confrontation with South Africa, which was another reason for his failure to win political support in Lesotho in its first election in 1965.

Significantly the people of Lesotho decided to put into power a man who was considered able to make coexistence with South Africa possible—Chief Leabua Jonathan. When he reminded them during the election campaign to "think of your stomachs," he was talking existentialist politics that the people understood. It seems clear that he won because the people approved his essentially conservative stance and his commitment to coexistence with South Africa—and therefore to the bread-and-butter issues of the day.

If the opposition party and its leader's subsequent quarrels with the South African ANC refugee leaders in Lesotho are considered, it becomes clear that after Mokhetle's heady platform rhetoric and his due obeisance in the direction of the OAU and Pan-Africanism, he suddenly realized the political naivete and the positive dangers of his politics to the very existence of Lesotho as an independent state in Southern Africa. It seems to have dawned on him that for Lesotho the only viable politics was perhaps the politics of dependence.

The 1970 Lesotho election results and subsequent reports indicate that Mokhetle's BCP party won the election, but that Chief Leabua Jonathan seized power by force with the acquiescence of the Republic of South Africa. People were most likely disenchanted with Jonathan's government, for Mokhetle was still Pan-Africanist and in this election, as always, he disdained the "politics of the stomach." It is easy to say today, with the help of hindsight and the experience of Mozambique, that Mokhetle's Pan-Africanist regime could have coexisted with the South African colossus and even extracted some concessions from it. Indeed, there are those who think that a Mokhetle regime might have been more efficient and have handled Sotho affairs with greater style and aplomb.

The Lesotho political picture is clouded, however, by the fact that it is difficult to talk at this moment of political activity or even of a political direction in the country. The positions of the political parties and of the King are ambiguous. Lesotho, like Swaziland, seems to be in a mire of political inactivity. Neither the head of government nor the King has indicated any kind of direction in terms of ideology or government policy, and, therefore, there is a deceptive and dangerous quiet in the country. Clearly the King is too weak at the moment to challenge the prime minister, and there does not seem to be any politician on the horizon who might act as a future rallying point. Serious political discussions can only be had with university students. The civil servants are timid and take protective cover under the protest that they are forbidden by law to be political.

Traditionally, Lesotho is oriented toward values, and customs, built around the time-honored rules and regulations whose central representative is King Moshoeshoe—a descendant of the warrior-diplomat King of the Basotho. King Moshoeshoe, like King Sobhuza of Swaziland, carries in his person the "mystical credentials of authority" that make him among the Basotho the unquestioned spiritual head of the nation and constitutional head of the government of Lesotho. Unlike King Sobhuza, King Moshoeshoe has, however, diluted his traditional authority and hold over the people and Lesotho affairs by adopting modernity. He is an educated man and his life style is modern (unlike King Sobhuza, who is traditionalism personified). This is an important distinction between Lesotho traditionalism and Swazi traditionalism.

King Moshoeshoe does not, therefore, exercise the political power and influence one would expect from him, nor does he wield the kind of sociopolitical power that even remotely resembles the power of the Swazi King. After abortive efforts to secure power, he was overshadowed by his prime minister and relegated to the position of ceremonial head of the government. His political powerlessness is seen by some Basotho as a commentary on his personality and political acumen rather than on the wishes of the people or even as a function of his constitutional position. Considering the initial advantages that he has over Chief Jonathan, that is, his "mystical credentials of authority" and his credentials as an educated man, his power-lessness seems to be due to his lack of leadership qualities.

There is not in Lesotho the same self-conscious traditionalism that per-meates the lives of government officials everywhere in Swaziland. The aver-age Mosotho does not extol the virtues of traditional ways or excuse personal or government behavior with the rhetoric of traditionalism; nei-ther are the schools and other state institutions used to propagate the ideology of traditionalism, probably because traditional life styles cannot be supported by the Lesotho traditional economy. Most Basotho have to go out to the Republic to earn a living either in the mines or on the white farms. That Lesotho is rapidly urbanizing can be seen by the growth of towns like Maseru and its immediate environs, like Mazenod and Roma. Further, there have been much greater educational advance and Christian impact on Sotho life now that traditionalism has been eroded. Perhaps this is why no threat to Sotho traditional life is perceived and no defensive mechanism developed by the rulers.

THE ECONOMY

In the summary of its study of the economy of the kingdom of Lesotho, the World Bank points out that Lesotho is one of the twenty-nine countries designated by the United Nations as "least-developed." It is unique among landlocked developing countries in that it is located completely within the borders of a single country, the Republic of South Africa. Despite its proximity to the vast mineral deposits within the Republic, Lesotho has few natural resources; currently only diamonds offer some prospect for mineral development. The country is largely mountainous, with less than 15 percent of the land area suitable for crop cultivation.

The summary also points to the structure of the economy, which reflects the dominance of subsistence agriculture and livestock raising (which con-tribute about half the domestic product), and to the critical dependence on migration of some 60 percent of the male labor force for employment in the Republic; at the same time the development of the domestic economy suffers from a severe shortage of skilled manpower. Economic links with the Republic have been forged mainly through sharing of a common currency, the Rand; membership in the Southern Africa Customs Union; the fact that the bulk of merchandise trade is with the Republic; and, more recently, the dependence on South African traffic in the rapidly growing tourism sector.

The National Development Plan (1970-71–1974-75) was the country's first systematic development program, and the investment allocations (such as for infrastructure, 40 percent; agriculture, 23 percent; and education, 14 percent) reflected the basic needs of an economy still at a very early stage of development. During the early years of planning, information on Lesotho's economic potential remained inadequate, and implementation capacity was itself a major constraint on growth. Recently the results of a number of sector studies (tourism, telecommunications, transportation, minerals, industry) have become available; improved knowledge of the country's economic potential will be reflected in the second National Development Plan, 1975-76–1980-81. Given the low level of development, the achievements of the first plan should be considered in terms of its progress in laying the foundations for sustained growth.

There have been a number of favorable developments since 1970. The economy emerged from more than a decade of stagnation; GDP grew at about 6 percent annually over the 1969-70–1973-74 period; technical and vocational training is being given greater emphasis in the educational system; the government's financial situation and implementing capacity have improved substantially. At the same time, however, certain structural weaknesses in the economy have persisted. Domestic employment remains inadequate for the rapidly growing labor force, thus strengthening the migration process. Soil conservation continues to pose a serious problem to increased agricultural production, the growth of which is less than that of population; this has led to a growing reliance on imported food supplies from South Africa. The government has recently strengthened institutional support to the agricultural sector by establishing produce-marketing and livestock-marketing boards. In addition, a program of rural development is being implemented that provides for a minimum package of inputs to farmers (fertilizer, seeds, extension services, credit, etc.) and offers some prospects for increasing agricultural productivity and for arresting the deterioration of soil.

A major objective of government policy during the plan period was achieved in 1973-74, when a surplus on the current budget was realized; until then, government finances depended on grants-in-aid from Britain.

The improved financial position was due mainly to the 1969 revision of the Southern Africa Customs Union Agreement, from which 60 percent of government revenue is derived. Good progress has also been made in building up and strengthening the country's financial institutions, which, since 1973, have been regulated by the Financial Institutions Act. Further legislation is soon to be enacted to regulate the operations of building societies and to establish an agricultural credit bank and a local insurance company. In 1975 the government introduced a deferred-payment scheme for migrant workers, under which 60 percent of the earnings of the workers will be repatriated to the Lesotho National Bank. Within two years a fund equivalent to about 75 percent of the government's current revenue, and about two and one half times its annual capital program, is expected to be built up; the scheme will substantially enhance the mobilization of domestic resources for development.

As regards external payments, the country's trade deficit has increased over the plan period. Though incomplete, relevant statistics show a decline in the growth of exports, while imports increased significantly. However, these deficits have been more than offset by workers' remittances and by unrequited transfers to both the government and the private sectors. Since Lesotho has no central bank and has free access to the reserves of the Rand monetary area, the normal balance of payments implications are not as relevant as would be the case if Lesotho had its own independent monetary system.

Projections of economic growth, according to the bank report, can be only illustrative, given the uncertainty of the migrant-labor situation and the limitations of available statistics. However, real growth in GDP of about 6 percent annually could be possible. It will depend mainly on the satisfactory performance of the agricultural sector and to a lesser extent on the implementation of substantial investments planned in mining and tourism. The growth in government financing in recent years is expected to slow down, largely because of a downward trend in receipts from the Customs Union Agreement; the current budget surplus of $14 million is expected to decline to about $2.8 million toward the end of the plan period. If, however, the negotiations currently taking place to amend the Customs Union Agreement are successful, the revenue outlook would improve substantially and the government would be able to transfer a portion of its expected budget surplus to the financing of its capital program. On the expenditure side, a government policy of fiscal restraint in current expenditure should be sustained, while its implementation capacity is expected to continue improving. Additionally, with sector knowledge now much improved and with a substantial technical-assistance program in operation, a growth rate in capital expenditure of about 10 percent annually should be attainable.

Lesotho's development challenge lies in reducing its dependence on the Republic for the employment of more than half of its male labor force. Government policy in this direction during the next plan period includes the establishment of a labor-intensive construction unit within the Ministry of Works. The purpose of this unit would be to deal with any reemployment arising from the emergency return of large numbers of migrant workers (as happened in 1974), to implement an ongoing program of labor-intensive public works, and at the same time to provide an opportunity for training in much-needed supervisory skills. Lesotho's unique circumstances call for a continuing search by the government for new approaches to the difficult task of development. Expenditure on labor-intensive construction should be considered an integral part of a long-term program of investment in the country's human resources; it could usefully be complemented by an in-depth study of the prospects for Basotho labor in Southern Africa.

The overall economic picture gleaned from the bank report is rather grim and raises serious questions about the economic health or long-term viability of Lesotho. It seems to suggest for Lesotho more than for any other Southern African black state a position of economic dependency that is bound to cramp its political style, if not completely compromise it.

WHITHER THE TWO KINGDOMS? FUTURE PROSPECTS

The "morning-after-independence" feeling that was experienced perhaps too dramatically by the leaders of the black states of Swaziland and Lesotho was that the external political and economic environment in which they operated had in no sense been altered by independence. Their geographical remoteness from independent Africa and their economic dependence on the neighboring state of South Africa were still important factors for their internal development and the international options open to them. From these facts their leaders drew certain conclusions that were reflected in their policies and the way they did business with their white neighbors.

Although these black states can now be discussed with the Africans as the focal point of analysis, this does not eliminate South African influence on their political and economic development. This is realism and does not in any way reflect the acceptance of apartheid and all it stands for. There is a universal hostility to apartheid policies of South Africa in all the black independent states of Africa, and the attempts made in the past to foist incorporation within the Republic upon what have become Swaziland, Lesotho, and Botswana confirmed the new countries' beliefs about the essential evil of that system.

But these states are caught in a cruel dilemma. The winds of change brought them to independence; the temper of the times demands militancy against all forms of colonialism in public and international affairs; and the states are importuned on all sides to show their allegiance to black Africa by adopting a rhetoric that fits those who are farther from South Africa. The ideological commitment to anticolonialism and Pan-Africanism required of them raises their most embarrassing problems both at home and abroad.

It was a matter of painful embarrassment for them to have to abstain from voting at the United Nations against South Africa because they fear the economic clout South Africa could administer with devastating effect. It is a matter of grief to them to refuse to commit themselves in the matter of refugees or to have to pretend that the sufferings of the blacks in the Republic are matters about which they are unconcerned. But they have apartheid all around them.

While recognizing the damage that may be done to the cause of their countries, the spokesmen of the three black states do increasingly speak their minds against South Africa, particularly at the United Nations, on the principle that morality is or should be the guiding principle in international relations. These people believe that they can and must maintain their political independence and integrity, and that there is no conflict between their political independence and their economic dependence on South Africa.

The countries' leaders fully realize the danger they are in, and thus they are deliberately exploring means of disengagement from South Africa. A first step in the disengagement process was to join the OAU and to commit themselves to supporting all OAU policies, which meant giving aid to refugees and even financing the liberation movements. The latest step has been to refuse to recognize the Transkei. These acts are perceived by South Africa as hostile.

Another aspect of the disengagement process, an economic one, indicates that at least some of the leaders of these black states have thought their strategies through very carefully. The states have linked themselves as much as possible to the African independent states north of the Zambezi, and they have also opened for themselves avenues for joining the East African Common Market and the European Common Market.

Thus, the Swazi have signed a series of agreements with black states to the north. In August 1967 they signed an agreement with Zambia under which Zambia would buy 25,000 carcasses of beef a year. Only recently they signed an agreement with Gabon to supply that country with beef. Soon after the devaluation of the British pound Swaziland signed an agreement with Uganda to take their wood pulp previously sold to Rhodesia. Kenya signed an agreement to buy beef and sugar. All of these agreements were concluded between June and August of 1969.

There is also a consistent pattern of disengagement in the area of foreign investment. The canning factory at Makerns in Swaziland has been awarded to the American firm Libby, and South African textiles must now compete with a Japanese textile factory in Swaziland. The Japanese have also agreed to participate in steel and mining activities, agreements signed toward the end of 1969. The Swazi have prohibited the use of Swaziland as a mere base from which wholly South African goods are passed on to other countries, like those in the European Economic Community, with which they have special arrangements. They insist on a 20- to 50-percent Swazi participation in any venture on Swazi soil.

In the field of transport the Swazi have a railroad to Mozambique, thus reducing their dependence on South Africa. Their motor roads are also well developed because all are important commercial arteries. They have recently laid great emphasis on developing air services. Future plans for development include a national airline that will be financed through the Tibiyo fund. The government of Lesotho is also involved in the same exercise, and for both countries internationally registered schedules will mean greater independence from South Africa by making it possible for visitors coming to either country to bypass South Africa. Mozambique and

Swiss interests have encouraged far-reaching plans in Swaziland to develop a shipping line based at Maputo.

Domestically, through the Tibiyo fund the Swazi nation now owns a significant part of the following major enterprises in the country: Havelock (asbestos) Mines (40 percent); Ubombo Ranches Sugar Mill and Cattle Holdings (40 percent); Swazi Iron Ore Development Co. Ltd. (20 percent); the Royal Swazi Spa and Holiday Inns Complex (31.5 percent); and Mhlume Sugar Mill and Estate (50 percent).

In the area of technical assistance both Swaziland and Lesotho have looked to international organizations. Thus, the United Nations Development Program has been asked to provide expert personnel either to consult or to train civil servants, who have replaced the South African experts who used to dominate this field of development.

Any attempt at understanding Lesotho and Swaziland must deal with the political options open to them. First and foremost, for both countries there is the problem of establishing acceptable constitutions that will lead them successfully to a political stability consistent with the economic and socio-cultural modernization now taking place. Clearly, both of them found the Westminster model bequeathed to them by Britain at independence unsatisfactory; hence, both independence constitutions were jettisoned.

It is clear from current talks and political activities that a constitution is now seen as a desirable, indeed necessary, instrument. What both countries seem to be looking for is a formula that allows for modernization and at the same time retains and protects what they regard as essential features of national identity. Unfortunately, the feature both seem to want to preserve entrenches aristocratic privilege along with one-man or one-party rule. This is clearly unacceptable to their young, rapidly urbanizing, and increasingly proletarian populations. Nor is there consent to this kind of arrangement from the significant intellectual and civil-servant sections of the population.

A possible alternative model, which has been tried in other parts of the African world, is for the constitutional arrangements to provide for the representation of traditional authorities either in one legislature as a percentage of the members (25 to 50 percent) or in a separate House of Chiefs similar to the British House of Lords. The tendency is toward the former.

It is obviously, however, merely a "holding pattern," and very soon the traditional sectors will disappear because the sociocultural trend is unmistakably toward modernity.

To support this claim of a clear drift toward modernity, proponents argue that there is a growing diminution of solidarities that favor kinship and clan affiliations and an increase in new types of associations based on common interests. Any attempts to perpetuate mechanical solidarities is bound to meet with strong resistance and ultimate failure. In Swaziland, for example, the critical issue is whether the Swazi National Council and the whole dual structure in government are relevant nine years after the departure of the colonial government apparatus to which the Swazi National Council was seen as a necessary countervailing force. Now that the modern independent government is run by the Swazi, the Swazi National Council has come to be viewed suspiciously as an anachronism that represents the vested interests of the aristocracy.

In both countries there seem to be some cultural difficulties with the Westminster constitutional model, especially with the concept of "the loyal opposition" because the opposition is seen and interpreted culturally as conspiratorial. The whole matter of the relations of the government and the opposition raises fears of a *coup d'état,* which seems to have been the result of the Westminster model in many states in the African world.

Speculation about the constitutional models likely to be adopted suggests that a version of the Tanzanian model might be adopted with different mixes of African socialism and the private-enterprise system. It also seems clear that new types of constitutional developments may have to await new types of leadership and thus will probably be inapplicable during the lifetime of the present rulers in these countries.

In the case of Swaziland the army will tend to be tied to the traditional arm of the government, because it is the traditionalists there who feel embattled. In Lesotho the army, if and when it does develop, will be a paramilitary police force capable of controlling internal disturbances. Unlike Swaziland, Lesotho does not have a potentially troublesome border. Swaziland borders on Marxist Mozambique, which is highly critical of what it calls reactionary governments. Coexistence between the two countries at the moment is clearly an uneasy partnership.

[8]

Conclusion

Looking to the Future

COLIN LEGUM

A STRIKING PHENOMENON of the liberation struggles in Africa north of
the Zambezi River was that in all but three countries independence was
achieved either with a minimum of violence or, for the greater part, with
no violence at all. By contrast, the only three countries to achieve full
independence so far by peaceful methods in Southern Africa (Lesotho,
Botswana, and Swaziland) are the three smallest states in the area, none of
which has a significant white resident population. Of the three countries in
the north whose independence was won through war, two (Algeria and
Kenya) had substantial white settler communities, while the third (Guinea-
Bissau) was part of the resistant Portuguese empire. This evidence indicates,
therefore, that the size of the local white population and the degree of
political and economic control in its hands have been major determinants
of the degree of violent resistance to the idea of majority rule. In Rhodesia,
and especially in South Africa, both of these elements are stronger than
anywhere else in Africa.

Angola and Mozambique have already bolstered the case of those who
argue that liberation in the white-dominated societies can come only
through an armed struggle. In Rhodesia, too, the critical factor of change

has been the growth of a serious guerrilla challenge. And in Namibia the only reason that South Africa did not carry out its own design for a Bantustan-type of independence was because of the potential resistance by SWAPO's guerrilla forces.

The easy conclusion, therefore, is that the necessity for an armed struggle will finally prevail in South Africa also and that this powerful and highly industrialized society will eventually disintegrate into violence. Such a confrontation driving the Republic's whites and blacks into opposing armed camps would dwarf all the other colonial wars fought in preindependence Africa except for Algeria. But while the possibility of a race war occurring in South Africa cannot be ruled out entirely, it is by no means axiomatic that what happened in the case of the Republic's immediate northern neighbors will be repeated in the last bastion of white supremacy on the continent.

The South African situation is completely different from that of any other part of the continent. It is a rich and powerfully armed country. Even more important, it is a country where the process of economic, if not yet of social, integration of the races has already gone so far that they are locked into interdependence. It was the refusal of the architects of apartheid to acknowledge the extent of this integration which not only resulted in a total failure to separate the races (except into residential zones) in the industrial cities and white rural areas, but sharpened the internal contradictions to the point where they have actually become a more serious threat to the maintenance of the present system than any challenge likely to come from an armed struggle. At best, the development of an armed struggle would only add another dimension to these internal contradictions.

Another major difference between South Africa and the former African colonial territories is that it ceased being a colony almost seventy years ago; it is therefore not dependent on decisions taken by a metropolitan power which, like Portugal, can decide to abdicate and withdraw its citizens. The size of its white community (more than four million) is greater than the combined white communities in the rest of Africa in the heyday of colonialism. White South Africans, especially the Afrikaners who have been rooted in African soil for over three centuries, have no other home where they might hope to find refuge. It is, at present, still unthinkable that these millions of whites will not continue to live in the country of their birth whatever the circumstances at the time of the transfer, or redistribution, of political power. No black leader of any consequence has ever publicly suggested that the whites should be "driven into the sea." Quite the contrary: black leaders have always insisted on the right of the whites to remain in South Africa, subject only to their willingness to abandon their *Herrenvolk* ideas.

Yet, as of now there is little prospect of white South Africans—and especially of Afrikaners—yielding to such a demand, at least not before the point has been reached where they begin to find effective power slipping from their hands. There are early signs that this possibility has begun to flicker through some minds; but the bulk of Afrikaners still believe, like Mao Tse-tung, that power springs from the barrel of the gun. Sad as this conclusion is, there seems to be no reasonable hope of white South Africans agreeing to negotiate meaningfully with the black majority while they still remain sufficiently confident of their own strength.

Is there, then, no reasonable hope that white South Africans will consent to a peaceful process of political change to move toward a nonracial society in which they would share a common home and destiny with blacks, through a federal or some other appropriate system? Any answer to this question must be heavily qualified. No, it is most unlikely that fundamental political change will come peacefully, but it could come without a totally ruinous conflagration. Yes, the idea of a federal or confederal solution might figure more urgently on the nation's agenda once the experiment of creating separate black states has proved to be a failure and if Western policies are altered to exert a positive influence in producing desired change.

For more than a decade most white South Africans have been led to believe that the policies of separate development culminating in the creation of eight or nine black independent republics and one white republic is the *only way* of safeguarding their way of life.

If the Bantustan experiment fails—as Gwendolen Carter convincingly argues in an earlier chapter it is most likely to do—white hopes will be busted and a desperate new search will begin for some, perhaps more realistic, alternative political system. Whatever it is—whether federal or confederal—its success can be assured only if blacks and whites sit down together at a conference table for the first time in their history. The longer this negotiated settlement is delayed, the surer the prospect of violence and of irreconcilable racial bitterness, and the less the chances for attitudes of mutual tolerance essential if there is to be any hope at all of a peaceful agreement being reached between the races.

It is still impossible to know which of the two likelier choices the Republic will be driven to take in response to the internal and external pressures building up against the present system. One strong possibility is that the entrenched white power establishment will resist to the bitter end, preferring to accept all the risks of serious violence, economic disruption, and the possible total disruption of the country rather than accept majority rule. The other possibility is that after considerable initial resistance (for, say, three to five more years), they will come to accept the necessity of negotiating a new constitutional settlement with representative black leaders to replace the Act of Union in 1910, designed by the two white communities, English-speaking and Afrikaners, without a single black representative being present at the conference table.

It is extremely unlikely, however, for the reasons stated earlier, that any serious attempt will be made to reach a negotiated settlement before the situation has become more violent and the economic system is actively threatened with paralysis and even collapse. This conclusion is based on an analysis of the white society's power structure. None of its leaders, or groups of leaders, is able to make the kind of autocratic decision that, for example, Charles de Gaulle made over Algeria if it touches on any fundamental issue affecting the continuation of the present system of white supremacy. In South Africa the vote on the possession of political power lies exclusively with the white electorate, the majority of which is Afrikaner. As of now, this electorate is still predominantly composed of diehard believers in the justification and invincibility of white supremacy, even under siege conditions. Even if the prime minister and his cabinet were to decide for hard-headed and practical reasons that a radical readjustment of power were urgently necessary (as some leading figures in the Afrikaner establishment are already convinced to be the case), they would likely be blocked by their own parliamentary caucus, which closely reflects the hard-line attitudes of the Afrikaner electorate.

A number of the most powerful Afrikaner leaders in the past have had this experience. For example, General J. C. Smuts decided during World War II that racial segregation had outlived the reality of the country's level of economic integration; his cautious attempts to edge the electorate toward softening segregation was a major reason for his defeat and for the election of the apartheid regime in 1948. Even such a commanding figure as the late Dr. H. F. Verwoerd was unable, at the pinnacle of his power as prime minister, to get his parliamentary supporters to accept the more radical proposals he believed necessary to give greater substance to the idea of the Bantu homelands, of which he was the principal architect. Today, even if Vorster were to throw his own considerable authority behind a more realistic approach to race relations, it is unlikely that he would succeed.

The critical factor in this situation is that of timing: to move too far ahead of how the white electorate perceives the reality of their power would destroy Vorster's leadership as completely as it did General Smuts'; to move too slowly, in terms of the blacks' perception of their own growing power, could result in destroying any hope of a more or less peaceful settlement of the country's problems.

If this analysis is correct, then the conclusion must be that the white electorate will not be ready to yield before it has suffered an extremely serious trauma such as the white Rhodesians experienced when they found themselves faced not only with a growing challenge from the guerrilla liberation movement and of economic strangulation, but also with an open disavowal of support from South Africa, the United States, and Britain.

One scenario of how such a trauma would occur in white South Africa might be scripted in the following way. Urban black violence (such as that sparked off in Soweto, the black dormitory city of Johannesburg) increases and becomes more difficult to repress, despite even heavier coercion; this further erodes the white community's confidence about the effectiveness of their physical power. The newly "independent" Transkei and other homelands develop as new bases of black power and serve to *sharpen the confrontation* between black South Africans and the white Republic. Since the basic assumption underlying separate development is that the "independent" homelands will serve to *diminish racial confrontation,* realization of this miscalculation comes as a profoundly disillusioning shock and leads to a fresh search for alternative policies. Meanwhile majority rule in Rhodesia and Namibia finally isolates the white Republic on the continent, and further boosts the morale and heightens the expectancies of black South Africans. They become more defiant, harder to control, and more demanding of early change. All these related developments make the Republic's basic instability more visible, intensifying the doubts among Western investors that had begun to develop seriously for the first time after the Soweto riots.

Previous assumptions about South Africa being a safe and profitable place for investment are revised and the Republic finds it increasingly harder (and more expensive) to raise new investment capital on the Euro-dollar market and from other Western banking institutions. (Currently South Africa needs $1.5 billion of new capital for its para-statal corporations' development programs alone.) A loss of Western confidence in the country's stability slows down the flow of new investment, which leads to increased black unemployment. This development not only contributes further to instability but leads to a reappraisal of the policies hitherto pursued by the United States and Western Europe. (This reappraisal has, in fact, already begun.) Now, South Africa finds itself isolated not only within the continent but more than ever from the Western community, its lifeline for economic support and defense against the "communist enemy." With the status quo beginning to crack, the communist nations increase the size of their commitments to the black challengers. The Western nations are faced with the choice of buttressing South Africa at a time when white power has already begun to slip badly or of identifying their interests as lying with the black and white forces demanding majority rule; the greater likelihood is that they will "tilt the balance to the blacks," as the Ford administration did over Rhodesia and Namibia.

Under these growing pressures the government declares a national state of emergency and proceeds to establish either a single-party state or possibly even military rule. Military rule could have two outcomes; either it could serve as a totalitarian instrument in hands of *ultras* determined on desperate resistance to any idea of concessions being offered to the black challengers, or it could become a Gaullist-type regime capable of making the kind of decisions that no government dependent on an exclusively white electorate would ever contemplate.

A second scenario proceeds along the same lines as the one above to the point where a military regime is established and opts for uncompromising, armed resistance and coercion. Such a stand would give greater credibility to the African National Congress' (ANC) preparations for an armed struggle; at the same time more young black militants inside the Republic rally to the ranks of the fighters. The ANC guerrilla bases, already being established in Mozambique, are also extended into Zimbabwe (Rhodesia), though most probably not to Botswana, Swaziland, and Lesotho. The homelands bordering on Mozambique (Kwa-Zulu and Gazankulu) come under external and internal pressures to provide facilities for clandestine guerrilla operations, to which the South African regime responds by moving its forces into those forward areas; this provokes even greater hostility from the homeland leaders and from the local populations. Hot pursuit of guerrillas into Mozambique follows; but even before it occurs, the Mozambican leaders prepare themselves for just such an eventuality and turn for support to strong external allies. The ANC-in-exile already enjoys strong Soviet backing; the Mozambicans, too, might decide (as Fidel Castro did) that when it comes to facing a powerful adversary, the Soviets have more to offer than the Chinese. The Soviet navy lands guerrillas by submarine along the Wild Coast of the Transkei. The last part of this scenario already forms the basis for contingency plans by South Africa, and it is also being examined by Mozambique. The worst nightmare of white South Africans—black *impis* (armies) armed with modern weapons, and backed by communists— offers a violent challenge to their way of life.

A third scenario, more hopeful but unfortunately less likely, opens with the Vorster (or military) regime reacting with the same kind of right-wing realism to its own situation at home that was displayed toward Mozambique and Rhodesia after the collapse of the Portuguese empire. Instead of waiting to be swamped by the kind of events already described, it begins to respond more quickly to demands for a new constitutional conference. The regime tries at first to confine the black representatives to the homeland leaders, but it is soon compelled to bring in the urban black leaders as well, although excluding the young militants and the banned Congress leaders. The willingness to begin negotiations helps to defuse the more militant opposition and wins strong Western backing for this more flexible approach. The very fact of white and black leaders negotiating about the country's future helps to condition white South Africans to accept the inevitability of a "shared society." (This is what has already happened to white thinking in Namibia.) It also strongly assists the cause of those white and black South Africans who believe that the country's future lies in finding agreement about a new federal or confederal constitution.

Faced with these three possible scenarios, what policy might one expect from the major Western nations if they hope to contribute constructively toward averting the violent disintegration of South Africa and, in terms of their own particular national interests, prevent the collapse of South Africa's economy and minimize the chances of anti-Western forces gaining power with the help of external communist support?

First, there should be a collective United States-European stand. This unity would prevent the Pretoria regime from exploiting Western differences, as they have managed to do up to now (for example, using the French as their major supplier of sophisticated weapons, aircraft, and warships). Second, there should be an unequivocable commitment to the principle of majority rule in South Africa. Third, there should be a collective Western stand in support of the idea of a national convention open to freely chosen white and black representatives for the purpose of negotiating a new constitution. At the same time there should be no outside dictation as to what form the constitution should take: that is a decision for the South Africans themselves. Fourth, Western governments should actively discourage any new capital investment from going to the Republic before there is a willingness to call a national convention; other practical forms of economic disengagement should also be considered. By collectively deciding on economic pressures, the Western governments could prevent South Africa from discriminating against the firms and investments of any one country. Fifth, the Security Council's arms embargo should be effectively enforced.

Once such a policy has been agreed upon, it would become possible to mount a concerted Western diplomatic initiative both by persuasion and by carefully calculated economic and diplomatic pressures to induce South

Africa to seek a negotiated settlement in much the same way as was done in Rhodesia and Namibia. By ending their present ambiguous policies toward South Africa, the Western nations would put themselves in a much stronger position to encourage change in the right direction and to appear in a more convincing role as champions of "the struggle for independence, for racial equality, for economic progress, for human dignity." (These aims were expressed by Dr. Kissinger in his speech in Lusaka in April 1976.)

While the crisis in South Africa persists, it is hardly feasible to try to forecast the political and economic future of a fully independent Southern African region. A settlement in South Africa would open up many exciting possibilities for developing the great human and economic potentialities of the region and for laying the foundations of a more stable political system. It would then be possible to look forward to an integrated economic community of Southern African states embracing all the countries whose economies and communications are so closely connected with, or even dependent on, South Africa—ranging from Zaïre, Angola, Zambia, and Malawi in the north to Mozambique, Rhodesia (Zimbabwe), Namibia, Botswana, Swaziland, and Lesotho in the south. The last three countries might even find their place in a new confederal structure of Southern African states. In human and economic terms everybody stands to gain immeasurably from the ending of the "unjust society in South Africa." However, at this stage it is pointless to speculate about the kinds of governments that might eventually prevail in countries like Angola and Mozambique, where the present Marxist regimes can only be regarded as experimental until a different political system has been evolved for the whole region. Nor is it possible to forecast what the relationship will be, after the crisis, between the West and the new states of Southern Africa. That depends very largely on the role the West itself chooses to play during the transition period.

South Africa, with all its tremendous potential advantages, unquestionably holds the key to peace and stability throughout the region. If its present rulers persist in their policies of apartheid, the outlook is for an embittering racial war, revolutionary upheavals, and the development of militantly African anti-Western attitudes that threaten not only the security of the large white resident communities and essential Western interests, but indeed the peace of the world. For all these reasons the events in South Africa in the years immediately ahead may prove to be of decisive importance.

International involvement is already inescapable. Since the nature of the struggle will be determined by a combination of internal and external pressures, it is crucially important that the Western nations, during this vital phase in the Post-Imperial Era, should not find themselves once again defending both the wrong and the losing cause. This is the time for a vigorous Western initiative that will not only match the initiatives of the communist nations but, more important, will live up to the expectations of all those South Africans who long to see the emergence of a just society and to see the present system transformed as peacefully as possible rather than to have to build a new society from the ruins of a violently disrupted country.

SUGGESTIONS FOR FURTHER READING

GENERAL

Davidson, Basil, Joe Slovo, and Anthony R. Wilkinson. *Southern Africa: The New Politics of Revolution.* London: Penguin, 1976.

Grundy, Kenneth W. *Confrontation and Accommodation in Southern Africa: The Limits of Independence.* Berkeley: University of California Press, 1973.

Legum, Colin, ed. *Africa Contemporary Record: Annual Survey and Documents: 1975–76.* New York: Africana Publishing Company, 1976.

Legum, Colin. *Vorster's Gamble for Africa: How the Search for Peace Failed.* New York: Africana Publishing Company, 1976; London: Rex Collings, 1976.

Legum, Colin, and Tony Hodges. *After Angola: The War Over Southern Africa.* New York: Africana Publishing Company, 1976; London: Rex Collings, 1976.

Nolutshungu, Sam C. *South Africa: A Study of Ideology and Foreign Policy.* New York: Africana Publishing Company, 1975.

1. RHODESIA

Bowman, Larry W. *Politics in Rhodesia: White Power in an African State.* Cambridge: Harvard University Press, 1973.

Kuper, Hilda. *The Shona and Ndebele of Southern Rhodesia.* London: International African Institute, 1954.

Lake, Anthony. *The "Tar Baby" Option: American Policy Towards Southern Rhodesia.* New York: Columbia University Press, 1976.

Palley, Claire. *The Constitutional History and Law of Southern Rhodesia, 1888–1965, With Special Reference to Imperial Control.* Oxford: Clarendon Press, 1966.

Ranger, Terence O. *The African Voice in Southern Rhodesia, 1898–1930.* London: Heinemann, 1970.

Shamuyarira, Nathan M. *Crisis in Rhodesia.* London: Andre Deutsch, 1965.

Sithole, Ndabaningi. *African Nationalism.* 2nd ed. London: Oxford University Press, 1968.

Todd, Judith. *The Right to Say No.* Stanford, California: Third Press, 1973.

2. MOZAMBIQUE

Chilcote, Ronald H. *Emergent Nationalism in Portuguese Africa.* Stanford, California: Hoover Institution Press, Stanford University, 1969.

Isaacman, Allen F. *The Tradition of Resistance in Mozambique.* London: Heinemann, 1976.

Machel, Samora. *Mozambique: Sowing the Seeds of Revolution.* London: Committee for Freedom in Mozambique, Angola, and Guinea, 1974.

Mondlane, Eduardo. *The Struggle for Mozambique.* London: Penguin, 1969.

Paul, John. *Mozambique: Memoirs of a Revolution.* London: Penguin, 1975.

Sousa Ferreira, Eduardo de. *Portuguese Colonialism in Africa: The End of an Era.* Paris: UNESCO Press, 1976.

3. SOUTH AFRICA

Adam, Heribert. *Modernizing Racial Domination: South Africa's Political Dynamics.* Berkeley: University of California Press, 1971.

Benson, Mary. *South Africa: The Struggle for a Birthright.* London: Penguin, 1969.

Carter, Gwendolen M. *The Politics of Inequality: South Africa Since 1948.* New York: Praeger, 1958–59.

Carter, Gwendolen M., Thomas Karis, and Newell M. Stultz. *South Africa's Transkei: The Politics of Domestic Colonialism.* Evanston: Northwestern University Press, 1967.

Karis, Thomas, and Gwendolen M. Carter, eds. *From Protest to Challenge: A Documentary History of African Politics in South Africa, 1882–1964.* 4 vol. Stanford, California: Hoover Institution Press, Vol. I (1882–1934), 1972; Vol. II (1935–1952), 1973; Vol. III (1953–1964), 1977; Vol. IV (Political Profiles), 1977.

Thomas, W. H., et al. *The Conditions of the Black Worker.* London: Africa Publication Trust, 1975. (Available through the African American Institute, 833 United Nations Plaza, New York City, 10017.)

Thompson, Leonard, and Jeffrey Butler, eds. *Change in Contemporary South Africa.* Berkeley: University of California Press, 1975.

Walshe, A. P. *The Rise of African Nationalism in South Africa: The African National Congress, 1912–1952.* Berkeley: University of California Press, 1971.

4. ANGOLA

Barnett, Don, and Roy Harvey. *The Revolution in Angola: MPLA, Life Histories and Documents.* Indianapolis: Bobbs-Merrill, 1972.

Butler, Herrick, Allison, et al. *Area Handbook for Angola.* Washington, D. C.: U.S. Government Printing Office, 1967.

Davidson, Basil. *In the Eye of the Storm: Angola's People.* Garden City, New York: Doubleday, 1972.

Marcum, John A. *The Angolan Revolution: The Anatomy of an Explosion (1950–1962).* Cambridge: MIT Press, 1969.

Wheeler, Douglas, and René Pelissier. *Angola.* New York: Praeger, 1971.

5. NAMIBIA

Dugard, John. *The South West Africa/Namibia Dispute.* Berkeley: University of California Press, 1973.

First, Ruth. *South West Africa.* London: Penguin, 1963.

Fraenkel, Peter. *The Namibians of South West Africa.* London: Minority Rights Group, 1974.

Horrell, Muriel. *South West Africa.* Johannesburg: South African Institute of Race Relations, 1967.

International Defence and Aid Fund. *All Options and None: The Constitutional Talks in Namibia.* Fact Paper on Southern Africa, No. 3, August 1976.

Landis, Elizabeth S. "Human Rights in Namibia," *Human Rights Journal,* Vol. 9, 1976.

Republic of South Africa. Report of the Commission of Enquiry into South West African Affairs 1962–63 (the so-called "Odendaal Report"). R. P. No. 12, 1964.

Republic of South Africa Department of Foreign Affairs. South West Africa Survey 1974. Published 1975.

Rogers, Barbara. *White Wealth and Black Poverty: American Investments in Southern Africa.* Westport, Ct.: Greenwood Press, 1976.

Segal, Ronald, and Ruth First, eds. *South West Africa: Travesty of Trust.* London: Andre Deutsch, 1967.

United Nations. *A Trust Betrayed: Namibia.* United Nations Office of Public Information, 1974.

Wellington, J. H. *South West Africa and Its Human Issues.* Oxford University Press, 1967.

6. BOTSWANA

Benson, Mary. *Tshekedi Khama.* London: Faber and Faber, 1960.

Dale, Richard. "Botswana," in C. Potholm and R. Dale, eds. *Perspectives on Southern Africa.* New York: The Free Press, 1972.

International Monetary Fund. *Surveys of African Economies.* Vol. 5. Washington, D. C., 1973.

Legum, Colin, ed. *Africa Contemporary Record.* Annual Reference Work. London: Rex Collings, 1976.

Sillery, Anthony. *Botswana: A Short Political History.* London: Methuen, 1974.

Smit, P. *Botswana: Resources and Development.* Pretoria: Africa Institute, No. 13, 1970.

Stevens, Richard P. *Botswana, Lesotho, and Swaziland: The History of the Former High Commission Territories.* London: Pall Mall, 1967.

7. SWAZILAND AND LESOTHO

Africa Institute Bulletin, Sept. 1968.

Khaketla, B. M. *Lesotho: 1970.* Berkeley: University of California Press, 1972.

Kuper, Hilda. *An African Aristocracy.* Oxford University Press, 1947.

Potholm, Christian P. *Four African Political Systems.* Englewood Cliffs, N. J.: Prentice-Hall, 1970.

Potholm, C., and Richard Dale. *Southern Africa in Perspective: Essays in Regional Politics.* New York: The Free Press, 1972.

Spence, J. E. *Lesotho: The Politics of Dependence.* Oxford University Press, 1969.

Stevens, Richard P. *Lesotho, Botswana and Swaziland: The Former H. C. T. of Southern Africa.* London: Pall Mall, 1967.

Index

About the Authors

Gwendolen M. Carter, Professor of Political Science and African Studies at Indiana University, was until recently Director of the Program of African Studies at Northwestern University and Melville J. Herskovits Professor of African Affairs. Her classic study of white politics in South Africa, *The Politics of Inequality,* has been followed by work on that country's racial policy of separate development in *South Africa's Transkei: The Politics of Domestic Colonialism,* of which she was coauthor, and of black politics in the four-volume series, *From Protest to Challenge: A Documentary History of African Politics in South Africa, 1882–1964,* of which she is a coeditor with Thomas Karis.

Tony Hodges is a journalist specializing in African affairs. He reported from Angola during the Angolan civil war for the London *Observer* and is the coauthor with Colin Legum of *After Angola: The War Over Southern Africa* (Rex Collings, 1976).

Elizabeth S. Landis is an attorney, a senior political affairs officer, and a former legal consultant for the United Nations Commissioner for Namibia. She is also vice-president of the American Committee on Africa, coeditor of the Liberian Code of Laws of 1956, and author of numerous articles on Namibia and South Africa.

Colin Legum, an Associate Editor of *The Observer,* is widely regarded as the doyen of British writers on Africa. Born in South Africa in 1919, he began his journalistic career at sixteen and joined *The Observer* in 1949. He has since followed closely the rise of independence of Africa and the emergence of the Third World. A number of his books on Africa have become standard reference works, including his annual *Africa Contemporary Record* and his history, *Pan-Africanism: A Political Guide.*

John A. Marcum is Provost of Merrill College and Professor of Politics at the University of California, Santa Cruz. Author of *The Angolan Revolution:* Vol. 1, *The Anatomy of an Explosion* (M.I.T. Press, 1969) and Vol. 2, *Exile Politics and Guerrilla Warfare,* forthcoming, he wrote the study on "Southern Africa after the Collapse of Portuguese Rule" for the Commission on Critical Choices for Americans appearing in Helen Kitchen (ed.), *Africa: From Mystery to Maze* (Lexington Books, 1976). A past president of the African Studies Association, he is a regular panelist for Africa on the PBS television series "World Press."

E. Philip Morgan is an Associate Professor of Public and Environmental Affairs at Indiana University. He helped establish the Institute of Development Management at the University of Botswana, Lesotho, and Swaziland, and he spent a year with the National Statistical Office of the Malawi Government. He edited *The Administration of Change in Africa* and has written articles on politics and development in Africa.

Patrick O'Meara is Director, African Studies Program at Indiana University, where he is also Associate Professor of Political Science, and Associate Professor, School of Public and Environmental Affairs. A graduate of the University of Cape Town, South Africa, he received his M.A. and Ph.D. degrees from Indiana University. He is author of *Rhodesia: Racial Conflict or Coexistence?*

Absolom L. Vilakazi was born in South Africa of Zulu parents. After training as an anthropologist, he came to the U. S. in 1958 and taught at Hartford Seminary Foundation. He worked for UNECA in Addis Ababa before joining the American University, where he is now Professor of Anthropology and International Relations.